PAT CONROY

PAT
CONROY

A Critical Companion

Landon C. Burns

CRITICAL COMPANIONS TO POPULAR CONTEMPORARY WRITERS
Kathleen Gregory Klein, Series Editor

Greenwood Press
Westport, Connecticut • London

Library of Congress Cataloging-in-Publication Data

Burns, Landon C.
    Pat Conroy : a critical companion / Landon C. Burns.
        p.   cm.—(Critical companions to popular contemporary
    writers, ISSN 1082–4979)
    Includes bibliographical references and index.
    ISBN 0–313–29419–4 (alk. paper)
    1. Conroy, Pat—Criticism and interpretation.   I. Title.
    II. Series.
    PS3553.O5198Z59   1996
    813'.54—dc20   95–39495

British Library Cataloguing in Publication Data is available.

Library of Congress Catalog Card Number: 95–39495
ISBN: 0–313–29419–4
ISSN: 1082–4979

First published in 1996

Greenwood Press, 88 Post Road West, Westport, CT 06881
An imprint of Greenwood Publishing Group, Inc.

Printed in the United States of America

The paper used in this book complies with the
Permanent Paper Standard issued by the National
Information Standards Organization (Z39.48–1984).

10 9 8 7 6 5 4 3 2 1

For Russ

without whose insistence
I would never have undertaken
to write this book (for which
I have cursed him), but without
whose impeccable taste in
editing (for which I have blessed
him) it would never have reached
publishable form.

Contents

Series Foreword

The authors who appear in the series Critical Companions to Popular Contemporary Writers are all best-selling writers. They do not have only one successful novel, but a string of them. Fans, critics, and specialist readers eagerly anticipate their next book. For some, high cash advances and breakthrough sales figures are automatic; movie deals often follow. Some writers become household names, recognized by almost everyone.

But novels are read one by one. Each reader chooses to start and, more importantly, to finish a book because of what she or he finds there. The real test of a novel is in the satisfaction its readers experience. This series acknowledges the extraordinary involvement of readers and writers in creating a best-seller.

The authors included in this series were chosen by an advisory board composed of high school English teachers and high school and public librarians. They ranked a list of best-selling writers according to their popularity among different groups of readers. Writers in the top-ranked group who had not received book-length, academic literary analysis (or none in at least the past ten years) were chosen for the series. Because of this selection method, Critical Companions to Popular Contemporary Writers meets a need that is not addressed elsewhere.

The volumes in the series are written by scholars with particular expertise in analyzing popular fiction. These specialists add an academic focus on their best-selling writers to the popular success that these writers already enjoy.

The series is designed to appeal to a wide range of readers. The general reading public will find explanations for the appeal of these well-known writers. Fans will find biographical and fictional questions answered. Students will find literary analysis, discussions of fictional genres, carefully organized introductions to new ways of reading the novels, and bibliographies for additional research. Students will also be able to apply what they have learned from this book to their readings of future novels by these best-selling writers.

Each volume begins with a biographical chapter drawing on published information, autobiographies or memoirs, prior interviews, and, in some cases, interviews given especially for this series. A chapter on literary history and genres describes how the author's work fits into a larger literary context. The following chapters analyze the writer's most important, most popular, and most recent novels in detail. Each chapter focuses on a single novel. This approach, suggested by the Advisory Board as the most useful to student research, allows for an in-depth analysis of the writer's fiction. Close and careful readings with numerous examples show readers exactly how the novels work. These chapters are organized around three central elements: plot development (how the story line moves forward), character development (what the reader knows about the important figures), and theme (the significant ideas of the novel). Chapters may also include sections on generic conventions (how the novel is similar to or different from others in its same category of science fiction, fantasy, thriller, etc.), narrative point of view (who tells the story and how), symbols and literary language, and historical or social context. Each chapter ends with an "alternative reading" of the novel. The volume concludes with a primary and secondary bibliography, including reviews.

The Alternative Readings are a unique feature of this series. By demonstrating a particular way of reading each novel, they provide a clear example of how a specific perspective can reveal important aspects of the book. In each alternative reading section, one contemporary literary theory—such as feminist criticism, Marxism, new historicism, deconstruction, or Jungian psychological critique—is defined in brief, easily comprehensible language. That definition is then applied to the novel to highlight specific features that might go unnoticed or be understood differently in a more general reading of the novel. Each volume defines two or three specific theories, making them part of the reader's understanding of how diverse meanings may be constructed from a single novel.

Taken collectively, the volumes in the Critical Companions to Popular Contemporary Writers series provide a wide-ranging investigation of the complexities of current best-selling fiction. By treating these novels seriously as both literary works and publishing successes, the series demonstrates the potential of popular literature in contemporary culture.

Kathleen Gregory Klein
Southern Connecticut State University

Acknowledgments

With special thanks to my friend, Joe Biscontini, who, some years ago, said, "You ought to read this guy Conroy—he's pretty good"; to my former colleagues, Janet Alwang and Elizabeth Buckmaster, who have been supportive in helping with everything from matters of grammar to listening for over a year to my complaints about the difficulties I was having in getting the book written; to Jan Elliott, who has been infinitely patient in guiding me through what must have seemed to him first-grade-level questions about how to use a computer; to the staff of the Delaware County Campus Library of The Pennsylvania State University, especially Jean Spahr and Susan Ware, for helping me assemble a microfilmed file of articles on Conroy that I never dreamed I would be able to access; to Barbara Rader for her efforts in gaining me quotation rights for Conroy's novels; above all, to Kathleen Gregory Klein, whose good humor and forbearance with my petulance deserve some kind of medal.

The Life of Pat Conroy

Donald Patrick Conroy was born in 1945, the eldest of Lieutenant Colonel Donald N. and Frances "Peg" Peck Conroy's seven children (there were also six miscarriages). Although Conroy—who as "Pat" is clearly and no doubt gratefully distinguished from his father—and his whole family seem given to hyperbole when they speak about the children's early years, there can be no doubt that the Conroys were nearly a casebook study in dysfunction: physical and psychological abuse from an autocratic father, almost annual moves dictated by military orders, constant tension between the parents, and neuroses in several of the children. So unhappy and destructive was life for the children in those years that Conroy's sister, Carol, is quoted as saying "the miscarriages were the lucky ones" (O'Neill 24).

Donald Conroy, a Marine Corps fighter pilot, according to the accounts not only by Pat, but also by a number of his siblings, was an authoritarian who treated his children as if they were Marine Corps recruits and physically attacked them and their mother with enough regularity to make them dread his presence. Their most pleasant memories are of the times when he was on overseas assignment and they lived with their maternal grandmother in Atlanta. Conroy says, in his Introduction to Mary Edwards Wertsch's *Military Brats: Legacies of Childhood Inside the Fortress*, that his father claims he exaggerates the terror he felt as a child but that he is reporting accurately:

> Mine was a forced march of blood and tears and I was always
> afraid in my father's house. But I did it because I had no
> choice and because I was a military brat conscripted at birth
> who had a strong and unshakeable sense of mission. (xix)

Colonel Conroy is clearly the model for Bull Meecham in *The Great
Santini* and reacted with predictable fury when he first read the book.
In his interview with Joyce Leviton, Conroy says that his father confirms
this by acknowledging that he threw the book across the room when he
reached page 233 (68). With Robert Duvall's softened and more sympathetic portrait in the movie version, Conroy senior became more mel-
low and began signing his Christmas cards, "The Great Santini." He
even claimed that he and Pat had earned Duvall an academy award
nomination. " 'He [Don] thinks,' says Conroy dryly, 'he made Robert
Duvall's career' " (Romano B3). Then in a typical Conroy-family reversal
or repression, Colonel Conroy, "in an interview with *Atlanta Magazine*
[1991] . . . dismissed his son's version of his youth, saying, 'Pat had an
ideal childhood' " (O'Neill 25). For a long time after that they were not
on speaking terms; then they came together publicly at a literary conference in Oxford, Mississippi, in 1994. Berendt reports that they were
superficially easy with each other, but they were wary and on edge (141).
Recently the Colonel has taken to joining his son at book signings and
inscribing copies, "The Great Santini" (Ahrens C2). On the surface, Conroy and his father seem to be friendly sparring partners, and in his
interview with Thomas Carney, Conroy jokes about his father's appearances on TV and radio shows (he says, with irony, that the Colonel is a
spokesman who gives his views on child rearing). Conroy claims that
their relationship is now a mutually satisfying one, but there is still a
bristling undercurrent in their exchanges:

> "What did it feel like to beat me as a boy, Dad?"
> "Felt good," says Don. "One of my pleasures." (Carney 113)

Aside from the abuse and the failure to express love for his family, a
number of other things about Colonel Conroy have left their mark on
his children. One of them is the emotional dislocation that comes with
the physical dislocations common to almost every military family; the
Conroys attended eleven schools in twelve years. Conroy describes the
effects in his Introduction to Wertsch's book. He says that he, and others
like him, were forever strangers and forever off balance:

I can engage anyone in conversation, become well-liked in a
matter of seconds, yet there is a distance I can never recover,
a slight shiver of alienation, of not belonging, and an eye on
the nearest door. . . . When Mary [Wertsch] writes of military
brats offering emotional blank checks to everyone in the
world, she's writing the first line of my biography. (Wertsch
xx–xxi)

Heroism is another part of Donald Conroy's life that Pat says he has
had to take into account in judging his father. He fought in three wars,
going to Vietnam twice. And Pat Conroy is no doubt paying tribute to
this side of his father's character when, in *The Great Santini*, as Bull Meecham's plane is going down in flames, he does not bail out but steers
his plane away from "populated areas." Conroy has said that the writing
of *The Great Santini* was in many ways cathartic for him and an expres-
sion of the love/hate feelings he has had for his father for as long as he
can remember.

Conroy's portrait of, and comments about, his father are often harsh,
but there is little about him that seems contrary to what can be seen on
the surface. An arrogant, abusive man, there was never anything subtle
or hidden about his personality. Conroy has said just the opposite about
his mother's inner versus her outer character. In an autobiographical
note, printed in *Book-of-the-Month Club News*, Conroy says that it took
him thirty years to realize that it was actually his mother who controlled
the household although to all appearances it was his father. He says she
"made Scarlett O'Hara [her favorite literary character] look shy and re-
tiring" (Stein D3). She stood between the Colonel and the children when
he abused them, and though he abused her as well, she was adamant in
her denial that he ever hit any of them. O'Neill recounts a typical episode
in which the children break into laughter as Bull, over six feet tall, is
about to slap one of the younger children who is crying because he has
fallen out of a tree. Pat receives the brunt of Bull's displeasure by having
a glass of milk thrown in his face that shatters and cuts him badly. As
his mother drives him to the hospital, she demands that he tell the doctor
that the children were playing touch football and that he fell and hit his
head on a water spigot (O'Neill 9).

This denial, which is reflected on in both *The Great Santini* and especially in the bitter portrait of Lila Wingo in *The Prince of Tides*, Peg Conroy insisted on as "family loyalty." Coming from a rural southern family,
she fully embraced the notion that a family, especially one with any pride

in itself, never allowed its dirty linen to be seen in public. While admirable in some respects, this repression and denial, says Conroy, also contains elements of neurosis and in extreme cases such as that of his mother, denials of reality on a larger scale. Her marriage to the son of a blue-collar Chicago family was probably fraught with dangerous cultural differences from the beginning, but in some ways Peg Conroy's own passion to "move up in the world" contributed to the tensions and discords in the family. David Toolan quotes Conroy as saying that his mother was a woman obsessed with a desire for a gentility she could never achieve (130). Nevertheless, Conroy admired his mother, a beautiful woman, who put the best possible face on the difficulties of being married to Donald Conroy and the annual disruptions of their lives as a new set of orders sent them to yet another town.

In a bit of timing that cannot have been accidental, Peg Conroy left her husband of thirty-three years on the day after his retirement parade. Conroy says their divorce was bitter; among other things "she presented the judge a copy of [*The Great Santini*] as 'evidence' of her husband's cruelty" (Ahrens C2). Although she remarried, she died of leukemia before the publication of *The Prince of Tides*. In his *Book-of-the-Month Club* note Conroy says that his mother asked him, as she was dying, to portray her in his next book, not as she was then, but beautiful as she had been in her younger days and that Meryl Streep be cast to play her part in the movie. Conroy acknowledges that he has made her beautiful in *The Prince of Tides* but that the portrait might not have pleased her.

It is hardly surprising that his conflicting emotions about his parents, as well as his own subsequent nervous disorders and those of his siblings, have figured prominently in his fiction. Many commentators have seen this personal trauma as the source of much of Conroy's most powerful plot, character, and thematic material. Joyce Leviton titles her profile, "Shaping His Pain Into Novels"; Ruthe Stein, hers, "Pat Conroy Reveals His Soap-Opera Life"; and David Toolan writes of "The Unfinished Boy & His Pain." Perhaps most succinctly Garry Abrams says in the *Los Angeles Times*, "Misfortune has been good to novelist Pat Conroy. It gave him a family of disciplinarians, misfits, eccentrics, liars and loudmouths" (5A1). He says that Conroy's education at The Citadel was from Sparta via Prussia and that his divorce and nervous breakdown sent him into intensive therapy. Although Abrams goes forward to speak of events before and after the publication of *The Prince of Tides*, he hits on what many have claimed is Conroy's ability to turn his personal traumas into literary gold mines.

After being graduated from high school in Beaufort, South Carolina, Conroy entered The Citadel in the fall of 1963, not because that was the college of his choice, but because that was the college his father ordered. So appalled was he by the sadistic treatment of first-year students (knobs), he called his father asking to come home. He told Leviton that his father's response was, "If you come home you'll be a pansy" (68). He stuck it out, and with the support of a man he came to admire, Lieutenant Colonel Courvoisie, Assistant Commandant of Cadets, and several faculty members, he actually came to a successful completion of his four years there. He found an outlet for his natural (rather than his military) talents by writing for, and editing, the college's literary magazine. Although he continued to loathe the military ethos of The Citadel and opposed the Vietnam War, Conroy does credit The Citadel with some of the most valuable lessons in his formative years. He knew certainly that he did not want a military career, Vietnam or otherwise. Wertsch quotes Conroy as saying that he started serving in the Marine Corps from the day of his birth and that he feels he had paid his dues.

But he credits The Citadel, again with a love/hate relationship like that with his father, for giving him a sense of self-control and a determination to be a writer with fierce integrity. He also, according to Frank Rose in his review of *The Lords of Discipline*, found here a theme of universal significance:

> What Conroy has achieved is twofold; his book is at once
> a suspense-ridden duel between conflicting ideals of manhood
> and a paean to brother love that ends in betrayal and death.
> (11)

Because of his myopia and color blindness, Conroy could not have become a pilot like his father even had he wanted to, and to gain at least temporary draft exemption, he returned in the fall of 1967 to teach at the Beaufort high school, from which he had been graduated only four years before. In those four years, however, an explosive change had taken place: racial integration. Conroy admits that he had grown up in a traditional southern culture of white supremacy, used words like "nigger" without a thought about their offensiveness, and gave little or no attention to the social upheaval that was about to come:

> My neck has lightened several shades since former times,
> or at least I like to think it has. My early years, darkened by

the shadows and regional superstitions of a bona fide cracker
boy, act as a sobering agent during the execrable periods of
self-righteousness that I inflict on those around me. . . . Those
were the years when the word *nigger* felt good to my tongue,
for my mother raised her children to say *colored* and to bow
our heads at the spoken name of Jesus. (*The Water Is Wide* 6)

During his years at The Citadel, these unexamined attitudes changed
considerably; but it was still with some insecurity because of his youth,
his inexperience, and his discomfort in not knowing how to deal with
an integrated student body, that Conroy went through his first year of
teaching. He found that he thoroughly enjoyed his classroom experience,
and he met three friends who were as passionately interested in politics,
the war, and philosophical values in general as he had become.

Then two things happened that caused a 180° turn in Conroy's racial
attitudes. The four friends went on a tour of Europe during the summer
of 1968; seeing firsthand the displays and gas chambers of Dachau forced
Conroy to rethink his preconceived notions of human relations. Secondly, the murder of Martin Luther King, Jr., in the spring of that year
and the angry reaction of the black students at the school made him
realize how misguided his earlier disregard for racial issues had been.
Like many a convert, Conroy now became such a vocal champion of
equality for blacks that he won the enmity of many among the all-white
faculty, including his former coach, who fired him as junior-varsity basketball coach because he thought Conroy favored "coloreds." He lobbied
for, and finally gained grudging acceptance of, a course in black history
even though he admits that he knew next to nothing about black history
and that the course was more symbolically than educationally important.

Although still in love with teaching, having become disaffected during
his second year at Beaufort with the largely reactionary faculty and the
tensions among the students, Conroy felt a desire for something more
challenging. Following an inexplicable failure to receive a reply to his
application for the Peace Corps and at the suggestion of his friend, Bernie
Schein, Conroy applied for the opening at the two-room elementary
school on Daufuskie Island. This was a small enclave, almost totally isolated (there was no bridge to the mainland), populated by several white
families (one of which "governed" the island almost as if it were a private fief) and a small group of blacks who had remained after factory
pollution from upstream destroyed what was once a thriving and pros-
perous oyster business.

In retrospect Conroy realizes several things about this one-year experience. His motives for taking the job were mixed, perhaps even misguided:

> At this time of my life a black man could probably have handed me a bucket of cow piss, commanded me to drink it in order that I might rid my soul of the stench of racism, and I would have only asked for a straw. . . . It dawned on me that I came to Yamacraw [Daufuskie] for a fallacious reason: I needed to be cleansed, born again, resurrected by good works and suffering, purified of the dark cankers that grew like toadstools in my past. (*The Water Is Wide* 114-15)

He also came to realize that, had he been more willing to work through the system rather than in a confrontational manner, he might have been able to remain and continue to work with these pathetic, nearly illiterate children. Yet, he also realizes that, given the mind-set of the school board and administration of the time, the isolation and poverty of the students, and his own limited educational resources, he could have made only marginal differences in their lives.

In spite of all the demands on his time and vigor in the academic year 1969–1970 on Daufuskie, Conroy seems to have had an enormous amount of youthful energy to spare. In September he fell in love with Barbara Jones, a Beaufort elementary schoolteacher and Vietnam War widow who was pregnant with her second child. They were married in October. Conroy continued to live on the island and return to Beaufort for weekends, but by November he realized this was unfair to Barbara, himself, and to Barbara's two-year-old daughter, Jessica. Thus, he began a daily commute by boat to the island, a tortuous journey through reefs, fog, and inclement weather.

Meanwhile, he began spending Saturday mornings in Charleston with Colonel Courvoisie writing what was to become his first published book, *The Boo* (1970). This book is really more a scrapbook than a biography, assembled like an album of sketches, anecdotes, reproductions of official memoranda and reports, cartoons, and photographs. Only in one or two brief sections is there sustained writing that suggests the prose stylist that Conroy was to become:

> *The Boo* in style and format is little removed from juvenilia, the language generally bland or affected, transitions weak or nonexistent. (Willingham 55)

But Willingham does note that, although "its literary merits . . . are neg-ligible," there are sections of *The Boo* that reveal Conroy's iconoclasm and offbeat humor.

Published by a small vanity press (McClure) for $1500 that Conroy borrowed from a banker in Beaufort, *The Boo* has remained in print and, although at one point banned by The Citadel, it later became required reading. When the manuscript for *The Water Is Wide* was ready two years later, this was something the local banker could not finance, and friends told Conroy that he needed an agent. Sam Staggs tells the story of Con-roy's search that ended in his finding the famous Julian Bach, who grudgingly agreed to read the manuscript. Since his father had refused to let Conroy take a typing course in high school because it was "sissy," he had to rely on friends to help him get the book ready to submit. He forgot, however, to tell them to use the same kind of paper, so they ended with a mishmash of onionskin, yellow foolscap, some lined sheets, and some pages shorter than others. Bach, says Conroy, thought it "was the most adorable hayseed thing he'd ever seen" and sold it to Houghton Mifflin for $7500. So naive was Conroy about the world of publishing that he thought that when Bach mentioned the figure he meant it would cost Conroy that amount rather than that the publisher would pay him. Somewhat sheepishly, Conroy says that Bach, to this day, thinks of him as a complete hick (Staggs 9).

The resulting modest success of *The Water Is Wide* gave Conroy the financial security to begin writing full time. When the book came out, the Conroys had not only Jessica and Barbara's second child, Melissa, but also a daughter, Megan, of their own. In addition, they had three black children from Daufuskie living with them while they attended Beaufort High School. Beaufort liked neither the book, which cast the board of education and the school administration in such a bad light, nor the Conroys' integrated household. Uncomfortable in this atmo-sphere, the family moved to Atlanta shortly after *Conrack* (1974), the Jon Voight film based on the book, appeared. (The name comes from the way some of the students pronounced his name, being unable to pro-nounce it as it is spelled.) Like the movie versions of all of Conroy's books, it was a financial success.

An even greater success than *The Water Is Wide*, Conroy's next book, *The Great Santini* (1976), was a true novel but one with such a highly autobiographical base that it blew "the Conroys apart. 'My whole family had a collective nervous breakdown'" (Leviton 68). His father's side of the family stopped speaking to him; his mother divorced his father after thirty-three years; Conroy's own marriage came apart, and he had a nervous breakdown. He says of his personal problems that he couldn't handle success and that Barbara couldn't handle his "craziness."

Even given the Conroy family's propensity to overstatement, Pat's description of his breakdown makes it seem to have been of epic proportions. He says that he couldn't write or sleep and that he "crawled" to his therapist's office "on my hands and knees" (Stein D5). Because of his Roman Catholic background, he was not prepared for the kind of revelations Marion O'Neill (his therapist) said were vital if she were to be able to help him. Conroy speaks of his divorce from Barbara in somewhat maudlin terms in his article for *Atlanta Magazine* (excerpted in *The Reader's Digest*), and no doubt this trauma contributed to his nervous/emotional collapse. Other accounts claim that his father's three-day disappearance and the fear that he had committed suicide after the publication of *The Great Santini* may have been the catalyst. In any case, the years of 1977–1980 seem to have been terribly troubling ones for him. Nevertheless, during this period of intense emotional distress, he managed to write and publish *The Lords of Discipline* (1980) and to meet his second wife, Lenore Gurewitz Fleischer, whom he married in 1981. He credits her with helping him find his emotional balance again and for at least ten years handling all his public business. A divorcée with two children, Lenore seems to have had an enormously steadying hand on Conroy, and they had another daughter, Susannah, of their own.

While *The Lords of Discipline* was a financial success, and again the movie version (although in this case not a very faithful adaptation) brought fame and dollars, nothing could have foretold the literary and commercial bonanza that came with *The Prince of Tides* (1986). Although by no means universally praised by critics, it became an overnight bestseller and went on to become the enormously successful movie, for which Conroy wrote a version of the script and worked with Barbra Streisand in the filming:

> So hot is "Prince of Tides,"—now the No. 1 paperback fiction best seller—that not even the last-minute rescheduling of the movie debut from September to December could stop it. (Max 84)

The enormous success of *The Prince of Tides* both as novel and movie proved to renew interest in Conroy's earlier work, and Bantam sold millions of copies stimulated by the popularity of *The Prince of Tides*.

In the years since *The Prince of Tides*, Conroy has become a literary celebrity. For example, at the 1986 meeting of the American Booksellers Association, Conroy was an enormously popular raconteur; indeed, he stole the spotlight from well-known personalities like Walter Cronkite and Carol Burnett. Among his other stories, he told one about asking Julian Bach (his agent) how he might sell more books. Bach is said to have answered by saying that he should include more sex. Conroy replied that he couldn't because his grandmother was still alive (Maryles 30). Or, when John Blades chose to ask a number of prominent authors how they would have handled the sequel to *Gone With the Wind*, Conroy answered somewhat flippantly that he would gladly have accepted the $4.9 million and given the book a distinctly southern gothic flavor. In his version Rhett Butler would have joined the Ku Klux Klan, but then "I would have had Rhett confess that he was gay and move to San Francisco" (Blades Tempo 5).

Conroy became intimately involved in a case in which Judith Fitzgerald, a Charleston high school teacher, was embroiled in an ugly controversy with a fundamentalist preacher over her assigning *The Prince of Tides* as optional reading for her eleventh-grade section of Advanced Placement English. The preacher, the Reverend R. Elton Johnson, Jr., demanded that the school board remove the book from Fitzgerald's students. Meanwhile, without endorsing Johnson's position on pornography, *The* [Charleston] *News and Courier* weighed into the imbroglio with an editorial saying "that because Conroy's works depend on the 'language of the gutter,' they are not literature at all. 'Real literature,' said the editor, 'has a far wider, far more appealing vocabulary'; he implored Conroy to write novels that 'soar like an eagle' " (White 18). Conroy fired back an angry letter to the editor in which he accused the paper of being "to American journalism what the Rev. R. Elton Johnson is to the Archbishop of Canterbury" (White 19).

The controversy became a cause célèbre that lasted for several months, and Conroy involved himself more and more as he sought to support Fitzgerald. He visited her classroom to talk, not so much about book banning as about the nature of good fiction. He wrote another long letter to *The News and Courier*, no doubt inspired in part by his own troubles as an English teacher eighteen years before, in which he applauded Judith Fitzgerald's integrity and teaching skill (White 20). The issue finally moved from the front pages, and, in a mealymouthed endorsement, the school board allowed that teachers had the right to assign "suitable" reading matter.

The incident, interesting in itself, shows also how passionate Conroy is on the subject of writing. He has always maintained that his writing is a way of expressing the " 'helplessness, tremendous anger and a need for revenge' that he felt as a child trapped in an abusive situation" (Romano B3). Willingham puts it in a slightly different way by saying that Conroy's life has been the major source for his fiction and that there is still a degree of "self-doubt" in both the author and the private man (58). On a less personal level, Conroy has spoken frequently about the need of the writer to "tell the truth," no matter how painful that truth is, and how he tries always to make each new novel more challenging than the last. "In each book, Conroy suggests that art begins when the artist recognizes the most natural state of mankind, always in need of grace, yet nevertheless ready to have its story told by the artist" (York 46).

With the money generated by *The Prince of Tides* the Conroys were free to live very much as they chose. For three years that was in Rome (which is the setting of a part of Conroy's next novel, *Beach Music*). Although there was a story that the Conroys had to leave Atlanta after Pat's fight with Lenore's former husband (for which Conroy spent a night in jail), Conroy brushes that aside as more a misunderstanding than a serious episode. It is true, however, that they wanted to escape the bitter custody battle over Lenore's two children and the civil lawsuit Dr. Fleischer (who became the model for Herbert Woodruff in *The Prince of Tides* [Carney 112]) brought against Conroy over the fight. After leaving Rome, the Conroys lived in San Francisco for several years where they were received with great pleasure by a society that is partial to famous authors (Stein D5).

While fame and fortune have come to Conroy, he still worries about problems of his character. He says that he would never hit his wife or children although he is sure that he has often frightened them:

> But one thing I've learned is that because I was raised by a violent man that I am a violent man, and violence exudes from me. (Epstein F12)

Conroy continues to wrestle with his personal demons, not the least of which is his volatile personality and his relationship with his equally volatile family. *Beach Music* (originally scheduled for publication in late 1990) was delayed for nearly five years as the result of several severe personal crises.

In the first place, the public appearances generated by the enormous

success of *The Prince of Tides* and Conroy's decision to write a screenplay
for the movie version of the book kept him occupied well into 1990.
Furthermore, there was the intimidating challenge of trying to surpass
himself with the new novel, while Doubleday, his publisher, began urging him to set a completion deadline. Already under these pressures,
Conroy suffered another blow as his second marriage unraveled; he
moved back to South Carolina while Lenore and their daughter, Susannah (upon whom Leah of *Beach Music* is based [Klein H4]), remained in
San Francisco. Conroy says that the divorce is primarily his fault because
he is unable to handle emotion, either good or bad, very well:

> I [Conroy's good friend, Tom Belk] think this divorce has
> put him at an all-time low point. His daughter told him she
> wouldn't even have dinner with him. (Guthrie 25)

In 1993 he was forced to have back surgery that for months afterward
kept him from sitting in a chair for more than very brief periods. Under
the weight of all these problems, Conroy suffered another serious nervous collapse that caused him to begin drinking heavily and made him
suicidal enough to think of buying a gun. Fortunately he returned to his
therapist, Marion O'Neill, who managed to bring him out of his depression and set him back to writing (Berendt 139). Then, when things
seemed to be going well again, and he was nearing completion of the
manuscript of *Beach Music*, he received the news in August 1994 that his
youngest brother, Tom, a paranoid schizophrenic, had committed suicide. Not only was this a devastating personal calamity, but in *Beach
Music*, using as he always does, a great many characters based on members of his family, Conroy had created a character based on this brother
and had written a draft of a chapter in which he commits suicide. Conroy, who had already had concerns about what effect this might have
on Tom, immediately decided to delete the section although he kept the
character in the novel.

With the booming popularity of *Beach Music*, Conroy set off on a
thirty-four-city publicity, book-signing tour, and although there was a
rumor as early as June 1994 that he had already negotiated the film rights
(Fleming 4), those were only finally settled in late June 1995:

> Paramount bought the rights for $5.1 million in a deal that
> also reportedly includes $1.3 million for *Ex*, a 1989 screenplay
> Conroy wrote with his friend Doug Marlette. (Martelle 6C)

Included in the same package was $700,000 for the adaptation for the screen of Thomas Wolfe's *Look Homeward, Angel*, a book Conroy has often cited as an inspiration for his own writing. Presumably, after the hoopla over *Beach Music* dies down, Conroy may well return to his modest house on Fripp Island, South Carolina (although he wants to maintain a presence in San Francisco so he can be near Susannah), where he will begin work on his next book. Berendt says that Conroy is not yet sure what that book will be about although he has been thinking for some time of a novel set in Atlanta. There is material that he reluctantly cut from *Beach Music* and stories that he has gleaned from other people:

> And there were incidents in his own life that he would write about in the fullness of time, when he was able to think them through and grasp their meaning. The suicide of his brother Tom would almost certainly be one of those. (Berendt 141)

Genres

Since Pat Conroy has written only a memoir and four novels (aside from the unclassifiable *The Boo*, 1970), and since in some ways they involve quite different subject matter, one might think that it would be difficult to place all his work in a familiar literary genre. Genre is defined in this context as a particular kind of literary work traditionally of major forms (such as tragedy, comedy, epic, lyric poetry, and the novel) that, until at least the late eighteenth century, had rather strict rules that authors were expected to follow; recently the term has been used more loosely, with less attention to "rules" and with a broadening into subgenres such as science fiction, mystery, the western, and the memoir. Actually, although superficially different, Conroy's works are strikingly similar and fit together in several overlapping genres including the autobiographical, coming-of-age, and southern gothic traditions.

Perhaps the strongest link in his work is the heavy dependence on autobiographical material (much of which is covered in the previous chapter). If there were a literary genre titled Autobiographical Fiction, Conroy would be among its foremost practitioners; indeed, Conroy has said that his family is the "theme of my life" (Smithsonian lecture). As a memoir, *The Water Is Wide* (1972), is by definition autobiographical. Like all memoirs, it focuses not only on the author himself and particular dates and events in his life, but on the world in which he has lived during the period covered in the book. *The Water Is Wide* is Conroy's

attempt to recount his year of teaching on Daufuskie Island, his reactions
to his pupils (and theirs to him) and his superiors, and what he learned
about himself, as well as what he experienced in his attempt to bring
these nearly illiterate children some degree of education, culture, and
knowledge of the world in which they lived. Although Conroy changes
the name of the island (from Daufuskie to Yamacraw) and some of the
names of the chief characters, *The Water Is Wide* is otherwise almost a
model of the form. This is not to say that it is as if a tape recorder's
cassettes have been transcribed. Conroy has obviously been selective in
his choice of incidents and the emphasis he places on them. Character
development has clearly been shaped and shaded by Conroy's desire to
make the book as readable as a novel. (Indeed, more than one critic,
including the astute David Toolan, mistakenly calls it a novel.)

   The Great Santini (1976) is, without question, a novel, but it is also a
very thinly disguised representation of Conroy's experience with his autocratic father, a Marine fighter pilot, during the year that the family
lived in Beaufort, South Carolina. In many interviews and comments,
Conroy has directly and angrily asserted that Bull Meecham is modeled
directly on his father, Lieutenant Colonel Donald N. Conroy. Lillian of
the novel bears a close resemblance to his mother, Peg, though Conroy
has said that his portrait of her in *The Great Santini* is not as accurate as
it should have been, because it was not until later that he learned it was
actually she, rather than his father, who ran the house in spite of appearances to the contrary.

   In obedience to his father, Conroy went to The Citadel and again he
acknowledges openly that the fictional Carolina Military Institute of *The
Lords of Discipline* (1980), situated like The Citadel in Charleston, bears
an uncommon resemblance to the real university. Pat Conroy/Ben Meecham has become Pat Conroy/Will McLean in this novel, and the figure
of Colonel Thomas Berrineau, the Bear, is clearly Lieutenant Colonel
Thomas Nugent Courvoisie, the Assistant Commandant of Cadets,
whom Conroy had memorialized in *The Boo*. Conroy has never com-
mented directly on the identities of the other characters in the book or
on its incidents. Indeed, he makes a very emphatic statement denying
any such parallels:

> This book is a work of fiction. No character is real, and no
> incident occurred as described in this book; no man or woman
> who lives within the pages of the book lives outside of it. . . .

Similarly, the actions I portray here are fictional archetypes
created from my own research, not actual events. (viii)

Since Will and the Bear are so obviously based on real people, it is hard
to know how far to trust Conroy's disclaimer. It seems likely that some
of the other characters, such as the roommates, do, in fact, resemble real
people.

Conroy's family has had a long history of mental/nervous disorders.
Carol, on whom Savannah of *The Prince of Tides* (1986) is modeled, is a
poet who lives in New York and who has had a series of nervous problems and has made several attempts at suicide. Conroy himself suffered
a serious collapse after the publication of *The Great Santini*. Thus, Tom
Wingo is yet another autobiographical version of Pat Conroy himself.
Susan Lowenstein is based, Conroy says in his interview with Ruthe
Stein, on the two women who helped him through the trauma of his
breakdown: Lenore, his second wife, and Marion O'Neill, his therapist.
The abusive father, Henry Wingo, is clearly reminiscent of Bull Meecham
in a number of ways, and Lila, a beautiful woman, who divorces Henry
after more than thirty years and marries a man she considers socially
and economically superior, is obviously based on Peg Conroy Egan.

Beach Music, too, is heavily dependent on autobiographical material.
Lucy McCall, who has divorced her husband of many years after raising
five sons and who is dying of leukemia, is yet another reflection of Conroy's mother. Jack of the novel is an alter ego of Pat, the eldest of the
Conroy sons, and John Hardin, like Conroy's youngest brother, Thomas,
is a paranoid schizophrenic. Even the occupations of the McCall brothers
in the novel are similar to those of the Conroy brothers in the real world.
The depiction, in this case almost parodic, of the abusive Marine Corps
father is transferred to Rembert Elliott, a minor character in his own
right, yet reminiscent of Donald Conroy and Bull Meecham of *The Great
Santini*. The town of Waterford seems remarkably like that of Beaufort,
and Jack's high school career in athletics mirrors that of Ben Meecham
and Will McLean.

Thus, Conroy's work is filled with people from his family and acquaintances, and he is quite open in his frequent public acknowledgment
of this. Moreover, in Conroy's case, all of his work belongs to what is
called the *Bildungsroman* tradition. This German term can be translated
as an "upbringing" or "education" novel. (Other nearly synonymous
terms are "coming-of-age" and "rites-of-passage" novels, though the latter covers a slightly larger scope.) It is a time-honored and widely used

structure, since the growing-up pains of a young man or woman, the passage from relative innocence to the often disillusioned experience of adulthood, is a universal phenomenon, and therefore something with which nearly every reader can identify. Furthermore, it allows the authors to explore the psyches of their characters and show how people, places, events, and relationships influence and help to shape their protagonists (the major character, often called the hero, of the novel—though in recent years that major character is often not really heroic at all and is more correctly termed the anti-hero). The list of famous *Bildungsroman*s would be a very long one indeed, and it would include the names of a wide variety of authors, especially if the term is interpreted broadly enough to include protagonists who may have reached physical maturity but still have much to learn about themselves and reality. Most critics would be comfortable in using the term to describe books that focus on the years in which the protagonist is under thirty, though that is a somewhat arbitrary limit. Thus, not only are Conroy's works autobiographical, they belong also in this coming-of-age category.

Goethe's *Wilhelm Meisters Lehrjahre* (*Wilhelm Meister's Apprenticeship*) (1795–1796) is usually considered the defining example of the genre. The tradition, however, can be traced back to the Middle Ages, and surely novels like Fielding's *Tom Jones* (1749) are classics of the type. (Purists might not include it because the literary term came into currency only after Goethe's novels were so named.) Dickens's *David Copperfield* (1850) is often cited as a model of the form as is Joyce's *A Portrait of the Artist as a Young Man* (1916). Works as diverse as Willa Cather's *O Pioneers!* (1913), Ralph Ellison's *Invisible Man* (1952), Doris Lessing's five-volume *Children of Violence* (1952–1969), and James Baldwin's *Giovanni's Room* (1956) are but a few of many distinguished novels that fit the definition. In plotting, these novels are frequently episodic, since the author wants to show the protagonist going through a series of experiences—such as an encounter with authority, sexual initiation, disillusionment with one whom she or he had previously considered a friend or mentor, or disappointment in the failure to achieve a goal long sought. The *Bildungsroman* has been a particularly popular genre with American authors, perhaps because many of them have seen parallels between characters coming of age and undergoing rites of passage and a nation, which at least until the middle of the twentieth century, was itself coming of age.

Conroy's *The Great Santini* and *The Lords of Discipline* are so obviously *Bildungsromans* that it is hardly necessary to explain why they are nearly textbook cases. Each covers a short period in a young man's life in which he goes through various experiences, trials, and tests in his passage from youth to maturity. *The Water Is Wide*, though a memoir rather than a novel, fits the same pattern. Conroy's experience in his year on Daufuskie Island is a sobering and enlightening one. He learns things about himself that are painful as well as salutary, and he learns a great deal about the ways in which power can be exerted by those in authority. If the events themselves in these three books were not enough to confirm them as *Bildungsromans*, the protagonists speak repeatedly about how naive they have been and how they have changed during the course of their initiation to the real world.

The Prince of Tides is a somewhat more complicated case, but even though Tom Wingo is over thirty-six at the present time of the novel, much of it has to do with the tales he tells Susan Lowenstein of his childhood, starting with the night of his and Savannah's birth and continuing through their youth and early adulthood. Though told in retrospect, these anecdotes and episodes are often serious, life-altering events and form the very heart of the novel. Presumably, what he tells Lowenstein is in an effort to help the therapist understand Savannah and her problems; a second reality is that Tom is, himself, undergoing therapy by telling Lowenstein these long-ago and often repressed stories of his growing up. Thus, even at thirty-six Tom Wingo is somewhat belatedly going through a series of learning experiences. David Toolan sums it up aptly:

> The healing love affair with Susan represents new territory for the hero and the author, Conroy's first bid at portraying a mature sexual relationship. (131)

Toolan goes on to say that Conroy makes us believe that this relationship could not have taken place had not Tom become a new man rising from the "death" of his former despair.

In *Beach Music*, after his wife's suicide, Jack McCall has retreated to Rome to avoid confrontation with his family, his in-laws, and his past. He has achieved a tenuous peace with himself and the world, which proves illusory when his mother's illness brings him home to confront all those issues that he has attempted to escape. Thus, in a sense, he too, at age thirty-seven, is undergoing rites of passage that he has naively thought he had put behind him. As is the case in *The Prince of Tides*, much of *Beach Music* is taken up with stories about Jack (and his friends) during their high school and college years. We are given, in retrospect, many of the episodes that constitute a coming-of-age story. By the end of the novel, after a series of healing events with his South Carolina relatives and friends, Jack returns to Rome with his daughter and Ledare, his new wife, and seems, perhaps more than any other of Conroy's protagonists, to have reached catharsis and reconciliation with himself as well as with others.

If asked what is the primary genre to which Conroy's work belongs, almost every critic would immediately reply, "southern." Many theories exist about why this region should have produced such a large and fertile group of writers (poets, playwrights, essayists, and especially short story writers and novelists), but among the things they have in common is a strong sense of place, a powerful identification with the land, both its rural areas and its historic cities. This may come, in part, from the region's agrarian history and, in part, from its turning inward in its long hostility to the Yankee North during and after the Civil War. Another strong link among these writers is a propensity for storytelling in its many forms that vary from yarns, legends, or family anecdotes on a small scale to the mammoth, nearly mythological saga of Faulkner's Yoknapatawpha novels. The names of writers in the southern school is long and illustrious: Edgar Allan Poe, Mark Twain (at least in some of his finest work), Kate Chopin, Katherine Anne Porter, Thomas Wolfe, Robert Penn Warren, and Eudora Welty would be only a few near the top of a very distinguished list.

Within the larger southern tradition there has emerged a group who are known as southern gothics. This group within a group has become so prominent that many commentators tend to think of it as the dominant form of southern writing today. The term "gothic novel" was given to a form of fiction very popular in the late eighteenth and early nineteenth centuries. Its chief characteristic was an emphasis on horror, violence, eccentric characters, and supernatural effects. Horace Walpole's *The Castle of Otranto* (1764), Ann Radcliffe's *The Mysteries of Udolpho* (1794), and M. S. (Monk) Lewis's *The Monk* (1795) are generally cited as landmark works in the field. Their eerie effects, suspenseful action, and mysterious, gloomy atmospheres were picked up by Poe (and, to some extent, by non-southern writers like Hawthorne and others) in the United States in the mid-1900s. After a period when southern writing turned to less sensational material, romance, and a kind of local color interest (as in the work of very different writers such as Joel Chandler Harris, Ellen Glasgow, James Branch Cabell, Hervey Allen, and Margaret Mitchell), the gothic element returned in a burst of invention and acclaim, beginning with William Faulkner's *The Sound and the Fury* (1929), *Absolam, Absolam!* (1936), and the Snopes trilogy (1940–1960). Following fast on Faulkner's critical success were authors like Carson McCullers, Flannery O'Connor, and William Styron among others. The gothic element came to be the hallmark of southern fiction. These authors' depictions of rape, incest, murder, and other forms of violence have given the school a reputation for melodrama and horror. Faulkner is certainly the most esteemed of the group (he won the Nobel prize for literature in 1949), but he has been followed by a long list, not so much of imitators, but of novelists who have used variations on his themes—Lillian Smith, Richard Wright, Walker Percy, Shirley Ann Grau, and many others. Along with the violence in their plots and themes, both major and minor authors of the school have concentrated on eccentric characters. Lamar York says that southern literature is about young people's rites of passage or about old people who have become senile; it is almost never about the middle class who live in the suburbs (46). And Conroy's mother, to whom he gives so much credit for his having become a writer, is quoted in the *Book-of-the-Month Club News* note as saying:

> All Southern literature can be summed up in these words: "On the night the hogs ate Willie, Mama died when she heard what Daddy did to Sister." (5)

Apocryphal as this statement may be, it is certainly a delightfully succinct parody of the excesses of the southern gothic tradition.

Especially with *Beach Music* and *The Prince of Tides,* and to a lesser extent with *The Great Santini* and *The Lords of Discipline,* Conroy takes his place firmly among the southern gothic writers. On the humorous side in *The Prince of Tides* there are Tom's grandparents, Amos and Tolitha Wingo, and their wonderfully eccentric and amusing escapades. On the far darker side are Henry Wingo's violence; the harrowing night of Tom and Savannah's birth; the rape of Lila, Savannah, and Tom by the escaped convicts; and Savannah's repeated suicide attempts. In the less horrific aspects of southern storytelling there are numerous anecdotes such as the rescuing of Snow, the white dolphin, and the depositing of a dead turtle in the Newburys' bed.

In *Beach Music* there are many sections that are pure southern gothic writing, but none is more clearly so than the tale of Lucy's childhood and the flight of her mother from the hills of North Carolina (Chapter Twenty-seven). So full of violence and mayhem is this section that it stands as a set piece, of gothic horror. Though not southern in their setting, the various stories about the atrocities inflicted on several Jewish members of the cast of characters during the Holocaust form another level of gothic description. Conroy seems almost obsessed with depicting in the most graphic terms scenes of torture, rape, and murder.

In addition to the gothic element, or, perhaps as a part of it, southern writing has become known for its ornateness and volubility. Faulkner was a unique stylist, famous for his long convoluted sentences, paragraphs that run on for several pages, and his often tortured syntax. Also well known for his style, although perhaps more for its prolixity and exuberance than for its intricacy, is Thomas Wolfe, an author whom Conroy acknowledges as his first literary "hero." He tells the story of Eugene Norris's (his high school English teacher), giving him a copy of *Look Homeward, Angel* for his fifteenth birthday; Conroy says that he was immediately enchanted with Wolfe's style and that during a trip to Wolfe's home in Asheville, North Carolina, he first became aware of the relationship between life and art (Epstein F1, F12). Wolfe, like Conroy, used a great deal of autobiographical material in this and other family-saga novels like *Of Time and the River* and *You Can't Go Home Again*; and he has proved to be an inspiration for numerous writers, especially beginning ones, in succeeding generations.

It is, then, Faulkner and Wolfe who have come to stand as the founding fathers of a large and prolific group of younger writers who have been identified as regional, in that they have lived in and written primarily about the South, have focused on eccentric characters from the area, and have incorporated a great deal of violence in their plots and themes. Moreover, many of them, while not stylists like Faulkner or Wolfe, have become known for their ornate and, some critics would say, inflated styles.

In his interview with Peter Gorner, Conroy confirms his recognition of the territory to which he belongs. Although critics label him a popular novelist, he would prefer to write like Wolfe and Faulkner if he were able. He says that he has tried to be more ambitious with each novel (3). Thus, Conroy is well aware of his literary roots and aspires to become even stronger in his chosen métier:

> "I am the son of a fearless man ... and a fearless woman. I want to go broader, and I want to go deeper. I wasn't raised to be afraid." (Logue 35)

It is clear that each of Conroy's novels thus far has been more challenging than the last and that he is striving for literary stature as well as popular success. Although he has won several minor, regional literary awards, he has not yet been nominated for anything major like the Pulitzer prize or the National Book Award.

There were scattered reviews of Conroy's books in nationally recognized newspapers and magazines before *The Prince of Tides*, but it was that book which brought him almost universal attention from the press and the public. The critical reaction to the novel was considerably mixed, but nearly every commentator noted that, with this novel, Conroy had firmly established himself as a major figure in the tradition of southern fiction. Many, like Brigitte Weeks, while admitting that there are lapses, says that Conroy is prodigiously articulate and that often:

> [T]he words are just right, cramming layers of meaning into a small sentence, as when Tom thinks of his grandmother's decline: "The capillaries of her brain seem to be drying up slowly, like the feeder creeks of an endangered river." ("Pat Conroy . . ." 14)

Gail Godwin is less enthusiastic, but she also acknowledges Conroy's power: "The ambition, invention and sheer energy in this book are admirable" (14). And R. Z. Sheppard notes: "Conroy can be shameless in his extravagances of language and plot, yet he consistently conveys two fundamental emotions: the attachment to place and the passion for blood ties" ("World" 97). Extravagant language, strong storytelling abilities, the vivid evocation of landscape, and unique characters— these are the quintessential qualities of southern fiction; and Conroy has captured and mastered them, beyond question, in *The Prince of Tides*. With *Beach Music* he confirms all the qualities of the earlier novel and has surpassed them.

One possible factor in the long delay in the publishing of *Beach Music* is Conroy's current interest in another genre, writing for the screen. When Barbra Streisand acquired the film rights to *The Prince of Tides*, she enlisted Conroy's aid in working on the script. He gladly accepted the $100,000 he was offered, and the producers liked his work, but they then turned to a Hollywood professional rewriter to whom they paid $500,000 (*Major 20th Century Authors* 680). In spite of this somewhat humiliating experience, he continued to work with Streisand on the picture (she was the producer as well as one of its stars), and Conroy has said that he found the work challenging and enjoyable. Although he acknowledges that the movie is more Streisand's than his, he nonetheless thinks it is a successful adaptation because she thoroughly understood the book (Stein D5). Perhaps because of his unexpected pleasure in working on the script of *The Prince of Tides*, Conroy has embarked on several similar projects. Among others, he wrote the screenplay for a television movie, *Unconquered* (shown in January 1989), a coming-of-age film set in the South of the 1960s—certainly material that would come naturally to the author of *The Great Santini*. It has been reported that Conroy will write the screenplay for *Beach Music* (Robertson E1), and he has undertaken to do the same for Thomas Wolfe's *Look Homeward Angel*. Conroy says that when he signed that contract:

> "[T]he first person I called was Gene Norris," he says, reminding us of the vital role one book and one teacher played in his life. (*The Literary Guild Entertainer* [2])

He wrote the Introduction for Mary Edwards Wertsch's *Military Brats: Legacies of Childhood Inside the Fortress* (1991). Ms. Wertsch claims that it was seeing the movie and then reading the book, *The Great Santini*, that gave her the idea for her own work, and she quotes extensively from the novel. She also acknowledges Conroy's aid and support throughout the process of writing the book. He told Sam Staggs some years ago that he was gathering a collection of nonfiction pieces, some of which he had written to help out friends, and that he "eventually . . . ended up with enough material for a book" (86). He is said to be coauthoring a cookbook (Wilson D2), certainly another natural for the man whose *Beach Music* is filled with descriptions of food and its preparation. None of these ventures has yet appeared in print, but obviously Conroy has been writing in spite of the personal problems he has encountered (see Chapter One) since the long-awaited new novel has at last appeared. With *Beach Music* (bought for book-club rights by the Literary Guild, which outbid the Book-of-the-Month Club by paying $1.1 million), Conroy is again on the best-seller lists. Foreign publishers are also already paying six-figure sums for publishing rights, since *The Prince of Tides* has been an enormous success in at least twenty-six foreign countries. Long before publication of *Beach Music*, Hollywood stars like Barbra Streisand and Kevin Costner were showing avid interest in acquiring screen rights, so all the signs point to another great fictional and financial success for Conroy with the new novel and film. There are major roles for at least a dozen actors (unless the novel is even more pared down than was *The Prince of Tides*), and there are scenic opportunities that will make a cinematographer ecstatic with long views of the South Carolina coast and the picturesqueness of Rome.

3

The Boo
(1970) and
The Water Is Wide
(1972)

The Boo (1970, 1981, 1988) is a curious book, more interesting today for the introduction Conroy wrote for the 1981 reprinting than for the substance of the book itself. Intended not as a full-scale biography of Lieutenant Colonel Thomas Nugent Courvoisie, Assistant Commandant of Cadets at The Citadel in the years 1961–1967, but as a tribute to Courvoisie's stern yet humane administration of his duties, the book is a young author's first attempt at writing for publication. Although feared by most cadets because of his formidable voice and his demands for strict compliance with the rules, Courvoisie was also much admired for his fairness, warm understanding, and generous support in times of trouble, either personal or academic. When Conroy found out that Courvoisie had been relieved of his job for being "bad for discipline," he was outraged since this was such a transparent ruse for demoting an officer who his superiors felt had become too popular and too highly esteemed:

> The Citadel cut the flow [of Courvoisie's love for the cadets] when they fired him, when they cut down one of their own sons in his prime. When they banished him from the life with his cadets it was not merely an administrative decision: it had all the sad elements of the death of unsung kings.
> The Boo had risen too high, too fast in the estimation of the

Corps. . . . He was emblematic of what was best, the very finest the Citadel could produce. He was fired because of human
envy, because his superiors could not bear the devotional esteem in which he was held by his boys. (xiii–xiv)

Courvoisie was sent to be the officer in charge of the warehouse, a
humiliating reassignment, and one which made Conroy and even the
ever-loyal Courvoisie so angry that they decided together to write a book
that would present a true picture of what it had been like during his
tenure as assistant commandant. The album they produced does per-
petuate the image of the Boo (the affectionate name given him by the
cadets) through a series of anecdotes, copies of memoranda, reports, cartoons, and photographs. Unfortunately, it is not a very well-written or
well-organized book. Affectionate and nostalgic as the portrait of
Courvoisie is, Conroy acknowledges that the book is really more important for what it taught him about how much he still had to learn before
he was to become a real writer.

In a 1981 Introduction to a new edition of *The Boo*, Conroy explains
not only his reasons for writing the book, but also his awareness of its
literary limitations. "It is a book without a single strength except the
passionate impulse which led me to write it in the first place" (viii).
A number of other interesting points come up in this Introduction. Conroy claims that *"The Boo is The Lords of Discipline* in embryo" (x) and that
he learned more about The Citadel in writing it [*The Boo*] than he did in
his four years there as a cadet (xii). He also says that Colonel Courvoisie
was a father figure, someone readers of *The Great Santini* (or Chapter
One of this book) will recognize immediately as a person to whom Conroy would respond positively:

He was the father of the Corps, the father who replaced the
ones all of us had forsaken, and still needed, when we left
our homes for college. Like all fathers, he was both prince and
tyrant; like all fathers, there were times when he failed and
betrayed us. (xiii)

Conroy says that he thought about an entire rewriting of *The Boo*, but
rejected the idea for several reasons:

I owe the boy who wrote this book the kindness of not condescending to the best he could do at the time. And it would

take too long, and there are other things I want to write about
now. (xv)

Nevertheless, Conroy says that when he wrote the chapter called "Me
and the Boo," he felt for the first time the sound of his voice as a writer.
There are one or two other passages in *The Boo* that give hints of the
writer Conroy was to become, and there are glimpses of the humor, the
rebelliousness, and the depth of feeling that have become Conroy trade-
marks.

Since the portrait of Courvoisie as Berrineau in *The Lords of Discipline*
is far more rounded and moving than the one presented in *The Boo*, and
since Conroy readily admits this first book's literary failings, one might
wonder why he has continued to reprint it. He claims, a bit sentimentally, that he still loves the book, not only because of his affection for
Courvoisie, but because it reminds him of his beginnings as a writer: "I
have tried to explain why this is not a better book. I hope that in the
explanation, you fully understand why I love this book with all my
heart" (xvi). He also says that he enjoys the way in which The Citadel's
negative reaction to the book (at one point it was banned from the campus for six years) served to make Courvoisie a greater hero and martyr
than he had ever been in reality. It might also be added that all the
proceeds from the book have gone to a gift fund honoring Citadel graduates killed in Vietnam and that a group of alumni organized a schol-
arship fund in Courvoisie's name:

> On what other college campus in America can they raise
> fifty thousand dollars to honor the man who handles the stu-
> dents' luggage and supplies the entire campus with paper
> clips and toilet paper? (xiv–xv)

An interesting footnote on this odd scrapbook of stories about Colonel
Courvoisie is that, while Conroy borrowed $1500 to have the book pub-
lished privately in 1970, twenty years later a single, first-edition copy
would sell for nearly that amount: "Pat Conroy's first book,'The Boo,'
sold very few copies as a vanity press edition, but it now goes for $1,000"
(O'Briant 11). No doubt Conroy's success with books like *The Lords of
Discipline* and *The Prince of Tides* accounts for this remarkable phenomenon, but it is an irony of book collecting and literary prestige that a
not-very-good book that would almost certainly be forgotten today, were
it not for its author's later fame, can command such a price.

The Water Is Wide (1972) is a very different matter, indeed. As a memoir it is a form of autobiography and, therefore, is not really susceptible to the same kind of analysis as is fiction, but there is here certainly something that resembles plot and character development and perhaps even theme. For one thing, the structure of the book is carefully planned to begin with events leading up to Conroy's taking the job on Daufuskie Island (called Yamacraw in the book) and to end with his being dismissed slightly over a year later. Thus, if not strictly a plot, the narrative does have a beginning, middle, and end. We see events unfold that pit Conroy against the school administration in Beaufort and a number of people on the island itself. While Conroy's attempt to teach the children forms the core of the narrative, from the onset there are episodes that complicate this main plot development. For example, from his first encounter with Mrs. Brown, the other teacher in the two-room school, Conroy realizes that they have very different attitudes about teaching, and this becomes a running conflict throughout the book. Another conflict arises as Conroy seeks to win the confidence of the adults on the island, starting with his efforts to get their permission for the children to go to the mainland for a party. His gradual winning them over becomes a kind of subplot that ends in their unanimous support in his battle with the school administration. The episodes at the end of the book (chiefly in Chapter Eleven), in which Conroy confronts Dr. Piedmont, the school superintendent, and the vividly rendered school board meetings, where Conroy is defending himself against Piedmont's various trumped-up accusations, constitute the suspenseful climax of the action and bring the memoir to a close.

Conroy is clearly the protagonist of *The Water Is Wide*. He is not only the main character, the narrator, and the figure around whom the action revolves, he is also the heroic center of the book. Ranged against him are the antagonists, some of whom are hostile from the beginning but most of whom only gradually emerge as his enemies. Mrs. Brown clearly falls in the former category. Piedmont; Ezra Bennington, the deputy superintendent; and Ted Stone, the island's most important white resident, are among the latter. It is as they learn of Conroy's liberal views, educational and political, that they come to see him as a threat to the status quo. Not all of the secondary characters, however, are antagonists. Though they play only rather minor roles, some are strongly supportive: Conroy's new wife, Barbara; his friend, Bernie Schein; Father Becker, the priest who helps arrange the Washington trip and offers the use of a summer camp; and Zeke Skimberry, who has been tireless in his efforts to transport the children to and from the island for the trips Conroy organizes for them.

The major theme of *The Water Is Wide*, like that of *The Great Santini* and *The Lords of Discipline*, is the coming-of-age, not only of a young man, but of an innocent liberal in the South of the late 1960s. He undergoes many of the tests and disillusionments that an idealist is bound to encounter. One of his first shocks is his initial meeting with the nearly illiterate students he has engaged himself to teach. Had he explored the situation a bit more fully, he might not have committed himself to a minimum of a year's assignment on Daufuskie Island, where there seems to be little hope of his achieving anything like the educational goals he had thought possible. He is stunned by the degree of violence, superstition, and ignorance among the adults of the island. He had not imagined that there could be, only a few miles from Beaufort, a group of people who were so isolated that they seem to be from a different age and culture. Though there is nothing to suggest that it is his first sexual encounter, he meets, falls in love with, and marries Barbara Jones. Most important, perhaps, Conroy has his initiation to the machinations of mediocre men who wield power but who feel threatened by anything or anyone who might challenge their authority. These are typical rites of passage, but they are given added force by the racial overtones (except for his marriage) that influence all of them. Racial themes appear in all of Conroy's books, but nowhere are they so prominent on the plot and character levels as they are in *The Water Is Wide*.

Most of the first chapter is taken up with Conroy's teaching experience at the Beaufort high school, the total change from his previous racial attitudes, and his restlessness. He felt that he wanted to do something more challenging than to continue in his old job with a largely conservative and unimaginative faculty and a student body struggling with the fact of recent integration. When he received no answer to his application for the Peace Corps, almost on a whim he applied for the opening on Daufuskie—knowing nothing about the students he would be teaching or the conditions under which he would be working.

There are ominous signs from the beginning, when Conroy is interviewed by Henry Piedmont and taken for his first visit to the island by Bennington. Piedmont is a pompous, self-important, religious zealot. Bennington is an elderly man, demoted by school district consolidation, who "looked, talked, and acted like a huge southern cliché, a parody who was unaware that his type had been catalogued and identified over and over again" (17–18). The first person Conroy meets on Daufuskie/

Yamacraw is Ted Stone, who, with his wife, runs the island by holding every existing public office. Conroy soon comes to learn that the Stones are political and racial rednecks of the most extreme kind, but he is forced to restrain his natural instinct to speak out against such attitudes because the Stones are the ruling power on the island. Finally, on this first trip, Conroy meets Mrs. Brown (who is black). She delivers him a chilling lecture on how the children must be treated:

> "Welcome overseas," she greeted me.
> "Thank you, ma'am. It is great to be here."
> "Ho, ho, ho. Don't speak too quick. You are in a snake pit, son. And them snakes are gonna start snappin' at your toes. You're overseas now."
> She then delivered a rather ferocious homily about handling of colored children by a teacher so obviously white. (25)

That these are the four people Conroy will have to work with most closely spells trouble ahead—especially since he is so temperamentally and philosophically opposed to their ways of thinking. All of them are narrow-minded and set in their ways. All of them think that teaching the children anything substantive is doomed to failure, and therefore the main requirements of the job are to maintain a degree of order in the classroom and to keep the children from reverting to barbarism outside it. It takes Conroy some time to learn just how formidable these soon-to-be opponents really are, but when he does, it is another part of his learning experience.

The first obvious blow that Conroy receives is the realization that these fifth- through eighth-grade children know almost nothing:

> With each question I asked I got madder and madder at the people responsible for the condition of these kids. At the end of the day [his first] I had compiled an impressive ledger of achievement. Seven of my students could not recite the alphabet. Three children could not spell their names. Eighteen children thought Savannah, Georgia, was the largest city in the world. . . . Four children could not add two and two. . . . Two children did not know how old they were. Five children did not know their birth dates. Four children could not count to ten. The four oldest thought the Civil War was fought between the Germans and the Japs. (37–38)

The bulk of the memoir is given to Conroy's innovative attempts to bring these children into the twentieth-century world and to the rudiments of the culture of the country in which they live. But he has enormous obstacles to overcome before he can even begin to achieve his modest aims. In the first place, the children are shy and reticent; they don't know how to react to Conroy's quite different approach to teaching. They speak a Gullah dialect that makes it almost impossible at first for Conroy to understand what they are saying, and they cannot pronounce his name—it comes out "Conrack." He quickly realizes that the prescribed textbooks are virtually useless (since the children can't read them), and that what he must do is devise alternative means for giving them a modicum of traditional curricular material. Even more important, though, is Conroy's realization that finding imaginative ways to give them a sense of the world that exists beyond the island, and perhaps most important of all, a sense of their own self-worth are his most challenging tasks.

Conroy is remarkably inventive in some of the things he does to awaken their interests and give them something more than the dismally unsuccessful, by-the-book and by-the-strap methods Mrs. Brown has used. Through their worship of James Brown (a popular singer of the day), for example, he leads them to an enthusiasm for classical music. He teaches them geography by using the news program from a portable radio as he points out on the map the places the announcer mentions. He engages their interest by engendering a kind of pep-rally mood, encouraging their attempts to participate in the "game" Conroy makes of learning experiences. Needless to say, this noisy enthusiasm arouses the ire of Mrs. Brown:

> Our pep rallies invariably ended when Mrs. Brown's large head would peer into the window and flash disapproving, desultory glances at me and the kids. The kids reacted as if a death's-head was in the window. After school Mrs. Brown would lecture me about the "proper way to conduct yourself around colored children." She repeated her offer to buy me a leather strap. I thanked her and told her that I was looking at a bull-whip in Savannah. (63)

During the course of the year, Conroy manages trips for them, over the protests and objections of his superiors and the suspicions of some of the children's parents: first to Beaufort for a Halloween party; then to Charleston for a Globetrotters' basketball game; and even to Washington,

D.C., where the zoo turns out to be the most popular attraction. He brings visiting performers (including his sister Carol, the poet) to the classroom to read and sing for the children, who respond with delight. These are minor victories in showing the children that there is a larger world than the island, but as Anatole Broyard says: "And, most memorable of all, he taught them to trust a white man and to believe that he cared about them" (33).

Conroy attempts to give his eighteen students some individual personalities: Prophet is the class clown; the twins, Samuel and Sidney, are among those whom Conroy considers almost hopelessly learning disabled; Mary comes closest to being a real student; Oscar is the class bully; Ethel and Cindy Lou are shy, fearful adolescent girls. For the most part, however, they form a homogeneous group of children who have been beaten and told that they are retarded by Mrs. Brown and who have been raised by superstitious, distrustful parents. That Conroy is able to instill in them a degree of spontaneity and curiosity is a remarkable feat in light of that background.

Almost more daunting than his attempts at teaching the children, are Conroy's encounters with the adults on the island. Violence of all kinds, but especially marital abuse, cruelty to animals, alcoholism, and general hostility to outsiders are norms rather than aberrations among the islanders. An abiding distrust of a white man—and one from the mainland at that—is a fact of life that Conroy has to confront when he tries to get their permission to allow the children to go on the trips he plans. Not only are many of the parents suspicious of anything "different," but they fear the simple matter of having their children getting in a boat and crossing the water. Again, only a few of these are individualized, but among the most interesting is Edna Graves, the island matriarch, whose dogs nearly kill Conroy when he first calls on her. He gradually wins her over, in part because the children have come to idolize him and in part because she despises Mrs. Brown. With Mrs. Graves's approval, Conroy has a valuable ally as he tries to reason with the others.

Yet if he wins some of his battles with the island mentality, he loses others. He is appalled at the way both adults and children treat animals, including their pets, and though the children nod their heads when he lectures them about this, they go home and continue the abuse they have always practiced. In a move calculated to teach the children something about love and compassion, Conroy finds some puppies that need homes. The children are at first delighted with the prospect of having dogs of their own, but when some months later Conroy visits one of the houses to which a new puppy has gone, he finds that the poor animal has become just like all the others on the island, and he regrets having initiated the project. In an effort to teach the boys something about "rules" and sportsmanship, Conroy encourages them to play football and basketball, to which they respond with great enthusiasm, but with total disregard for "rules" and fair play. When he tries to put some order in their games, the children react as if *he* is the one who fails to understand the nature of the game. Conroy is, of course, discouraged by these failures, but he has the good sense also "to measure the importance of small victories" (161).

Meanwhile, changes are taking place in Conroy's personal life that will have profound effects on his work on the island. He falls in love during the fall of 1969 with a Vietnam War widow, Barbara Jones, who has one child and is pregnant with a second. They are married in October. For a time Conroy continues to live on the island during the week and return to Beaufort for the weekends, but this arrangement proves a strain on family life, and his quarters in a rat-infested house on the island are certainly less than satisfactory. Thus, he begins a daily commute to the island. While there are pleasures and the opportunity for meditation in the solitary journey during pleasant weather, in the bitter cold of January and the impenetrable fogs that follow, the daily trip proves to be a torture:

> The river remained temperamental and full of surprises. When I was certain that the cold was my most formidable enemy, I was challenged one morning by a prowling, spectral nemesis that crept along the lowcountry as silent as an egret's flight—the fog. . . . I had no compass and hoped that the routine of the daily commute would be enough to deliver me to the island. But the deeper I went into the soul of the fog, the more helplessly lost I became, the more confused, and the more panicked. (188)

In spite of these natural obstacles, Conroy perseveres and is seldom late for classes, even though he has to fight the elements and once grounds himself on a sandbar.

Ironically, it is a few instances of being late and the money needed for gas for the boat that provide Piedmont and the rest of the administration the opening wedges they use to humiliate Conroy and finally to fire him. He had written a vehement letter to Piedmont soon after he arrived on the island, complaining of the conditions he has found there. This "insubordination" has obviously displeased the superintendent, but it is not until spring that Conroy becomes aware of the growing hostility.

Piedmont appoints a rabid racist, Howard Sedgwick, the principal of the Bluffton high school, as supervisor for the Yamacraw school: "I now had to deal with a principal who acted as though she wanted to be white and an administrative head who was sorry there were blacks" (196). From here on, it is open warfare with Piedmont, Bennington, and Sedgwick on one side (with Mrs. Brown as their passive ally) and Conroy on the other. In his youth and impetuosity he writes another letter to Piedmont announcing that he will appear before the board of education to protest Sedgwick's refusal to pay for the gas. He also sees this as an opportunity to inform the members of the conditions on the island that they would certainly never learn from Piedmont and Bennington.

His request to appear is refused because Piedmont controls the board. The warfare escalates as Sedgwick and Bennington continue to use the gas bill for the boat as their weapon, but by some clever manipulation, Conroy negotiates an uneasy, and what turns out to be, a very short-lived truce.

In a lull before the final storm, Conroy engineers, over considerable opposition and logistical problems, the exhilarating trip to Washington in May:

> The one goal I developed the first week that never changed was to prepare the kids for the day when they would leave the island for the other side. Their experience in driving oxen, cleaning fish, and catching crabs could not be classified as excellent preparation for the streets of large cities. Anything I could construe as relevant to the day when they would leave the island had a place in the classroom. (248)

The trip to Washington seems a perfect, if small, adventure in an effort to fulfill that vow Conroy has made to himself. Again, he has trouble convincing the parents and must go to Dr. Piedmont in order to gain permission over Mrs. Brown's denial. Although their hosts in suburban Washington are a bit bemused by these odd children, they are unfailingly generous and hospitable. The trip turns out to be an enormous success, and Conroy's depression about his miniscule achievement in teaching the children and his ongoing difficulties with the administration is temporarily relieved.

During the summer Conroy has the use of a playground and swimming pool in Beaufort to which he and Barbara bring seven of the children each day, and things seem to be going well. Then the axe falls! Sedgwick calls to announce that he has been fired because Piedmont has refused to pay the bills for the gas and has "had a lot of complaints about you" (266). Conroy immediately confronts Piedmont and insists on a meeting with the board of education. Meanwhile, he and his friend, Bernie Schein, enlist the parents on Yamacraw Island to initiate a petition in Conroy's favor, even though many of them need help in signing their names.

The rest of *The Water Is Wide* is given over to the ongoing battle between Conroy and his adversaries, Piedmont and Bennington, and the majority of the board whom Piedmont controls. The description of the board meeting is a strong piece of courtroom-like reporting, with the drama of statement and counter-statement and the noisy audience pleas in Conroy's behalf (from, among others, three black mothers, including Edna Graves). Finally, in executive session, which Piedmont hoped to sway in his favor, the board votes to support Conroy:

> But the victory, if one could call it that, was ephemeral and elusive, a brief and strident shout atop a mountain that was more noise than substance, more smoke than flames. Piedmont and I had locked horns in a furious encounter, separated by an insurmountable gap of thirty years. The victory strengthened my belief that a man could speak the truth to his elders, to the new scribes and pharisees, and not be crucified or vilified because of it. . . .
> But that was when I was young. (278)

As the new school year begins, although he has told Piedmont that he wants to spend only this one more year on the island, Conroy is full of ambitious plans for more trips, and the new Vista volunteers have great success with the children. Even Mrs. Brown seems more subdued. Then the final war erupts as Piedmont fires Conroy for "disobeying instructions, insubordination, conduct unbecoming a professional educator, and gross neglect of duty" (285). When the people of the island hear about this they vow to strike the school. But they underestimate the weapons in Piedmont's armory. Truant officers arrive the day after the boycott begins, threatening fines and jail sentences. Another man comes to tell one woman that, unless her children return to school, her welfare checks will be stopped. Conroy even receives a notice that the draft board is reclassifying him I-A. He realizes that he and the people have no way to resist these kinds of pressure and calls off the boycott. He tries one more appeal before the board, which this time reverses its former decision, and the case finally ends in court, where once again the verdict is against him.

Part of the change of heart on the part of many of the board members, Conroy knows, is because he and Barbara have agreed to allow three of the island children to live with them while they go to Beaufort High School:

> Some ugly talk circulated behind our backs and some felt this ugly talk encouraged Piedmont to place my head on the chopping block. Indeed I had trouble choosing my most heinous crime. I had embarrassed Piedmont in front of the board, and had brought niggers into my home. It looked as though the Old South was still alive and well. (287)

Thus, in the form of a memoir about his year of teaching on Daufuskie Island, Conroy has done far more than merely describe chronologically what happened. Though they may not be three-dimensional characters, he has presented vivid portraits of at least a half a dozen personalities such as Edna Graves, whose fierce integrity contrasts so pointedly with the self-serving lies and underhanded tactics of men like Piedmont and Bennington. It would have been easy, in his anger, to make total villains of men like these, but Conroy, to his credit, says:

> I also saw that Piedmont and Bennington were not evil men. They were just predictably mediocre. Their dreams and aspirations had the grandeur, scope, and breadth of postage stamps. . . . They did not feel the need for redemption, because they had already been redeemed. The only thing they could not control was their fear. (299)

He comes to feel pity for Mrs. Brown: "a woman victimized by her own insecurity. She wanted so badly to be accepted by whites" (301). And he can even forgive Ted Stone, who sabotaged the boat that was to have brought witnesses from the island to Conroy's trial.

In addition to these character portraits, Conroy has touched on many aspects of the theme of southern racial attitudes. He speaks about the mediocrity of so many of the people in power (including the politicians who listen, pretend sympathy, and then do nothing) and the way they use that power to manipulate events to their advantage. But what is obviously the most important thing in the book, even beyond his tales of what happened, is his recognition of, and report on, how this year has been an incredible learning experience for him.

Almost all of the final chapter of *The Water Is Wide* is devoted to Conroy's self-analysis and what he has learned from the experience. Among many things that he must learn is to compromise, control his rash temper, and develop a degree of diplomacy. His ego has interfered with what should have been his priority—to remain with the children on Daufuskie, even at the cost of some face. Although it is primarily in this last chapter that Conroy recognizes so much about what brought about his downfall, scattered through the book there are brief moments of insight: from the early recognition of how retrograde his racial attitudes had been to his realization that when he and Bernie brought the children to Beaufort for parties, it may have done more for their own efforts at "do-gooderism" than any substantive good it did for the children. He admits that he has a "bleeding-heart theory of discipline" (175), and that, somewhere short of Mrs. Brown's strap, he might have done more to "civilize" the children with a sterner hand. If, during the course of the year, he has seen some of his naiveté and mistakes, he has also learned something of his strengths:

> Piedmont could not scare me. Nor could Bennington. Nor could the assembled board of education in all its measly glory. For in crossing the river twice daily I had come closer to more basic things. . . . The river, the tides, and the fog were part of a great flow and a fitting together of harmonious parts. (267)

Although this self-confidence receives some severe blows during the latter part of the book, he comes, after his initial fury at the inequity of his being fired (and the way in which it was accomplished), to a calm recognition that he has had an enriching experience no one will ever be able to take away from him. (He also displays, in passages like the one above, hints of the prose stylist he is to become.) In a final bit of poignant self-knowledge, Conroy says:

> Of the Yamacraw children I can say little. I don't think I changed the quality of their lives significantly or altered the

inexorable fact that they were imprisoned by the very circum-
stance of their birth. I felt much beauty in my year with them.
For them I leave a single prayer: that the river is good to them
in the crossing. (302–03)

The Water Is Wide is a remarkably resonant title for this book in which
Conroy explains in so many ways the gulf between the island children
and the rest of the world. When Mrs. Brown says, ''Welcome overseas,''
she means something entirely defeatist. Conroy's effort, from the very
beginning, is in trying to help them bridge the gap and prepare for their
eventual, and almost inevitable, crossing of that water. The water is both
real and metaphorical: it is educational and cultural as well as geograph-
ical. His personal battles with Piedmont and the school board quite aside,
Conroy has made heroic efforts in his attempts to bring the Yamacraw
children into a twentieth-century realization of where they are going to
have to live.

In an analogy that certainly should not be pushed too far, there are
some fascinating parallels between *The Boo* and *The Water Is Wide*. Both
protagonists have been fired from their jobs because, in one sense, they
have done them too well. Their superiors are embarrassed by the popularity and success that these men have had, which the upper echelons
see, correctly, as reflections on their own failures in leadership. The cases
differ in the degree to which the superiors are responsible for the catas-
trophes that have ensued from their lack of imagination and integrity,
but the parallels are obvious. Mediocre and mean-spirited men at the
top have felt threatened by the imagination, the boldness, and the refusal
to compromise of their juniors. They have used their power to rid themselves of the objectors, but their victories are Pyrrhic. Courvoisie becomes
a legend at The Citadel, and Conroy is inspired to become a writer. Both
men, one a hardened veteran of many encounters with authority, and
the other, a brash young man who has much to learn about himself and
his relationship to those who hold his destiny in their hands, maintain
their integrity in the face of intense efforts to break it down; and both,
to their temporary discomfort, suffer the results of their resolution. In
the end, however, they prove to be far stronger in matters of accounta-
bility and honor than their titular superiors.

The Great Santini
(1976)

The Great Santini (1976) is a developing writer's first work of fiction (Conroy was thirty-one when it was published), and it is immediately recognizable as a coming-of-age novel. It covers almost exactly the year in the life of Ben Meecham in which he struggles to achieve maturity and establish his own identity as he turns eighteen, is graduated from high school, and is required to assume the role of "man of the family." It is also a thinly veiled autobiographical account of the conflict between father and son, a theme which is frequently a major element in the novel of initiation. Thus, *The Great Santini*, in plot, character, and structure has many parallels to novels like Lawrence's *Sons and Lovers*, and Joyce's *A Portrait of the Artist as a Young Man*. In theme it echoes darker versions of the story such as *Hamlet*, *Oedipus Rex*, and Mary Renault's *The King Must Die*.

Among several secondary themes, *The Great Santini* explores the curious rituals of military male bonding, particularly in the U. S. Marine Corps; the negative effects on family solidarity and security in the nearly annual transfers of armed service personnel; race relations and their terrible effects in the rural South of the 1960s; the pinched mentality and morality of Roman Catholic catechism and education; athletics as a metaphor for manhood; and, most especially, the psychology of a man who is a symbol of all that is most admired in a fighter pilot, but who is, at the same time, a symbol of almost all that is worst in a husband and father.

NARRATIVE POINT OF VIEW

Conroy uses conventional, third-person, omniscient narration in *The Great Santini*, but does from time to time narrow that focus so that we see events through the eyes of, and experience the emotions of, individual characters. That is to say, to a limited extent we get inside the person's mind instead of observing her or him only from the outside. This happens primarily with Ben, occasionally with his father, Bull, and once or twice with Lillian (Ben's mother). In a slightly different way, dialogue is often so revealing that a character's psyche, such as that of Ben's sister, Mary Anne, is exposed in all its pain and insecurity, although nothing about these problems has been explicitly stated.

Good examples of Conroy's going into Ben's mind occur when he analyzes the play of others on the basketball court, when he fantasizes about a sexual encounter with Ansley Matthews, and most poignantly, at the end of the novel, when he accepts his father's death and its implications. Since Bull is not an introspective man, there are fewer cases in which we are privy to his inner thought, but one of the most revealing occurs at the beginning of Chapter Twelve, when he realizes, but doesn't fully understand why, achieving his lifelong dream of becoming a squadron commander is not as satisfying as he had expected it would be. Almost any of Mary Anne's acerbic verbal exchanges with Ben or her father reveals the inferiority complex and bitterness of this unhappy girl.

Another aspect of narrative point of view (which also determines, in part, the structure of the novel) is Conroy's use of discrete chapters focusing on Bull and his life as a Marine, interspersed with the chapters focusing on Ben and the events that shape his character during this critical year of his life. Of the thirty-four chapters in the novel, eight are devoted almost exclusively to Bull's military duties, his activities as squadron commander, his wild carousing in off-duty hours, and the pride he takes in his role as fighter pilot. These chapters are scattered through the novel in no exact pattern, but this separation of material about Bull as Marine from material having to do with his life as husband and father serves several important symbolic and thematic purposes. It emphasizes his near total commitment to his professional life; his family is merely an adjunct to that, often an annoying one, in spite of his insistence on their being a model of Marine Corps decorum.

More damaging to the portrait of Bull that emerges, these chapters often focus on the puerile behavior of grown men who, in drunken abandon, or even without the excuse of drunkenness, behave like crude schoolboys: the revolting incident of simulated vomiting in Chapter One; pulling down the pants of a startled corporal in a latrine in Six; the drunken brawl in Twenty-six. Bull's behavior and that of the other "mature" men is so disgustingly immature that it helps to elevate Ben's hesitant, but far more constructive, reactions to the challenges he faces: his intervening to protect Sammy Wertzberger from the attack of Red Pettus, the school bully; his determination and sportsmanship on the basketball court; his courageous attempt to help Toomer Smalls in Chapter Thirty-one. The stark contrast of these scenes underlines Bull's arrested development in spite of his blustering "Stand-by-for-a-fighter-pilot" melodramatics while Ben is quietly but rapidly developing into a sensitive, brave adult with admirable attitudes and values.

PLOT DEVELOPMENT AND STRUCTURE

The plot of *The Great Santini* is a linear, episodic one covering significant events in the year—from the early summer of 1962 to the late spring of 1963—when Ben (about halfway through the novel) celebrates his eighteenth birthday. It begins with Bull's airborne return from overseas and ends with his death in a fiery flying accident. Thus, the novel is framed and formally structured by Bull's arrival and departure.

Aside from the counterpart of the chapters focused on Bull, the major pattern of the plot is a series of episodes in which Ben is tested, reacts either positively or in embarrassment, and emerges somewhat stronger, and certainly wiser, for the experience. For example, after Bull has imperiously arranged a date for Ben with Ansley Matthews, and he has grudgingly but dutifully done what his parents want, she shamelessly deserts him to go off with her steady boyfriend. Ben's first reaction is one of humiliation and anger; but when Sammy appears and convinces him that it is she who has behaved badly, Ben, if only subconsciously, has gained a degree of self-respect. When, through his skill and long hours of practice, Ben makes the basketball team, it is another important step in the achievement of his identity, but he accepts the position with humility; he feels more in common with the boys who failed to make the team than with those arrogant members of it that he will be joining. A traumatic learning experience occurs when, against all his natural instincts of sportsmanship, Ben obeys Bull's command to "hurt" an opposing player. As he deliberately fouls Peanut Abbott and breaks his arm, Ben knows immediately that he has behaved disgracefully and that he deserves his punishment of being barred from athletics for the remainder of the year. From this mistake and the good advice of the high school principal, Mr. Dacus, Ben has learned, not only that he should never betray himself by behaving dishonorably, but also that when his father or anyone else urges him to do something he knows is wrong, he should refuse.

Along with tests such as these, there are chapters devoted to traditional rites-of-passage thresholds that Ben crosses: learning to fish and hunt with Toomer's guidance, coming to a realization of his sexual maturity, critically examining religious formulae that he had heretofore accepted without question, realizing that his own instincts about when a prank has gone too far are better than Sammy's. Thus, *The Great Santini* is a classic novel of initiation, plotted in the same episodic way as *Huckleberry Finn* and *The Catcher in the Rye* although it deals with a slightly older boy and the problems Huck and Holden will have to face some years hence. While this kind of plot development works well for putting Ben through a series of tests, it, almost of necessity, leaves other plot elements unresolved. For example, when Bull flies off to Cuba, since there seems to be a threat of invasion or war, there is no follow-up (as there would be in a more organically developed plot) to explain the outcome.

Otherwise, the plot of *The Great Santini* is a conventionally structured one. We are given explicit signals about the turn of the seasons: the family's move to Ravenel (in reality, Beaufort), South Carolina, takes place in August; there are several chapters devoted to Christmas festivities; Ben's disgrace and dismissal from the basketball team occur in February; the high school prom takes place in April; and Bull dies in May. There is no doubt that Conroy has deliberately framed the novel this way; the ending in late spring is a clear way of announcing Ben's emergence into "new life." In keeping with the *Bildungsroman* tradition (defined in Chapter Two), Ben arrives at the end, if not finally, at least more than tentatively, in control of himself and his identity:

> And for the flight-jacketed boy on the road to Atlanta, he
> filled up for the first time, he filled up even though he knew

the hatred would return, but for now, he filled up as if he would burst. Ben Meecham filled up on the road to Atlanta with the love of his father, with the love of Santini. (536)

CHARACTER DEVELOPMENT

As in any good novel, the characters in *The Great Santini* are revealed through their actions and their words far more often and more power- fully than through description by the omniscient narrator. In a contin- uous interplay of action and character, Conroy presents the major and most of the secondary figures. Ben Meecham, for example, is shaped and developed by the events in which he becomes a participant, but to some extent he becomes involved in those events and behaves as he does be- cause of the values and attitudes he has already embraced. The early episode in which he intervenes on behalf of Sammy Wertzberger shows Ben acting courageously (egged on by Mary Anne) in confronting Red Pettus; at the same time it gives him a measure of esteem and confidence in the new school environment in which he needs to establish himself. In any given situation Bull Meecham acts as he does because of the per- son he is, but the person creates those same situations. His shameful ordering of Ben to foul an opponent, for example, is the aggressive Bull of fighter pilot fame. And, while Ben is humiliated by what he has done, Bull is delighted because he believes it will show the college scouts that Ben is a fighting player.

Ben is clearly the protagonist (main character, "hero") of the novel. On one level, he is a normal, likable, adolescent boy, with the problems, confusions, and energies that go with being seventeen. He has acne; he is timid and inexperienced but increasingly interested in girls; he is more and more resistant to the narrow, unrealistic Roman Catholic positions on religious faith and sex; he puts great emphasis on athletics and his success in them; and he has begun to seek an identity of his own (no longer content merely to be his father's son). In combination with the tests of his manhood and values that are the major episodes of the plot, the primary factor in defining Ben's character is the contest of wills with his father that has existed as long as Ben can remember, but which comes to a climax in this year. Known to psychologists as Oedipal conflict, this very common struggle between father and son takes its name from the mythological Greek king who unknowingly kills his father and marries his mother. Although he occasionally says he wishes his father were

dead, Ben doesn't really want that so much as he wants the release from
the constant tension between them that Bull's assignment to another
overseas post would bring. Yet, Ben, at least subconsciously, knows that
he must break the hold his father has over him if he is ever to become
a man in his own right. While there are no overt sexual overtones in
Ben's relationship with Lillian, there is a clear bond between them that
excludes Bull, and, to some extent, the rest of the children.

For seventeen years Ben (and indeed the whole family as it has grown
to include three other children) has been almost totally dominated by
Bull's autocratic rule. Ben has grown up a sensitive, intelligent boy, but
a very insecure one because he has been shaped and disciplined in the
military-style conformity and lack of emotion his father insists upon and
because he has been consistently denigrated by Bull's notions of how
best to train a "hog." As Lillian has attempted to protect the children
from some of Bull's most crude, aggressive behavior, she has instilled in
them some sense of gentleness and culture; but it is Bull who has set the
tone for, and has demanded the absolute obedience of, the whole family.

Now, as Ben is gaining physical maturity and a growing need for
independence, he is for the first time able to challenge Bull's dominance.
For example, through the years Bull has trained Ben in the skills and
nuances of hard-fought basketball competition. But until now Bull has
always beaten Ben whenever they have played one-on-one in contest.
(Indeed, Bull has never lost to Ben or anyone else in the family in any
competition.) In this summer of his eighteenth birthday, Ben at last beats
Bull in basketball. The symbolic victory here is more important than the
physical one, since Ben has for the first time broken his father's
heretofore invincible power and control.

In an even more dramatic and significant event, Ben, again goaded by
Mary Anne, for the first time flagrantly disobeys his father's direct order
by going to the assistance of his friend Toomer Smalls. As it turns out,
this episode demands enormous courage and physical prowess, but the
defying of his father's command is an even more important step in Ben's
escape from Bull's dominance. This traumatic incident shows Ben at his
best; his loyalty to his friend overrides his personal fear, and he is inventive in doing his best to rescue Toomer. In spite of his heroic efforts,
he fails to save Toomer and must cope with removing his body from the
vortex of savage dogs that has killed Red Pettus and would do the same
to Ben were he not clever and brave beyond his years. This event, which
comes late in the novel, brings together the themes of personal test and

conflict with the father, so in proving himself here, Ben has made large strides in his journey toward manhood.

Finally, in Chapter Thirty-two, Bull arrives home from an orgy of drinking at the officers' mess and proceeds to a physical battering of Lillian and the younger children. Led by Ben, they overpower him, and he staggers out into the night. Seething with anger, Ben goes in search of his father, finds him passed out on the town green, and manages to guide him home. But, in this episode, Ben rises for the first time above his hatred for his father:

> Twenty minutes before he would have spit on this obscenity in the grass or thought he would have done it. Now he was trying to resuscitate the hatred he had felt in the kitchen. But it would not come. . . .
> He heard himself saying, unbelieving, unwilling:
> "I love you, Dad." (489–90)

In this mature realization and reaction to Bull's insufferable behavior, Ben has become a dignified man while Bull is shown in his helpless, deplorable childishness. Ben is not fully conscious of all of this (and certainly Bull is not), but it marks an irreversible change in their relationship. Later, at the very end of the novel, when Bull dies in the plane accident, one of the townsmen turns to Ben and says, "You become [*sic*] a man this morning, Ben" (523). But this is only the final, symbolic event in the process that began with the basketball victory and reached its climax when Ben showed his maturity in dealing with his extremely immature, drunken father.

Yet, if Ben has survived and grown in the tests of his manhood among his peers and, partly through his own strength and partly through Bull's death, "won" the Oedipal conflict, there is one other, perhaps even more daunting, barrier to a fully achieved, independent personality. As Mary Anne constantly reminds him, his excessive desire to be good, to please, is not only annoying, but, more important, a flaw in his character. Until the very end of the novel Ben fails to understand her criticism, but in his coming to a realization of the truth in what she has been saying, he has at least made the step without which he would never be able to conquer this weakness.

Lamar York explores in depth this theme (which runs through Conroy's work) in his essay, "Pat Conroy's Portrait of the Artist as Young

Southerner." York focuses on the way this desire to be liked, this need for approval, is an impediment to the artist's absolute need "to tell the truth," no matter who may be hurt or offended, but he also analyzes it as Ben's most serious weakness. It takes no great psychological insight to recognize how this quest on Ben's part came about: with a father who has shown nothing but contempt for everything the boy has done or tried to do, it is only natural that the child would develop a desire to please, to gain a word of praise or at least approval. Furthermore, as Ben says repeatedly, he simply wants to stay out of Bull's way, and the easiest way of doing that is to do what his father demands. Thus, it is Bull, in his harsh, unbending attitudes, who has created this need in Ben. On the other hand, Ben, who has always seen himself as Mary Anne's greatest ally, comes at the end to realize that he has actually hurt her:

> Because he had been afraid, he had said "yes" to everything his parents wanted, had let himself be sculpted by his parents' wishes, had danced to the music of his parents' every dream, and had betrayed his sister by not preparing them for a girl who would not dance. (533)

Ben is too hard on himself, but the element of truth in this moment of introspection is painful for it undermines one of the things in which he has taken pride. The next step, moving to eradicate the flaw, will be even more painful and difficult since it will require a near total readjustment of some of his values. We can only speculate about whether or not he will be able to do so, but two things are certain: (1) this bit of self-knowledge is as important as anything else that has occurred in Ben's coming to manhood; and (2) that he has begun to grasp and regret some of the less admirable implications of his past behavior is a hopeful sign that he will continue to grow.

While it may be an oversimplification to say that the lack of this kind of self-knowledge is the chief reason for Bull Meecham's failures as husband, father, and, ultimately, human being, it is certainly among the things that have made him what he is. Clearly Bull is the novel's antagonist (the opponent of the protagonist) in that he makes his family's life an ongoing torment by treating them as if they were Marine Corps recruits. His severe insistence on military discipline and order in the household would almost be a joke if it were not so damaging to the emotional and psychological fabric of their lives and if it were not such an obvious clue to the hollowness of Bull's character. Time and again Lillian and the children are the victims of his anger, his insensitivity, his egomania, and his brutishness. The man is incapable of, or so insecure that he fears, any display of affection and normal familial warmth. He has become so imbued with what is almost a parody of the Marine Corps ethos of rigid discipline, iron-willed refusal to show any inner feelings, and delight in one-upmanship that he fails to make any distinction between his relationships in the military and those with his wife and children.

Lillian, in one of her more intimate conversations with Ben, puts Bull's character in perfect profile:

> "Your father has taken the whole mythology of the Corps, or what he interprets as the mythology, and entwined it with his own personality. . . . The Marine Corps takes a small ego and makes it gigantic; it takes a large ego and then steps back to see how large it can grow." (240)

Moreover, Bull is the worst kind of authority figure—one who insists on absolute control of the behavior of his subordinates but one who exercises none over his own. He is so aggressively competitive that he plays Chinese checkers with his younger daughter, Karen, as if it were a duel to death with enemy aircraft. If Lillian sums him up in one way, Mr. Dacus does so in another:

> "Your father is the dream of a high school principal or a deputy sheriff. He believes in the institution over the individual even when the individual is his own child. That's why he's such a good Marine." (441)

Conroy uses Bull as the foil against whom Ben must struggle to gain his own identity, but he is clearly interested also in the psyche of Colonel Meecham as a representative of what may have been superb in a World War II and Korean War fighter pilot, yet is so sadly lacking in a man functioning in any other role. How does a person, even a not very well-educated, insensitive one like Bull Meecham, come to be the near ogre he is in the novel? Something is obviously wrong with a man who feels exhilaration in running over turtles on the highway, who calls himself the invulnerable Great Santini to remind everyone of what he takes to be his awesome achievements, who takes delight in embarrassing enlisted men and black cleaning women, who inflicts physical damage on his children when they displease him.

Robert Burkholder, in his article, "The Uses of Myth in Pat Conroy's *The Great Santini*," offers some interesting suggestions in answer to these questions. Burkholder posits, but does not follow through to all the logical implications of, the hypothesis that Bull, for several reasons, has become frozen in the mythos of the fighter pilot as he was twenty-odd years before. Because he lacks the inner resources to change with the times and lacks the vision even to see any reason for doing so, his military career is in jeopardy, and he fails to distinguish between what may have been appropriate in a fighter pilot and what is appropriate as a husband and father. Bull clings to an obsolete myth of Marine Corps valor, bravado, and invincibility as a mask to disguise the emptiness beneath the facade. Ben rightly says that his father is acting a part, and two of his superiors, as well as his best friend, tell him that his behavior is outdated and destructive.

What emerges is at once a damning critique of an unexamined military mentality and, ultimately, of a pathetic man empty at the core. His delight in his self-appropriated sobriquet, The Great Santini, and his nickname, Bull (gained by having served at El Toro air base in California and his having a bull-like physique) as opposed to his given name, Wilbur, reveals a great deal about a man with a severe identity problem. That he could seriously compare his responsibilities as squadron commander to those of God; that he could play "war" games with his children oblivious to the physical harm he could do them, to say nothing of the emotional harm; that he could take pride in being offensive and inconsiderate—these and many other examples expose a man of badly flawed character and almost no self-knowledge.

There are rare moments when the mask drops away and Bull shows a warmer, even tender side: his determined effort to find Ben a spot on a Little League team; his playing a reindeer on the roof at Christmas time; his insistence that Mary Anne have a new dress for the high school prom. But these are indeed rare moments, and even many of them are tainted by their perhaps subconscious intent of self-promotion rather than genuine concern for others. Still, both the wise Mr. Dacus and Lillian insist that Bull really loves his family but is simply incapable of, or disdains, showing it in conventional ways. By the end of the novel, Ben has come a long way toward accepting this paradox, which Lillian, and most interestingly, Mary Anne have understood for a long time. In spite of his gallant, final gesture in steering his burning plane away from a populated area, the portrait of Bull Meecham that remains is one of a person who may have achieved legendary status as a fighter pilot but whose failures in the more important aspects of manhood have been enormous.

Of the other characters in the novel, only Lillian and Mary Anne are three-dimensional. Lillian, a Southerner, comes from a cultural heritage quite different from Bull's working-class, Chicago background. Indeed, the values of these two cultures are in many ways antithetical. He comes from a rough, every-man-for-himself, Roman Catholic neighborhood where only physical, athletic interests are seen as appropriate for the male and where "nice guys finish last." She, advocating perhaps a bit naively, the old southern code of refinement, honor, and gentility, tries to instill in the children an appreciation of good manners, a love of literature and the other arts, and a consideration for others. Thus, even aside from Bull's special brand of brutishness, there is a continuing tension in the family as mother and father try to mold the children in their opposing value systems. Lillian's strategy is not only an attempt to pass on what she believes to be critical attributes, but to keep the children from being shaped completely by Bull's cold, anti-intellectual, self-serving philosophy.

In addition to enduring the constant bluster and arrogant issuing of orders, sometimes even the physical abuse that Bull heaps on her, another burden that falls to Lillian is acting as a buffer between Bull and the children in the continuing battle between them. As she frequently tells Ben, she is always in the middle, a difficult role she must play on an almost daily basis. Ben and the others have learned never to cross Bull unless their mother is present, for only she can blunt his violent temper and the physical damage he is capable of inflicting on them. Lillian's sympathies are usually with the children, but she must often pretend to support her husband while trying to soften his rigid, unreasonable demands.

In order to continue in her difficult position, both as wife and mother, Lillian, as Burkholder points out, has formed a protective shield of her own. As a convert to Roman Catholicism, she has adopted exaggerated positions on matters of prayer and faith. Her shrine, which Mary Anne calls Our Lady of the Fighter Pilot, includes, along with traditional icons, a plastic model of an F-8 fighter plane. Her unshakable, romanticized southern values (her favorite book is *Gone With the Wind* and she identifies with Scarlett O'Hara) are a form of denial. But by far the most blatant lie in her protective shield is that Bull has never physically attacked her. We see several instances in the novel itself (and Ben reminds her of a number of other episodes) in which Bull hits and kicks her. She simply denies that it has happened. She tells Ben at least twice that if Bull ever treats her again as he has just done, she will leave him, but both Ben and Lillian herself know that this is not true.

All these form a facade that is at once pathetic in its transparency and self-deception and admirable in its power to sustain her in the difficult roles she must play. She is unquestionably devoted to her children and, in spite of the turmoil and pain he makes of their lives, to Bull. Lillian emerges, then, as a valiant woman (Mary Anne calls her Saintly Lillian) with an inner strength belied by her surface beauty and by her willingness to compromise her integrity for the sake of keeping the family a viable, if always troubled, unit.

Mary Anne is undoubtedly the most complex and tormented character in the novel. Ben's problems with growing up and with his father are, if traumatic, fairly straightforward conflicts. They are relatively easy to understand both in their sources and in the solutions they require. Mary Anne's conflicts are much deeper and resistant to resolution. She is at once the overweight, nearsighted, ungainly daughter of a beautiful woman and a stern, insensitive father. In Ben's critical self-examination at the end of the novel, he says he has always thought this to be the cause of her inferiority complex and bitterness. Surely he is at least partly correct in that analysis. But by the time of the events in the book, Mary Anne's problems have become a neurosis. She talks to Ben several times about suicide, and both he and she know that, at the moment, this is a form of self-dramatization. In combination, however, with other signs of emotional instability, these threats are ominous signs for the future.

Unlike Ben, Mary Anne refuses to "play the game" of trying to please her parents. She is the ugly duckling, and instead of trying to ameliorate that disadvantage by being cooperative, at every opportunity, she takes the opposite action of doing or saying something to annoy or anger her parents and even her siblings. This behavior is, of course, a kind of self-fulfilling invitation to more unhappiness. She mocks her mother's religion and her father's self-importance. She cannot resist taunting her younger brother, Matt. It is true that Ben, who, however awkwardly, looks to her as a soul mate and thinks of himself as her protector, is, in fact, the cause of some of her distress since she cannot or will not behave as he does. But to whatever degree he hurts her, the fault is unintentional. Mary Anne's problems come from much more profound personality troubles than having a straight-arrow brother.

Because she has renounced any attempt to play the docile daughter, Mary Anne is far more audacious than Ben: she more openly mocks what

Conroy sees as the banal Roman Catholic dogma than Ben, who is only beginning to question; she confronts her mother with the bases of their conflict; and, in two crucial incidents, it is she who goads Ben into courageous action. Admirable as these forthright positions may be, they are at the same time self-defeating. The more she thumbs her nose at convention and traditional behavior, the more isolated she becomes.

Mary Anne retreats into a kind of esoteric, intellectual cocoon, but she, of all the characters in the novel, has the most accurate insights about the psyches and reactions of the other members of the family. She knows that Lillian's pious bromides are a sham and that, actually, Bull in all his boorishness and cruelty is the more honest of the two. She knows, and finally shames Ben into acknowledging, that his efforts to please and keep out of trouble are weak and unworthy stances. Mary Anne speaks often of becoming a writer, and it seems as if she has, in her intelligence, her love of words, and her keen knowledge of human nature, many of the qualities that would make her a successful one. Yet, at the end of the novel, there seems to be little that would suggest a change in her personality. Bull's death gives Ben, and to some extent Lillian, a new freedom, but Mary Anne seems trapped in her neurotic insecurity.

Of the secondary characters, several are important for the roles they play in Ben's development, and several are important in showing that not all good Marines are caricatures of the sort that Bull is. Toomer Smalls, a black man, lame and halting of speech, is one of the most obvious of Ben's several surrogate fathers. Physically he is the opposite of Bull, but in his quiet dignity, he is the more admirable man. He teaches Ben to hunt and fish and gives him a feeling of confidence with nature. Lillian wisely encourages this bonding of Ben and Toomer, for she knows that what Toomer can give Ben are valuable attributes of the southern tradition she so venerates and also that it is the kind of relationship Ben will never find with Bull. Toomer is warmly regarded by most of the white people of Ravenel, but he becomes a victim of a red-necked, bigoted minority. Like Ben, Toomer has always aimed to please others and to avoid conflict, but when pushed too far by Red Pettus, he reacts with more than justified anger and strength. This proves to be the catalyst for the episode that ends in death for both Toomer and Red, but it is also, indirectly, the catalyst for Ben's most important act of courage and independence.

Among other surrogate fathers, the high school principal, Mr. Dacus, is an extremely affecting figure. He too is everything that Bull is not: a former athlete, but one with a keen sense of sportsmanship; a man who

knows when harsh discipline is in order and when sympathetic support
is called for; a sensitive judge of character and a wise counselor. Mr.
Dacus applauds Ben for standing up for Sammy Wertzberger and for his
success on the basketball court in ways that are much more encouraging
than Bull's gruff, grudging criticism. Perhaps the most telling episode,
however, is when Ben is in jail and Bull not only hits him but believes
the crude sheriff's very strained accusations about what Ben has done.
Thanks to Sammy's knowing the right person to whom he should turn,
Mr. Dacus uses the considerable force of his personality to get Ben released. Even more important than the physical act is Mr. Dacus's fatherly
belief in the boy and his emotional support at a difficult moment:

> "I'm cold," Ben said looking out toward the river.
> "Why didn't you tell me, pissant," Mr. Dacus said. He put
> his arm around Ben and pulled him close to his body. It was
> not the hardness of the principal's body that amazed Ben; it
> had something to do with the realization that he had never
> been held this closely and lovingly by a man. Slowly Ben put
> his arm around the man's waist as they turned toward the
> Dacus home. (442)

Ben's godfather, Vergil Hedgepath, is another surrogate father and is
Bull's best friend; but, unlike Bull, he knows when Marine Corps she-
nanigans are appropriate and when they are not. This makes him, along
with Bull's superiors, Luther Windham and Joe Varney, a man who has
had the ability to grow and change. It is no accident that of these four
contemporaries, the other three have been promoted while Bull has been
passed over. Bull sneers at Varney's polished speech and refined tastes,
and he resents Varney's insistence on the protocols that go with the difference in their ranks. Vergil, like Varney, has the qualities that make
him capable of commanding men with a quiet voice and steel-hard resolve—ultimately more effective and becoming in a senior officer than
the yelling, cursing drill-sergeant approach that Bull adopts.

In the large cast of minor characters, a few are used to comment on
the social and psychological climate of Ravenel and, therefore, of the
world in which Ben finds himself. Sammy Wertzberger, as a Jew and
non-athlete, is the object of ridicule and harassment by the rough, redneck element of the school led by Red Pettus. Sammy adopts a jaunty,
defensive attitude, but the unrealistic fantasies he creates are in sharp
contrast to Ben's more thoughtful, measured responses. Against his

better judgment, Ben participates in the Tom Sawyerish attempt to blackmail Junior Palmer, the deputy sheriff, and lands in jail for his foolishness. Worse, Sammy's efforts at sexual conquest lead to the rape of Emma Lee Givens and, ultimately, to Toomer's death. As Ben survives and grows, Sammy, for all his charm and ingratiating self-deprecation, must be exiled to New York for his youthful, but nonetheless serious, indiscretion.

Red Pettus is not only a significant player in several of the episodes that test Ben's mettle, but also the representative of a whole underclass of the bigoted and ignorant. He is a bully of the ugliest sort and the only real villain in the novel. Conroy embodies in him the worst elements of southern racism. He is the antagonist against whom Ben must struggle to prove to himself and others that, like Mr. Dacus and Vergil Hedgepath, he has a power that is stronger than brutality and vicious anger.

Two more of the positive minor characters are Ben's English teacher, Ogden Loring, and Toomer's mother, Arrabelle Smalls. Loring is an eccentric and a total surprise to Ben after his experience with nuns as by-rote teachers. Ben's horizons are expanded enormously by this gifted man's totally different approach to education, and he comes to realize that Loring, in all his non-traditional, "crazy" techniques, is the best teacher he has ever had. Arrabelle embodies all the strength, poise, and dignity of the old southern black. (She is a direct literary descendant of Faulkner's Dilsey—"They endured.") Lillian says that Arrabelle and Toomer represent what was best in the old southern tradition of mutual respect that existed between cultured whites and their black servants. Whatever flaws there may be in that vision, there is also an element of truth. Toomer's death suggests that in some ways for the better, but in some ways for the worse, Arrabelle's generation is the last that will maintain that relationship.

THEMATIC ISSUES

In addition to the major coming-of-age theme in *The Great Santini* and the examination of Bull Meecham's character as an exaggerated representative of Marine Corps machismo, Conroy touches on a number of secondary themes, at least two of which are directly related to Bull's career. One is the unreflective continuation of drinking bouts that most college fraternity boys outgrow by the time of their graduation. The strange and childish antics of grown men drinking together until they are no longer rational is depicted in vivid detail in at least three lengthy scenes in the novel. These rituals are so central to a certain type of Marine's idea of solidarity that it is impossible to see them as anything but Conroy's harsh comment on yet another level of the Marine Corps mythos. Bull and others like him believe that somehow it proves their masculinity and camaraderie to "drink all night, puke all morning, and fly all afternoon" (87). There is something false and demeaning, Conroy is saying, if this kind of male bonding is the level at which these men have stopped growing and the level at which they think true courage and esprit de corps are to be reinforced.

Another effect of military life more damaging to the stability of the family is the nearly annual dislocations caused by duty transfers. The rootlessness caused by constant moving manifests itself in several ways. There are the obvious burdens of packing and unpacking, living in houses that are always temporary quarters, and adjusting to new environments. It means that the children have to start over making friends in a new school nearly every year. All the Meecham children, but especially Ben and Mary Anne, have come to dread the opening months of school because they will be outsiders, and it will take them half the year to make new friends and establish a presence, all of which will be lost six months later when the cycle repeats itself. A more subtle effect is psychological. This lack of a sense of belonging anywhere makes it hard to build a sense of identity. Ben is at a critical stage of asking, "Who am I?" Finding answers to that difficult question is made more difficult if one has no sense of roots. If there is no security in home, school, or community, especially for a young person, there is going to be a concomitant lack of security in self.

Other themes that Conroy touches on include a very unfavorable view of Roman Catholic education both in and out of the classroom. In the hands of the feckless, alcoholic Father Pinckney and the shrewish Sister Loretta, what seems to Ben and Mary Anne an already unrealistic approach to matters of sex education and faith becomes a travesty. In this instance Conroy uses satire for his attack on what seems a self-defeating, rigid catechism in answer to the genuine questions and problems of teenagers. Intended to instill obedience and allegiance to Roman Catholic dogma, Sister Loretta's sterile, humorless diatribes have precisely the opposite effect on sensitive, inquisitive minds like Ben's.

Another area, and in this case the mentor is a credible, admirable one, is the value of sports as a training ground for the building of character. Bull is a strong advocate of sports as a way of developing aggressiveness and a "killer instinct" in young men, but it is Mr. Dacus who succinctly says why it is that athletics are an important part of a young person's development:

> "It's very important, Ben. Sports show you your limits. Sports teach humility. Sooner or later the athlete becomes humble no matter how good he is. But he plays until he has reached as high as he can." (441)

Clearly, competitive athletics give the individual an opportunity to develop stamina but, more important, to develop either estimable or reprehensible traits of character. In the course of the novel, Ben shows both, but his one instance of unsportsmanlike behavior (provoked by Bull) is an aberration in his otherwise instinctive good nature. Thus, athletics become a kind of metaphor for manhood. Bull, an ungraceful loser and a savage competitor even with his own children, is revealed in part by his attitude toward sports. Mr. Dacus; Ben's Little League coach, Dan Murphy; and Ben himself are also partly defined by their notions, quite different from Bull's, about the importance of the game.

Conroy's most troubling secondary theme is the still ugly, destructive racial bigotry and hostility existing in the South of the early 1960s. Bull and nearly all the other white males use racial and other ethnic epithets without a moment's thought. Far more insidious is the active hostility of rednecks like Red Pettus and the latent animosity of even the more moderate white population (and clearly in this instance Ravenel reflects a general southern ethos). When Emma Lee Givens is raped by a black man, an instant Ku-Klux-Klan mentality takes over the town. No black man is above suspicion, and one would almost certainly have been lynched or taken as a scapegoat had not Toomer's death diverted attention from the search. Conroy doesn't pursue this plot thread to its conclusion, but the fatal confrontation between Red and Toomer is, in fact, an offshoot and a dramatic enactment of it. While on the surface, except for the angry restiveness on the part of the population represented by Red Pettus, all is calm and tolerant, there is an atavistic racial abhorrence lying just beneath that surface that can be inflamed by even a suggestion of black male aggression against a white female—or almost any other infraction of what are seen as proper roles for blacks to play.

The tranquil beauty of the riverfront town; a warm, mutually supportive relationship like that of Ben and Toomer; the cracker-barrel folksiness of Hobie's breakfast counter are all undercut by the eruption of vigilantism after Emma Lee's rape. Sammy is forced to leave town since he is believed to be responsible for the situation; Red Pettus is released from any restraints on his swaggering hostility; and Toomer is the innocent victim of this mania. Conroy shows how this malignant force touches every aspect of the town's existence and mars its otherwise alluring serenity.

STYLE AND LITERARY DEVICES

Conroy's style in *The Great Santini* is, for the most part, very serviceable and realistic. Except for periodic bursts of lyricism, the prose is straightforward and undecorated. This works well in setting the characters and plot in motion quickly and establishing the bonds and tensions in the Meecham household. The autobiographical basis of much in the novel is clear, and this doubtless contributes to the authentic ring Conroy gives to anecdotes and dialogue. The action is seldom slowed by long passages of description or introspection. While there are instances of both, the major focus of the novel is on action and reaction rather than on more subtle aspects of character and motivation. Thus, *The Great Santini* confirms in some ways Conroy's self-effacing claim to being a shallow writer (Staggs 86). At the same time, it also supports his claim to being primarily a storyteller. The "story" moves forward without flagging, and the unencumbered style is one of the major elements that helps to accomplish that.

On the other hand, *The Great Santini* is not a mere page-turner. There are aspects of Conroy's style that give the novel depth and a richer texture than is suggested by the adjective "shallow." Although somewhat self-conscious, there are a number of lyrical passages that create mood and provide a background against which action is set. For example, between the report of Bull's plane being down and the arrival of Joe Varney to tell Lillian the news, Conroy inserts a set piece of poetic description:

> Ravenel began to wake in earnest at six in the morning. Hobie made his way through the gloom of River Street to open his restaurant. Ed Mills woke to arthritic cramps that made each morning a matins of pain for him. . . . The earliest birdsong whispered through the streets. The time was marked down and all eyes turned eastward toward the waters and breakers along the barrier islands. . . . It was the time when night trem-

bled before the coming resurrection, when the air sighed like
a lover, when the first fingers of light came stealing out of the
abyss to find the secret, soft places. Light and dark groped for
each other in the birthing of dawn. Dawn spilled, mist-filtered,
into each window, into each leaf, into the river, into each creek
and into the eyes of Ben and Mary Anne. Light danced quick
in the river and the marshland, as quick as death or the snap
of a claw. (517)

There may be something a bit heavy-handed in this juxtaposition, but
there is also testimony to Conroy's ability to write in a lambent prose
voice as well as in his storytelling, action-dominated one. There are numerous passages in the novel like this, several especially notable ones
being descriptions such as that of the journey to Ravenel, Ben's meditation on the death of his Little League coach, his bracing for the battle
with Bull after his return from Mess Night at the Officers' Club, and his
rhapsodic portrait "of the God of Ben Meecham":

> Ben would give Him the sweetness of Lillian, the dark, hon-
> est eyes of Arrabelle, the soft virility of Mr. Dacus, the birth-
> mark of Pinkie on his throat, and Ogden Loring's upcountry
> drawl. Ben would give Him the shoulders of Vergil Hedge-
> path, the innocence of Karen, the spoon and tears of Mary
> Anne, the high-pitched laugh of Sammy, Matt's intensity, and
> the loyalty of the Gray. And Ben would put his God on a
> street like River Street and he would have his God lift his
> voice in the holy song of Toomer. The hands of this God
> would be bright with flowers that would never die and this
> God would sing and stutter and limp along an alleyway and
> pass judgment in the land beside the river. He would hold
> mercy in a bouquet of azaleas and he would listen to Ben.
> (535)

Although Conroy uses imagery, allusion, and other literary devices
sparingly, he uses them to good effect: an extended analogy of Bull's
temperament to stormy weather conditions; Vergil Hedgepath's comparison of Bull's manic personality to Henry V's St. Crispin's Day speech;
an extraordinary simile that likens the host in communion to both the
birth of a child and the creation of the universe; war imagery scattered
throughout to underline the battle between Bull and his family.

In addition, there are other stylistic devices that Conroy uses for a variety of purposes. For example, when Bull is at home, time is usually reported in military fashion. It is natural that Bull would use this terminology, but when the omniscient narrator says that Bull's alarm clock sounded at 0300 hours, it helps to establish the military atmosphere that Bull has imposed on the household. When he never calls his children by name, but rather calls them "sportsfans" and "hogs," these impersonal and distant terms help to define his cold, authoritarian attitude toward them. When Lillian is vexed with Bull (which is much of the time), she uses an exaggerated southern accent in calling him "Sugah," knowing this will grate on his distaste for all things southern and anything that hints of sweetness. The Meecham children have denigrating nicknames for each other (e. g., "feces face," "midget"), and these create a solidarity among them in their battle with Bull. Mr. Dacus's calling Ben "pissant" is an affectionate parody of Bull's "hog."

Finally, while Conroy does not rely heavily on symbols, there are a few that are obvious and effective. One of the most significant is the flight jacket that Bull gives Ben on his birthday. It is the one Bull wore during his heroic bombing raids in World War II, and it is clearly a symbol to him of his greatest moments of glory. In one sense his giving the jacket to Ben is one of those rare gestures on Bull's part that shows he really does love his son, but in another, Bull is also hoping that Ben will be reminded of his father's fame every time he wears it and would like to mold Ben in his own image. When Bull hands the jacket to Ben and the boy tries it on, it seems "much too large for him" (224). By the end of the novel, as Ben wears it for the drive away from Ravenel, it seems to fit perfectly. Obviously Ben has not grown so much physically in six months as he has in confidence and responsibility. In the drive itself and especially in the way Ben orchestrates it, he has become the man of the household, and ironically, in many ways he assumes exactly the same rituals and authority that Bull used to exercise. Between these two scenes involving the flight jacket, Ben wears it the night he disobeys his father and goes to Toomer's aid. During this critical episode, the jacket is badly torn by one of Toomer's dogs, and this might indicate that the old relationship between Bull and Ben has been severely torn. That Ben continues to wear it and that Bull does not have the grace to express his admiration for his son's own heroism suggest that both may, at least subconsciously, recognize the change.

Among several less complicated symbols, the most poignant is Mary Anne's flicking tears out of a silver spoon on Bull's neck during the drive to Ravenel and repeating the same prank on Ben as he drives the car away at the end. It is a mark of Ben's growing awareness and sensitivity that it is he who recognizes the symbolism here:

> "Hey, cut it out, Mary Anne," Ben said angrily. "I'm not Santini." That he had invoked his father's nom de guerre surprised him. . . . The tears hit again in the purest form of grief and protest.
> His anger subsided, for it was Mary Anne and at that moment he knew she would always fling tears at men who sat in front seats and all the men in her life. Her weapons would always come from her eyes and her tongue, from her face. (533)

Mary Anne, who will never attract men as Lillian has done, tries to establish a position of her own, seemingly indifferent and contemptuous, but transparently unhappy in the role she finds herself playing.

A FEMINIST READING

Bull Meecham is so close to being a caricature of the prototypical "male chauvinist pig" that feminist literary critics might find him hardly worth their time in addressing. His swaggering, male supremacist attitudes, his contempt for women as anything except sex objects, his physical abuse of Lillian and his daughters, and his total attention to Ben and ignoring of Mary Anne and Karen are only the most obvious of his retrograde qualities. It is clear, however, that Conroy finds this side of Bull's character as repugnant as a feminist critic would. Thus, unlike Kate Millett's attack on D. H. Lawrence, Henry Miller, and Norman Mailer in *Sexual Politics*, feminist critics would direct their fire not primarily at the author, but at the characters of a socio-psychological mindset that has been responsible for some of the worst aspects of our patriarchal society's devaluation of women.

Beyond a fierce attack on male-dominated linguistic usage such as "man" used universally as a suffix ("businessman," "chairman," "mailman"); as the generic term for the human race ("all men are created equal"); and "he" or "his" as the pronoun to follow a singular antecedent (all endorsed by grammarians until fairly recently), feminist literary criticism takes many forms. Its most obvious concerns range from a special interest in female writers and their female characters to an ex-

amination and critique of historical male dominance in the writing and
analyzing of literary works to the way in which the presentation of characters, both female and male, reflects attitudes and realities in the society
of the day. They take special interest in works they see as "helping
women understand their lives" (McMahan et al. viii) and "writers concerned with feminist issues and ideas: power and powerlessness, the
sexual double standard, the quest for identity, the unfair demands for
nurturing, the need for money and personal liberty, the importance of
work in achieving selfhood" (McMahan et al. ix).

An early, but still useful, definition of feminist literary criticism is to
be found in Annis V. Pratt's "The New Feminist Criticisms: Exploring
the History of the New Space." Pratt outlines eight somewhat overlapping areas of interest and investigation for feminist literary critics. In
summary: 1) Stereotypical—images of women in literature, such as
women in the novels of men like Lawrence and Mailer; 2) Archetypal—
the psycho-mythological development of the female hero as in Virginia
Woolf's *To the Lighthouse*; 3) Textual—are there distinct male and female
styles reflecting distinct sexual sensibilities?; 4) Contextual—historical
and sociological examination of women's roles in literature—literature
as document; 5) Ideological—an examination of women's roles in literature from a nonliterary body of theory such as Marxism, existentialism,
Zen, etc.; 6) Bibliographical—an investigation of the careless or deliberate
relegation to obscurity of female writers simply because they were female; 7) Spadework Criticism—reviving forgotten women authors and
determining why they were forgotten; 8) Phallic Criticism—exposing
sexism in male critics (177).

This particular focus in literary criticism grew out of the Women's
Liberation Movement, stimulated by books like Betty Friedan's *The Fem-
inine Mystique*, Simone de Beauvoir's *The Second Sex*, and Kate Millett's
Sexual Politics. In an attempt to do many things, from raising consciousness about the inferior status of women in western society to achieving
equality in hiring and compensation to enacting laws that give women
power in education, business, and government, the Women's Movement
has been responsible for enormous changes in almost every aspect of our
culture. Although they see their achievement as significant, they by no
means see the battle as won. For example, the Equal Rights Amendment
to the Constitution has yet to be ratified, and there are obvious vestiges
of prejudice in many areas of business and the professions (frequently
called "the glass ceiling"). Thus, the Women's Movement remains an
active and influential force, spearheaded by groups like the National

Organization for Women, striving for identification and the eradication of remaining areas of gender bias. Located primarily in academic institutions, feminist literary critics see their role in this movement as calling attention to past and present instances of female victimization, not only by specific males in their lives, but also by the norms of the society in which they live.

It is, of course, the characters as reflections of women's positions in the early 1960s and the way they have been shaped by the mores of the times that would be one of the chief interests of feminist critics of *The Great Santini*. And if they did not dismiss him out of hand, it is Bull who would be a large and vulnerable first target. His attitudes and behavior, from his casual reference to women as "split tails" to his physical abuse of Lillian are a paradigm of all that feminists see wrong with American male-dominated society.

When Bull is on overseas assignment, Lillian is responsible for running the household and disciplining the children; the instant he returns, he seizes that role, and Lillian reverts to her task of mediating between Bull and the children. For Bull there is no sense of shared responsibility in raising the children and ordering the family's priorities. At the same time, he takes no interest in maintaining the house by drying a dish, pulling a weed, or mending a dripping faucet. He tries to reverse any evidence of interest in the arts, refinement, or sensitivity that Lillian has been able to instill in the children while he has been away. Mary Anne claims, rightly on the evidence in the novel, that he never once has had a conversation with his children; what exchange there is consists of Bull's orders and the children's protests or assents. The level of communication with Lillian is scarcely any different. Bull speaks *ex cathedra*, and she can and does frequently protest or criticize, but it seldom makes any difference in the outcome.

His idea of involvement with the children is to play "war games" with them, using real swords and fireplace implements. He shuts out any complaint or attempt at real dialogue, as when Mary Anne, in trying to get his attention, says she is failing three subjects in school, he completely ignores what she has said and replies that good grades are the only thing that a girl can hope to achieve. He can be unabashedly cruel as in his treatment of defenseless enlisted men under his command or in his refusal to stop the car long enough for Matt to urinate. In his frustration at losing to Ben in basketball, he repeatedly hits the boy on the head with the ball in an effort to break his spirit and make him cry.

If *The Great Santini* is a virtual litany of Bull's flaws as seen by a fem-

inist (or almost any other kind of) literary critic, his role as a fairly typical, if obviously exaggerated, male in his society would receive more
serious attention. In the early 1960s the Marine pilots' world was a
strictly masculine one, but it was really only a heightened and more rigid
reflection of the general pattern of masculine dominance and exclusivity.
For example, Lillian's description of the wives at the Marine Corps Birthday Ball would not be greatly different if she were describing a party of
lawyers, doctors, or industrialists:

> Lillian stood at the center of a large group of 367 [Bull's
> squadron number] wives. . . . She saw women who smiled too
> much or drank too much and these were the women ordered
> to have a good time by their husbands. There were women
> who clung to her and laughed at her every joke, and admin-
> istered to her every whim, and she knew these were the am-
> bitious women who were driving their husbands forward in
> the ranks. There were many others who could not be shuffled
> into convenient categories, but it was because they were
> skilled at hiding the signs of their satisfaction or their discon-
> tent. Whatever their story, these wives were appendages,
> roses climbing on the trellises. Their roles were decorative on
> this night and on all others. (271)

When Bull says that women's mission "is to love the fighter pilot, cook
good meals, police up the house, and raise superior children" (254) or
that he wants his daughters "to be fine pieces of tail for their husbands"
(255) or when Mary Anne asks if girls can be real Meechams and Bull
answers that, because she is a girl, she is "a simple form of Meecham"
(400), these are, of course, the crude responses of this particular boor.
Yet, they unfortunately reflect only slightly exaggerated attitudes of a
large segment of the society of the period, and they have by no means
disappeared a generation later. More sophisticated, better educated men
might be embarrassed to express such opinions openly or might pretend
that these are not their true values at all, yet the lingering, unacknowl-
edged existence of such attitudes may be even more insidious than the
bald, unapologetic fatuousness of blustering men like Bull Meecham.

Such behavior has been thoroughly explored and excoriated by the
Women's Movement generally, and feminist literary critics in particular,
for twenty-five or more years. Thus, what can be said about Bull and
the near parody of male chauvinist attitudes he represents is by now
nearly a cliché. This is not to say that such men and such attitudes no

longer exist; it is merely that the exposure and censure of them is no longer very new or controversial.

More interesting, because somewhat less familiar and more complex, as a focus for the feminist critic of *The Great Santini* would be a study of the two major female characters, Lillian and Mary Anne. This analysis would consist of several parts: beyond their superficial roles in the Meecham family and plot, what do they reveal about women's positions in the larger world of American society in the early 1960s (see Pratt's Number 4 above)? How, and to what degree, have the men in their lives specifically and the patriarchal society generally shaped their personalities? From what perspective does the author present these women and acknowledge the influences on them by that society? What are their reactions to the roles that in some part they have been assigned and in some part they have chosen to play?

Examined through this lens, Lillian Meecham is a more complicated and contradictory character than she might otherwise appear. Though not a member of southern aristocracy, Lillian clings to many of the values of gentility, sensitivity, and decorum that are its hallmarks. Her marriage to a Marine from a blue-collar, Roman Catholic Chicago background is almost prima facie a union doomed to conflict. Her assertion that he swept her off her feet in spite of the fact that she had many other suitors must be accepted at face value, but Bull's personality is so blunt and overbearing that it seems odd Lillian could not have read the danger signals from the beginning. When Bull is not physically abusing her, he is verbally relegating her to chattel status, and it seems she might easily have been able to predict this before she married him. The answer, feminist critics might posit, is that women of Lillian's generation were not sensitized to the damage men like Bull were capable of inflicting on their wives and families. Too easily impressed by a man who sent her roses every day for two weeks, she ignored the more ominous aspects of his character.

Worse still, Lillian in large measure "buys into" the male view of women's roles. As she urges Mary Anne to wear clothes that would be more flattering, she reveals her acceptance of female stereotyping:

> "A woman has one job. To be adorable. Everything else is just icing. Dressing nice to catch a man's eye is part of the game. . . . "That's what every woman wants," Lillian said harshly, "or should want. . . . Maybe everybody would like you better

if you weren't so know-it-all. It's best for a woman not to know so much." (396–97)

She repeatedly urges Mary Anne to be more accommodating to the norms of female appearance and behavior, and she refuses to acknowledge Mary Anne's wrenching complaints about the conflict between them. As a beautiful woman who has never lacked for attention from male admirers, she fails utterly to appreciate or sympathize with (in fact denies the legitimacy of) Mary Anne's claims of being unloved by her mother because she is physically unalluring. In an otherwise sympathetic, attractive character, this is a serious blind spot of Lillian's and another flaw in her mask of denial of anything that disturbs her attempt to create a "perfect" world. It is also largely responsible for Mary Anne's failure to find any support in her obvious cries for help and understanding.

On the other hand, a feminist critic would admire Lillian's valiant efforts to counteract Bull's worst aggressions. She fights, not often very successfully, to protect the children from his overbearing, insensitive attacks. She admits, especially to Ben, that Bull is a vulgar, brutish philistine. (This only serves to inflame Ben's own conflict with his father.) Yet she claims that she stays with him for the sake of the children. Despite the triteness of such an excuse, in Lillian's case it has some validity. She is a woman of her times: loyal to the commitment she has made; alternately outraged by the indignities that Bull heaps on her and proud of her status as the wife of a senior officer; dignified under the trials he inflicts on her and in his death; resourceful enough to be seeking a job (with no observable skills) at the end of the novel. Lillian Meecham, is, by feminist standards, too easily accepting of the male dominance of her life and the values that implies while remaining deaf to Mary Anne's obvious appeals for a mother's loving attention. Yet she is a strong woman who bears her burdens stoically and tries to give her children antidotes to their father's severity.

Mary Anne, although only sixteen, is an entirely different woman. Lillian can be understood largely by her background and her generation. So too, to some extent, can Mary Anne, but the vast difference between their physical attributes on the one hand and Lillian's failure to appreciate and deal with that difference on the other, account to a large extent for the hostility that exists between them and for the bitter neuroses of this unhappy girl. Mary Anne, as Ben says, is the victim of a beautiful mother and a cold father, and though he later says that his own behavior has contributed to her unhappiness, his original assessment is valid. Lillian is indeed "saintly" in her refusal to acknowledge serious flaws in her attempt to create an ideal family. But Lillian's "saintliness" and self-deception are too mawkishly contrived for an intelligent, sensitive girl like Mary Anne to accept. She is too bruised by her father's disdain, too hurt by her mother's ignoring of her, and too self-conscious about her own physical unattractiveness to have much chance of developing self-confidence. And to some extent all of these factors are offshoots of the male-oriented value structure.

It is true that if Ben were not such a model of good behavior (Mary Anne calls him Golden Boy), Mary Anne's rebellion would not seem so willful and disconcerting. Yet, it is chiefly a cry for an interest in her concerns and attention to her problems that motivates her in her attempt to gain some interest from a family dominated by an autocratic father and the achievements of the elder son. Matt and Karen are yet too young to be conscious of the psychological bruises that will almost certainly come their way. Mary Anne, however, is an extremely intelligent, sensitive young woman who knows exactly the sources of her distress and who, unfortunately, has neither parental understanding nor surrogates such as Ben's Mr. Dacus to give her guidance and support.

Mary Anne's fascination with esoteric "dead" words, while an amusing hobby that gives her some small sense of identity and individuality is, nevertheless, disturbing, for it is an entirely introspective interest and a pursuit of that which is obsolete and deceased rather than something forward and outward directed. She may become, as she often says, a writer, but she may, as she also says, commit suicide. A feminist critic would see much of Mary Anne's plight as the result of the society's misplaced values in relation to women—from its emphasis on physical attractiveness to its ignoring of women's interests in favor of those of the male siblings to its refusal to take seriously any role for them save that of wife and mother to its pushing aside any challenge to those values. Mary Anne, as Ben presciently predicts, will always be at war with a male-dominated society for she is doomed, given the values of that society, to be a desperately unhappy woman, and she is not one who will accept that role without protest.

The Lords of Discipline
(1980)

It is an extraordinary (some might even say wonderful) irony that in 1995 The Citadel, virtually undisguised in *The Lords of Discipline* (1980) as Carolina Military Institute, was, more than twenty-five years after the events of 1966–1967 described in the novel, once again engaged in a bitter battle of exclusion. Shannon Faulkner fought through the courts for two and a half years to become the first fully-integrated female in the heretofore all-male cadet corps of The Citadel. That she had been permitted to attend classes but not admitted to cadet status was a diversionary tactic that The Citadel had hoped would diffuse the issue. (Two informative articles about the struggle are Susan Faludi's "The Naked Citadel," and Catherine S. Manegold's "The Citadel's Lone Wolf: Shannon Faulkner.")[1]

Because of its setting (The Institute/Citadel), *The Lords of Discipline* immediately calls to mind Calder Willingham's 1947 novel, *End as a Man*. Like Conroy, Willingham was a graduate of The Citadel, and The Academy is also a scarcely disguised version of his alma mater. The characters and themes of the two novels bear some resemblances, but there is no suggestion that Conroy borrowed from Willingham (actually the two novels are as notable for their differences as for their similarities). Rather, both authors emphasize the ways in which institutions like The Citadel attract and mold certain types of characters and even breed, because of the fierce military ethos, certain kinds of behavior and underground cabals, groups bent on release from the rigorous discipline on campus or, more insidiously, to protect the "purity" of the institution.

Lucian K. Truscott's *Dress Gray* (1978) is another novel that, in light of its setting at West Point and the attempts to purge a cadet because of, in this case, his sexual orientation, bears some striking parallels to *The Lords of Discipline*. Not only is there the official and unofficial campaign to "cover up" the scandal of David Hand's murder by another homosexual cadet, there is the background of the Vietnam War and the bitter divisions it spawned. Truscott carries his indictment of West Point and the military hierarchy even further than Conroy does his of The Citadel, but the two novels share a caustic vision of the hypocritical efforts of top echelon officers to suppress evidence and even encourage sadistic attempts to intimidate those who might expose the truth.

Also, because of its West Point setting and the time it treats (the class of 1966 and its experiences, first as cadets and later as officers in Vietnam and after), Rick Atkinson's nonfictional *The Long Gray Line* (1989) shares some of the same interests as *The Lords of Discipline*—especially in its first section dealing with the class during its four years as undergraduates. Although this is a work of journalism, Atkinson writes with a novelist's use of dialogue, characterization, and plot development, thus making the book move like a work of fiction and engaging the reader on an emotional level that is remarkable in factual reporting.

Finally, another work of nonfiction bears a resemblance to *The Lords of Discipline*, in this case not for its military background, but because of its social commentary. Like Conroy's novel and its portrait of the sinister decadence of Charleston society and especially of the families who live SOB (South of Broad), John Berendt's *Midnight in the Garden of Good and Evil* (1994) lays bare the hypocrisy, false values, and corruption of a similar aristocracy in Savannah.

However interesting these parallels may be, *The Lords of Discipline* is without question another coming-of-age novel, but it is so different from *The Great Santini* and *The Water Is Wide* in every way that, as Frederick Crews says in his review in *The New York Times Book Review*, it is hard to believe that the book was written by the same author. In every aspect—narrative point of view, plot and character development, themes, and style—*The Lords of Discipline* is so much more sophisticated that it represents a quantum leap for Conroy as a writer. Whereas there are many tests of manhood posed for Ben Meecham, they are of a completely different and simpler order from those posed for Will McLean. While Will inherits from Ben many character traits such as his desire to please and his fundamental good nature, he is so much more complex and intellectual than Ben that the relationship between them is of minor interest (save that they are both Conroy alter egos). If one knows Ben, then one can see certain things in Will that are reminiscent; if one does not know Ben, there is no difficulty in recognizing Will immediately as an extremely sensitive, intelligent, courageous young man in his own right.

In *The Lords of Discipline*, Will McLean has presumably confronted and passed the tests of manhood that Ben Meecham passes in *The Great Santini*. We know very little of Will's boyhood before he arrives at the Institute in summer of 1963, save that it sounds as if he comes from a family very like the Meechams—stern father, refined mother, and an ongoing father-son conflict. It is tests of manhood of a totally different order that Will must face in his four years at the Institute—ranging from the physical, emotional, and fortitudinal in his plebe year to the social, sexual, and moral in his final months before graduation—that form the backbone of this rites-of-passage novel.

Because of its in-depth characterization, its multi-layered plot, its stylistic variety, and its thematic complexity, *The Lords of Discipline* marks Conroy's entry to the front ranks of popular fiction writers, and its achievement began the enormous popular and critical success he enjoys today.

NARRATIVE POINT OF VIEW AND STRUCTURE

To begin with, *The Lords of Discipline* is Will McLean's first-person narrative, a much more demanding and restrictive point of view than the omniscient narration of *The Great Santini*. This means that the reader may know nothing that the narrator has not himself done, seen, or heard about, a decision that puts considerable restraints on the author and forces him to use a series of devices to include necessary information gleaned from sources when Will has not been present. Conroy is clever enough to keep these to a minimum, as in having Colonel Berrineau and Colonel Reynolds tell Will things he could hardly have discovered on his own. He is also scrupulous about maintaining this point of view, whereas some novelists, having chosen first-person narration, "cheat" or use very awkward devices to introduce vital exposition.

In addition to this restriction of narrative point of view, Conroy introduces at least three levels of remove from the most immediate "present" of the novel. In the first of these in the Prologue, Will speaks from a considerable distance in time:

> I WEAR THE RING.
>   I wear the ring and I return often to the city of Charleston, South Carolina, to study the history of my becoming a man. (1)

We are not sure just how far this voice is removed from the voice of Will McLean who relates the rest of the novel, but we know that it is long enough to have given him perspective on the events that comprise the heart of the book. Furthermore, as Will relates time present, both in his senior year (1966–1967) and, at another remove, his plebe year (1963–1964), he frequently reverts to the retrospective voice of the Prologue: "In the 1960s, to be liberal was one infallible way for a Southern boy to attract the attention of his family and friends" (89).

The major time frame is the first-person narration of Will McLean relating the events of his senior year, the present of the novel. These too are told in the past tense, but a much more immediate past tense—as if they had happened a few moments or at most a day or so before. These sections, I, III, and IV form the frame of the novel, the nine months in which Will McLean grows from a wisecracking, skeptical outsider amid the oppressively cohesive and conformist senior class to a bitter, cynical survivor of a terrible struggle with disillusionment, betrayal, and evil on several levels. Part I covers the days in September 1966, when Will has returned early to the Institute as a member of "the cadre" (seniors assigned the duty of "breaking in" the new plebes) and the first weeks of their fearsome initiation, climaxed by the suicide of John Poteete, a plebe so tortured that he kills himself rather than return to his family admitting that he had been broken by "the system."

Abruptly, Part II is given as a flashback (the second remove from the main "present" of the novel) to the nine months of Will's own plebe year (1963–1964), introduced by the voice of the Prologue—Will McLean a number of years after his graduation. This inventive and successful manipulation of chronology (and the structure of the book) serves several important purposes. By interrupting the narrative flow of the novel to tell in such vivid and brutal detail the events of that traumatic experience so long afterward, Conroy throws them into a highlighted perspective and emphasizes what a profound impression they made on him:

I was not the same boy who had awakened to reveille that morning. . . . The cadre had ripped civilization from my back as though it were nothing more than strips of skin. They were going to change us all into men by reducing us to children again, by breaking down every single vestige of civilization and society that we had brought to protect and sustain us. They would tame us like beasts of the field before they remade us in their own fierce image. (151)

Conroy's technique here is almost parallel to a psychiatrist's cutting through layers of time and experience to reach the ultimate source of what has formed one's personality as it is years later. This account of the sadistic brutality exercised by the cadre of Will's plebe year helps to explain Will's refusal to take an active part in the brutality of his classmates in their reenactment of it three years later.

Another thing achieved by this flashback is to allow Conroy to expose many aspects of the system that Will deplores and despises without dwelling on them at length in the present, where other matters of character and plot are being developed and are moving rapidly forward. That is to say, this seeming digression (which is by no means of secondary importance) allows the pace of the novel's main action in Parts III and IV to move steadily, even inexorably, forward without pauses to introduce aspects of the Institute life that Conroy finds so appalling. This chapter, set out of chronological sequence, helps us to understand the incredible bonding that has taken place among the four roommates that we see in the other chapters (and therefore sets us up for the terrible shock of the events that will shatter those bonds in Part IV). It shows us their coming together, the growth of their mutual dependence and affection, and the playful as well as supportive nature of their relationship. Thus, in an isolated chapter, Conroy avoids having to dwell elsewhere on why these four men are so closely bonded. Finally, it is the core having been revealed that makes the intervening years of 1964–1966 unnecessary to report on in detail. Conroy's telescoping of time is, then, an economy, allowing him to skip over two years without the reader's feeling that vital information has been ignored.

There are only minimal references to Will's family and the years immediately before he enters the Institute (the third remove in time). We learn just enough about his mother's insistence that he obey his promise to his dying father about attending the Institute to cover all we need to know about him before September 1963.

PLOT DEVELOPMENT

If the plot development of *The Great Santini* was a straightforward, linear one, that of *The Lords of Discipline* is quite different. Like the earlier novel, the primary, unifying plot line is Will's coming-of-age, but this is a journey from relatively naive boy to disillusioned man, from open, trusting, carefree youth to bitter, ambivalent, driven adult who feels compelled to report not only on the events of his four years at the Institute but, equally important, the effects of the system on both those who succeed and those who fail.

While Will's maturing constitutes the main cord of the plot in *The Lords of Discipline*, this is presented primarily through at least five major, interrelated strands in the complex set of events and issues that make up Will's story. Although some of these may be more integral to his coming-of-age than others, it would be a foolish exercise to attempt rating their importance in Will's development. Without any suggestion of such ranking, one of the first of these threads that the reader is made aware of is Will's appointment by Colonel Berrineau (the Bear) as the monitor of Thomas Pearce's (the Institute's first black cadet) progress during his initial year. Berrineau knows (a) that Pearce will be singled out for special harassment by the cadre and others; (b) that it is vital for public relations and political reasons that Pearce succeed; and (c) that, because of his maverick, liberal status, Will McLean is the ideal choice for the task. Through a secret communication system, Pearce can report to Will any untoward threats or attacks on him, and Will can alert the Bear. It is not until late in the novel that this plot element erupts in all its violence, but it is introduced in the opening pages.

Another aspect of Will's maturing that is introduced early is his relationship with the St. Croix family, one of Charleston's most aristocratic. Through his roommate, Tradd, Will comes to be treated at the St. Croix mansion almost as another son. For a boy of modest means from rural Georgia to be accepted by this wealthy, socially elite family is both flattering and educational. Although Abigail St. Croix sometimes acts almost flirtatiously with Will rather than as a surrogate mother, it is through her that he comes to his abiding love of Charleston and to a knowledge and appreciation of art, gardens, antiques, and music. This relationship also comes to its climax only at the end of the novel, but it is an important element throughout.

It is while visiting Tradd and his parents that Will meets Annie Kate

Gervais, and this not only sets in motion another, important part of Will's rites of passage, but leads to some of the most salient comments on the hypocrisy, deceit, and false values of the Charleston aristocracy. Will's love for Annie Kate grows in spite of her mercurial temperament and treatment of him. Although she is pregnant with another man's child, it is with her that Will loses his virginity and his heart. In spite of the fact that he alone stands by her during the long difficult months before the delivery of the dead baby, she immediately rejects him in favor of a return to her social ambitions, thus introducing one of the many variations on the theme of betrayal that reverberate throughout the novel.

The bonding of Will and his three roommates, Tradd St. Croix, Mark Santoro, and Dante (Pig) Pignetti, provides a special plot component of its own, but the relationship of the roommates is also an important element on several other levels as well. Male bonding is, of course, a major theme in the novel as it depicts the whole Institute ethos, but the intense solidarity among these four boys from vastly different backgrounds is treated with great care and attention. From their initial reasons for coming together, through their blood ritual affirmation of brotherhood, through their pranks and mutual support in moments of crisis, to the terrible shattering of their union at the end, Conroy concentrates a great deal of time and space to showing these four young men together, their individual personalities, and their feelings for each other. This is doubtless done in large part to make the events at the end of the novel as surprising and poignant as possible, but it also serves to emphasize another aspect of the theme of betrayal, the experiencing of which is one of the most important elements in Will's coming to manhood.

If by plot, one thinks of suspenseful action as well as events which reveal character and theme, then Will's attempts to discover whether or not the legendary "Ten" (a secret society dedicated to purging the corps of undesirable cadets) really does exist and then to identify its members and expose their sadistic torture of individuals they deem unworthy of "wearing the ring" is of great importance. Conroy builds this plot line very carefully by introducing ominous hints of the Ten's existence and activity early in the novel. Even when Will is still a plebe, there is the suspicious disappearance of a cadet who involuntarily urinates in response to harassment, but it is not until the suicide of Poteete that Will begins to see a pattern that makes him think that the Ten does in fact exist and its members do in fact behave as legend has it. In the final section of the novel, as Pearce is attacked and Pig is driven to suicide, the major action is devoted to Will's and the Bear's efforts to discover exactly who is involved, what is going on, and how best to expose and thereby stop it. Indeed, the last twelve (of forty-nine) chapters are devoted almost exclusively to this plot thread, which involves a series of shocking revelations, terrifying physical violence, sudden reversals, and ultimate acts of betrayal on the part of at least four of the major characters in the novel. Conroy crafts this section so carefully that it reads very like a novel of intrigue and suspense—without, however, sacrificing attention to theme and character.

Thus, on the level of plot development alone, *The Lords of Discipline* is a sophisticated work of fiction. The various threads are intricately interwoven with characters prominent on one strand having substantial roles on one or more of the other strands. Especially in the final chapters, Conroy uses expert techniques in building tension and suspense (e. g., Chapter Thirty-eight when Will spies on the Ten's torture of Pearce, his discovery by the villains, a chase down the beach, and his rescue by Pig and Mark; Chapter Forty-five as Will and Mark break into Commerce St. Croix's library and read his secret journals; Chapter Forty-seven when Will and the Bear confront General Durrell). Yet, in the end, despite Conroy's creation of a gripping, suspenseful line of action, *The Lords of Discipline* is most memorable for its creation of character, its prose style, and its disturbing themes.

CHARACTER DEVELOPMENT

In a novel with well over sixty named characters, *The Lords of Discipline* is remarkable in giving at least twenty of them more than "walk-on" roles. While perhaps only seven or eight might be defined as fully three-dimensional figures, another ten have an individuality that is important: they are actors in critical plot incidents or they are representatives of distinct personality types within the cadet corps or Charleston society. They, therefore, have roles on the thematic level. Yet another ten appear frequently enough to be recognizably differentiated from the mass of characters (chiefly cadets) who, while named, really have no roles to play beyond populating the barracks, the basketball court, and the Friday afternoon dress parades.

In his Author's Note at the beginning of the book, Conroy claims somewhat disingenuously that no character or action in the novel is based on an actual person or event. There is very little question that at least two of the characters are not even very thinly disguised portraits of real people. Will McLean is Pat Conroy's alter ego (just as Ben Meecham was in *The Great Santini*) and the Bear is a carbon copy of The Boo, Lieutenant Colonel Thomas Courvoisie, to whom *The Lords of Discipline* is dedicated and whose character Conroy presented in his first published work. While many of the events of the novel may be fictionalized, that in no way alters Conroy's larger purposes:

> At the Institute the making of men was a kind of grotesque artistry.
>
> Yet I am a product of this artistry. And I have need to bear witness to what I saw there. I want to tell you how it was. I want precision. I want a murderous, stunning truthfulness. I want to find my own singular voice for the first time. I want you to understand why I hate the school with all my power and passion. Then I want you to forgive me for loving the school. (6)

These words come from the mouth of Will McLean, but the ventriloquist is Pat Conroy. Especially the words about finding his own voice and speaking with murderous truthfulness recall what Conroy says in his Introduction to the second edition of *The Boo* about the writer's need to report things as they are without regard to who might be hurt or offended.

Will writes in the Prologue that when he looks at pictures of himself during his cadet days, he scarcely recognizes the person he was. So totally did the Institute, and especially the events of his senior year, change him that the man who is telling the story some years after his graduation is haunted by his need to describe the "Taming" of plebes so savage that it drives some to physical breakdown and suicide and the discouragement if not the actual destruction of individuality demanded by the system. He feels also the need to expose the military ethos of the Institute (many would claim even more authoritarian and unyielding than at West Point) and the hypocrisy, corruption, and viciousness at the highest levels of administration and in the alumni. That in doing this he also traces his development from somewhat callow youth to courageous, hardened man is by no means coincidental. Thus, the story told in *The Lords of Discipline* may be, on one level, a cathartic indictment of all that Will hates about the Institute, but on another, it is a classic tale of the loss of innocence.

Will, even before he arrives at the Institute, knows himself to be an outsider, a rebel, as a result of the long-standing conflict with his ultra-conservative, authoritarian father. He already has a nearly reflexive re-action against compelled conformity and gratuitous cruelty. As a result, it is hardly surprising that within days, if not hours, of his arrival at the Institute, he realizes he does not "belong." He abhors "the system," which in addition to its physical abuse of the plebes, attempts to reduce them to unthinking robots.

Early on, while attempting to avoid attracting undue attention to him-self, Will draws inward; he becomes a loner and vows to resist any temp-tation to relax his moral condemnation of what is going on. In several instances (such as the spitting on Bobby Bentley) he fails in his resolve and behaves like the rest, but these are rare, isolated cases, and, even at the moment of his action, he reviles himself for betraying his principles. As the year goes on, Will's silent refusal to accept the system grows bolder, and his irreverence erupts when he publishes a humorous but scurrilous poem about the seniors in his company. This brings down on him the full force of the Taming (the most violent form of physical and psychological abuse the cadre can inflict) with two results. First, there is Will's development of a fierce inner strength and resolve: "They had promised to make a man out of me and they were doing it. They were making a mean and angry man" (184). The second result is that Will survives, but with a public reputation as a cynic and a dissenter, looked on by all save his roommates and his basketball teammates (and even they sometimes have their doubts) as a dangerous disparager of tradition and the Institute itself.

Meanwhile, the other important event of Will's plebe year is his forg-ing of the steel bond of friendship among his roommates. Will and Tradd St. Croix declare their friendship during a mutually supportive effort to survive Hell Night. Their linking with Mark Santaro and Dante Pignetti is a somewhat more calculated move of self-protection (since the two Italians are among the strongest men in the class); but the developing relation to and love for each other in the resulting quartet (which is largely the result of Will's initiative), provide some of the most tender, some of the most humorous, and some of the most heartrending mo-ments in the novel.

By his senior year, Will has settled into the routine of his role among his classmates. They and the Bear know him as an iconoclast, openly hostile to the military ethos, a liberal among conservatives, an individual who refuses any appeal to solidarity if it violates his intellectual reason or his moral code (he alone refuses to sign a pledge of military service in Vietnam). Partly because of his prowess on the basketball court and partly because of his integrity—in spite of his being perceived as an eccentric by most of his peers—Will has established an identity that is guardedly tolerated by all but the most extreme militaristic faction of his class. Thus, it is with a mutual understanding of the reasons for the choice that Will accepts the Bear's charge to look out for Pearce, neither of them suspecting the Pandora's box of violence and evil that will evolve on that front.

Otherwise, at least at the beginning of the year, Will is almost smug in his close relationship with the St. Croix family; excited, perplexed, and frustrated by his growing love affair with Annie Kate Gervais; and troubled by what he sees as a repetition by his own classmates of the sadistic treatment that led to the disappearance of Bobby Bentley in his plebe year and now to the suicide of John Poteete in the fall term of his senior. There is a calm before the storm for Will in Part III (although Conroy carefully plants hints of trouble to come): "It began to rain and I could see lightning embroidering the sky with violent, jagged silver. 'It's Satan setting the table,' my grandmother used to tell me" (230). And then there are the fast-moving events of Part IV when Will, backed by Mark and Pig, sets out on his relentless pursuit of the Ten. No longer the trepid young man of his earlier years, he is now a resolute, almost reckless pursuer of what he knows to be evil, with its tentacles reaching through every level of the Institute's hierarchy of administration, alumni, and cadets.

If his survival of the plebe-year Taming made Will McLean a man in one sense, his betrayals by Annie Kate on one level, by General Durrell on another, and by Tradd and Abigail St. Croix on two other and even more intimate levels are the stuff from which bitter men are made. As we have learned in the Prologue, Will *is* a bitter man, but that bitterness is tempered by his realization that his years in Charleston and at the Institute gave him strength and understanding, indeed, "made him a man," though perhaps not in the sense that the Institute uses that phrase in its creed. One of the most affecting scenes in the novel is the final one, when Will asks the Bear to sign his diploma so that it will have on it the name of a man he respects:

> He handed back the diploma without signing it. "There already is, Bubba," he answered. "There already is."
> And he pointed to my name. (499)

As in the case of the various subplots in *The Lords of Discipline*, it would be difficult to rank the next five or six most prominent characters in order of their importance. Certainly the Bear is a major figure throughout. In his dedication Conroy pays tribute to Berrineau/Courvoisie, and in his depiction here (as well as in *The Boo*) it is not difficult to understand why Conroy so esteems this gruff, hard, but fair and caring man. Universally feared because he is stern and exacting, he appears when and where he is least expected. The Bear is representative of the Institute's more benign regimen of discipline and order, so that, while the cadets dread his surprise visits, they nonetheless respect him because, unlike others in authority, he plays no favorites and does his job because he believes in its importance, not because its power is ego inflating.

What makes the Bear unique, however, is an entirely different side of his character. He is colorful, witty, and humane. His ever-present cigar, in its malodorousness, often serves cadets as an early-warning signal of his approach (and he is well aware of this), and his voice is legendary in its volume and its ferocity. He has a mischievous, imaginative turn of mind and the unusual ability to banter and joke with the cadets, even accepting humorously pointed jibes, without ever compromising his position as their commandant. If he is feared and respected by the cadets, he is also known as the person to whom they can turn in time of trouble, personal or scholastic. The Bear calls them his lambs, and, in several ways, he is a very good shepherd.

Although personally Berrineau would have preferred that the cadet corps remain all white, he knows the Institute is long overdue for integration and that it is his task to see that it happens with a minimum of disturbance and publicity. (It is an interesting footnote that, long since retired, Colonel Courvoisie, who oversaw that first integration in the 1960s, strongly opposes the admission of Shannon Faulkner in the 1990s, and it is another interesting footnote that, as Berendt says [110], Conroy took delight in "twitting" The Citadel once again by giving a dinner party in her honor.) The ability to distinguish his personal feelings from his duty to the institution is a mark of his integrity and good judgment—in direct contrast to those of General Bentley Durrell, the president of the Institute.

Except for a brief time when Will has been tricked into believing that the Bear is, himself, a member of the Ten, they work together relentlessly to expose the secret society and its machinations. It is typical of the Bear's sincerity that he removes his Institute ring and gives it to Will in order to protest the lie that he is in league with the Ten. In the final confrontation with General Durrell, the Bear shows his true courage and incorruptibility. At the cost of a career that has been his lifelong pride, he defies Durrell's attempt to expel Will and Mark and rejects the bribe the General offers to coax him to betray Will. He stands by Will to the very end:

> "Your job is extremely important to you, is it not, Colonel?"
>
> "Yes, sir, you know it's important to me."
>
> "Very good, then. We have struck a deal Colonel?" the General said.
>
> "You can kiss my ass, General Durrell," the Bear replied.
>
> "You would betray the Institute, Colonel?" the General whispered harshly.
>
> "No, sir," the Bear said without emotion. "I would never do that. Would you, sir?" (479)

The Bear is one of the most appealing characters in the book. A man of absolute integrity, he stands as a symbol of all that a wearer of the ring should be, as opposed to the many others who wear it while their conduct is in blatant contradiction of what it stands for.

Of Will's roommates, Tradd St. Croix's character is the most complex and the most fully developed. Coming from a rich, cultured family, he has tastes and manners that set him apart from the average cadet. His slight build and his artistic interests draw taunts of effeminacy from his own father, and these are intensified by his peers, who nickname him the Honey Prince. Though there is absolutely no evidence to support these suggestions that he is an effete homosexual, the name sticks and causes Tradd enormous pain and embarrassment. On the other hand, there is often a sanctimonious prissiness about him and more than a hint of snobbishness. He is also the ultimate Judas figure in the novel. During the first half of their senior year, Tradd behaves with his roommates as he always has, slightly aloof but otherwise an unquestioned member of the brotherhood. Then, as Will's concern about Pearce and his pursuit of the Ten increase in the spring semester, there are subtle changes in Tradd's attitudes and behavior. Conroy is much too clever to make these changes giveaways to what is happening, and on a first reading of the novel, one might overlook them entirely. On rereading, however, one can see Conroy's careful planting of ominous signals. As early as Chapter Twenty-six, when Will tells the Bear that the roommates will cover for him in looking in the library for Pearce's messages while he is away on basketball trips, Tradd is caught by the Bear watching them intently. Neither Will nor the Bear thinks anything of it at the time, but it is the first of a series of hints that Tradd may be something other than he seems.

As Will's attempts to expose the Ten come closer to their climax, it becomes obvious that Tradd is drawing apart. It is later made clear that it was Tradd who alerted the Ten to Will's spying on the night of Pearce's torture and that it is he who made the call that set the authorities onto Pig in his foolish syphoning of gas from Will's car. While the reader does not yet know the extent of Tradd's treachery, his exaggerated sympathy for Pig and his reaction to the "10" painted on their door are ever clearer signs that something is amiss. During this time Tradd has disingenuously tried to discourage any belief that the Ten even exist; and, near the end, when Will and Mark are about to be expelled, Tradd urges them to resign, ostensibly to avoid humiliation, but actually to lessen the danger that they will discover his membership in the Ten and his despicable betrayals.

Finally, it is revealed that, along with his other deceits, Tradd is the father of Annie Kate's child. He has abandoned her because Abigail has dictated (and he has failed to protest) that there is no possibility of their marrying—Annie Kate's family is simply not socially acceptable to the St. Croix. The penultimate chapter of the novel (Forty-eight) comprises Will's harrowing confrontation with Tradd and Abigail, when all of Tradd's perfidy is laid bare and he cravenly tries to justify himself. This chapter (coming as it does immediately after the episode in which Will and the Bear courageously confront General Durrell) makes Tradd seem especially pathetic in his spineless self-pity. An insecure boy from the beginning, in part because of his father's denigration and in part because of the razzing of his classmates, Tradd has taken a dishonorable, shameful path to acceptance by joining the Ten, and at their insistence, betraying his sworn brothers. At the end, after Will's merciless exposure and rejection of him, Tradd is a broken man, friendless and disgraced, while Will, throughout the novel and especially at the end, has grown in dignity, even gaining a kind of heroic stature.

In contrast to Tradd, Mark Santaro is a heroic figure, although on a less dramatic level than Will. A young man whose enormous physical strength is matched by his loyalty and moral courage, he too makes Tradd's behavior seem all the more venal. Mark serves as a stabilizing force in a room that is described by many of their peers as a zoo and a lunatic asylum. Among his many virtues, Mark's "gruff gentleness"

(231), his down-to-earth humor and sense of proportion, and his attempts to save his roommates from their follies both small and large, identify him as the center of gravity among the four "brothers."

Mark is a young man of Italian background, open, guileless, and instinctively generous, genuinely committed to the ideals of the Institute, and unafraid of emotional display:

> He kissed me again on both cheeks and with no self-consciousness at all looked into my eyes with benign tenderness and said, "I love you, Will." . . . I answered, "I think you're a gaping asshole." We had said the same thing. (37)

Mark's awakening to the insidious nature of "the system" is slower than Will's, but when it comes, it is fierce and determined. He takes the lead in engineering the hair-raising extraction of information about the Ten from Daniel Molligen (an alumnus whom Bobby Bentley has identified as one of his tormentors) and, having urged Will not to pursue his spying mission, along with Pig, rescues him from the Ten on the night of Pearce's torture.

Mark is not so sensitive as Will, and he says he doesn't really care about Pearce, but he has instinctively noticed something phony and patronizing about the St. Croix's hospitality, and therefore doesn't often join Will at their dinner parties. It is he who spots the incriminating familiarity between Molligen and Commerce St. Croix. While he is less quick and intellectual than Will, Mark Santaro is observant and loyal, an enormously likable, sympathetic character. In his final words about Mark, conveying the fact that he has been killed, Will's testimony to this courageous, self-effacing man is moving without being maudlin.

The fourth roommate, Dante Pignetti, is perhaps the least successfully drawn of the major characters. Although Pig is colorful in many ways, Conroy comes close to making him a caricature rather than a fully rounded character like Will, Tradd, and Mark. Another Italian, but of an extremely volatile, undisciplined nature, Pig, at least until the final moments of his life, is defined by several eccentric characteristics. Like Mark, he is extraordinarily strong and versatile in the skills of wrestling and karate, but unlike Mark, he has almost no self-control. He is a fanatic about bodybuilding and vitamins as panaceas for all problems—physical, mental, or emotional. He is also a fanatic about the photograph of his girlfriend, Theresa. He goes berserk if anyone uses foul language in her [the photograph's] presence, and against all logic, claims that she is offended by such crudity. On the other hand, there is an engaging appeal in Pig's blind loyalty to the roommates. It is he who initiates the blood ritual in their plebe year, and it is he who fights in their defense first and asks questions, if at all, later.

In spite of Pig's simplified character, there is an ingenuous charm in his "vast artlessness" (216), and there is genuine pathos in his gratitude to the roommates for their generosity and tolerance of his volcanic temperament. Like Mark, he doesn't really care about Pearce, but he cares enough about Will to risk his graduation and even his life in rescuing Will from the pursuing Ten. Pignetti, a poor boy with pride, makes the fatal error of syphoning gas from Will's car (which he knows Will would forgive) because he is ashamed to ask for more handouts from his roommates. But he is incredibly naive to do this when he knows that he, Mark, and Will are under constant surveillance by members of the Ten in an effort to find ways of driving them out of the Institute before they can gather the necessary evidence to expose the group and its inquisition of Pearce. Pig's trial before the Honor Court is one of the poignant subclimaxes of the novel. Will brings himself to lie in Pig's defense and even Tradd tries to minimize Pig's flagrant offense (though, of course, it was Tradd who set the whole case in motion). Pig's "Walk of Shame" is an agony for Will, who knows that it has been rigged by the Ten, though he is as yet unable to prove it. For Pig it is the ultimate humiliation, and he commits suicide by marching in front of the 11:42 train rather than face the disgrace he would undergo with Theresa and his family.

Pig's death is for Will, and by extension for Mark, the final galvanizing motive for exposing the Ten. Will becomes a man obsessed and exacts appropriate revenge when he serves Abigail and Tradd St. Croix water from the Ashley River where Pig's dismembered body fell, and when, contrary to the tradition that a shamed cadet's name shall never again be mentioned, he spits in General Durrell's face the name, "Dante Pignetti," as he accepts his diploma.

Pig is not a three-dimensional character, but he is extremely important for a variety of reasons. He provides comic relief in his fight with the mauler at the county fair and in his quixotic defense of Theresa's purity. More important, he is the primary victim of the Ten's totally amoral tactics in eliminating "undesirables" and thus becomes a martyr. His fierce loyalty to Will and Mark is inspirational for Mark, who gives General Durrell "the finger" in the climactic chapter of the novel, and for

Will, who vows to and succeeds in exposing the villains and the evil that brought about his dear friend's death.

Of the remaining characters, Annie Kate Gervais is one of the most important in Will's coming-of-age and in Conroy's exposure of the false values of the decadent Charleston society. Although her unwanted pregnancy may well account for some of her petulant irritability, her contradictory attitudes and treatment of Will, and her bitterness toward the world, there is no question that she has been a spoiled child, raised on the snobbish values of her equally supercilious mother. At various times she simply denies that she is carrying a baby and claims that her nine-month exile from the world is a period that will not exist once it is over. So that no one in Charleston will know of her condition, Abigail St. Croix, in collusion with Mrs. Gervais, arranges an elaborate charade in which Annie Kate was to have been attending the University of California at Santa Barbara but is in fact in hiding, first in her own house in Charleston and later at the Gervais family's beach house on Sullivan's Island. It is here that Will goes every weekend to give her company and comfort, and it is here that his love for her is consummated.

Annie Kate is pathetic in her isolation and in her dependence on her alcoholic mother. Still, she is ultimately cruel to Will while desperate for his friendship and company. She nearly laughs in his face when he offers to marry her, and at the same time she begs him not to desert her. Once the baby is gone, she immediately reverts to her Charleston social attitudes and dismisses Will with cold, heartless disdain. She goes off to California (this time really), leaving him hurt and puzzled by her indifference to his feelings; and, without comment, she sends him the box of sand dollars they had so lovingly collected on the beach (most of them broken in the shipping). Although there have been fleeting, superficial hints that she has learned something from her experience ("My whole life is one huge ugly lie" 291), it is only at the end of the novel when Annie Kate writes Will a letter, that there is any sense (and it is not a very strong one) of remorse for what she has done. Finally, there is a marvelous irony in that the snobbish Annie Kate and her mother, who considered Will McLean not good enough for her, should be "out-snobbed" by Abigail St. Croix.

Will doubtless falls in love with Annie Kate in large part because, as Abigail, Tradd, and Will himself acknowledge, he has a strong desire to make himself needed by others. Abigail puts it succinctly when she says that she knew that Will would feel sorry for Annie Kate and that he couldn't resist coming to her aid. She sneeringly suggests that his need to pity people is a weakness that, in part, accounts for his fondness for her. But, if this weakness in him is responsible for this chastening first experience with a woman, it is only part. In spite of her faults, there is a charm in Annie Kate when she chooses to allow it to surface, as when she and Will are walking on the beach collecting sea shells. His rejection by this sad, selfish girl is yet another aspect of his passage to manhood, and his reaction to it—essentially a stoic acceptance—again shows his maturity and strength.

A far more duplicitous woman adds to his pain and disillusionment perhaps even more severely than does Annie Kate. Abigail St. Croix, like her son in his hypocrisy, turns out to be a very different person from the charming, vivacious woman who captures Will's affection at the beginning of his plebe year. From his earliest days at the Institute, Abigail treats him almost as her escort rather than her son's roommate. She makes no pretense of having a fulfilling marriage with Commerce and turns to Will for long walks through Charleston and talk of the arts, antique furniture, and horticulture, which Will finds fascinating as he halfway falls in love with this worldly, poised, intelligent woman.

At first Conroy leads us to believe that there is nothing insincere in Abigail's attention to Will, but when her true character is revealed at the end of the book, it is impossible not to conclude that she has encouraged Will's closeness to the family because she has realized that his clean-cut, physically strong, open traits would make him an ideal comrade and protector for Tradd in the rough and harsh male world of the Institute. Be that as it may, Will thoroughly enjoys his frequent visits to the St. Croix mansion, and in many ways, they constitute another part of his education.

Until we learn that Abigail has deliberately arranged what seemed like a chance meeting between Will and Annie Kate, we have not been aware of her ruthless, conniving character. This crass exploitation of Will's good nature to protect Tradd from having to accept his responsibility as the father of Annie Kate's child is the first, and perhaps the most serious, of her manipulations. Rapidly, after that revelation, we learn that she refused even to consider Tradd's marriage to Annie Kate because Mr. Gervais had come from North Charleston, "the wrong side of the tracks," and in the final confrontational scene, we see her in her ugliest patronizing role as she tries to appeal to Will's ambitions by suggesting that Tradd will be able to help with introductions and influence.

In the Prologue Will has spoken of his mother as a woman who is like those who have become known as "steel magnolias" (a term that has gained currency from the play, *Steel Magnolias*, by Robert Harling). It describes the outwardly passive, helpless southern female, who gives the appearance of complete dependence on the men in her life, but who actually rules the family with a hidden power the men are hardly aware of. Will says that it has taken him years to realize it was his mother who controlled the McLean household (as Conroy does elsewhere about his own mother), when to all appearances it was his father. Abigail St. Croix is a steel magnolia with the added force of social position, influence, and enormous wealth. Of the many betrayals Will suffers at the end of the novel, hers may be one of the most cruel.

Among the remaining characters of importance to the plot and thematic issues, even though they are not of major interest in their own right, Commerce St. Croix is one of the most prominent. A hypocrite in several ways, he pretends to despise Charleston society, yet is wedded to it; he makes fun of his classmate, Bentley Durrell, yet both are members of the Ten; in his travels he is regularly unfaithful to his wife; and his secret journals, of which he is inordinately proud and protective, are actually, among other things, a record of the membership and atrocities committed by the Ten. Commerce is a harsh father, a representative of many of the nearly congenital weaknesses that have come from an inbred aristocracy, and a mean-spirited man who pretends conviviality with Will primarily to humiliate his son.

Commerce's less affluent and almost impotent parallel is Annie Kate's mother, Mrs. Gervais. An alcoholic, who refuses to sell either of her run-down houses because to do so would be to admit publicly that she is in "reduced circumstances," she is, like her daughter, capable of an almost total rejection of reality. That she can believe owning two shabby properties is not so much an admission of reduced circumstances as selling one in order to restore the other reveals a kind of blind faith in a social code that is antiquated and transparently fake. She lives "in mortal dread that someone who mattered, someone prominent in the thinly oxygenated heights of Charleston society, would spot Annie Kate." (231). She constantly asks how Annie Kate could have done this (the pregnancy) to *her*, with more concern about her own social position than about her daughter's distress and welfare. She sneers at Will's bourgeois background but imperiously "allows" him to help Annie Kate through her ordeal. While Commerce is a decadent avatar of an obsolete aristocracy, Mrs. Gervais is a pathetic, but complaisant, victim of its false values and misplaced priorities.

General Bentley Durrell, the president of the Institute, is important because in his position of power, he is a prime mover and supporter of the Ten, thus an ultimate villain by cooperating in their atrocities. He has gained his rank and fame, it is widely known, from his indifference to the number of casualties among his men, just so long as he has gained credit for a "victory." A vain, ambitious man, it is he who has encouraged the increasing harshness and savage abuse of the plebes with his claim that the more severe the test put upon them, the stronger they will be as the "men" he means to have as graduates of the Institute. The full measure of his meretriciousness does not become clear until the final confrontation with Will and the Bear. Here, in his attempt to bribe the Bear into betraying Will, is an unambiguous display of his hypocrisy.

Among the many other secondary characters, most are important as representatives of a type. Gardiner Fox, for instance, is the worst of his in his nearly pathological, sadistic treatment of the plebes. General Durrell and Fox are used as flagrant examples of leaders in "the system" in part to make it obvious why Will so despises it. Less important, but still products of it, are sycophants like John Alexander and his own toady, Wayne Braselton; young men whose egos are exaggeratedly inflated by their power over others such as Frank Maccabee and Philip Blasingame; and unquestioning adherents like Cecil Snipes and Cain Gilbreath.

Yet, among the preponderance of unsympathetic characters at the Institute, there are several who are memorable because they are victims of "the system" like Bobby Bentley and J. M. Poteete, or because they are humane, reasonable young men in a culture that has largely driven out these qualities in its survivors. Lance Hemphill, a senior on the basketball team when Will is a plebe, intervenes to save him from the worst of the Taming and gives him the valuable advice that in the large scheme what is happening at the moment is "bullshit." The basketball team's manager, Bo Maybank, a boy too short to play on the team, is nevertheless the best basket shooter of them all and has a hero worship of Will. One of the most affecting moments in the novel comes when Will, being borne aloft after the victory over VMI, later realizes that he should have lifted Bo up to join him in the celebration. Long before Bo is killed in Vietnam, Will learns that physical stature has nothing to do with fortitude and moral stature.

SETTING

As Frederick Crews says, Conroy's evocation of Charleston is so powerful and emotionally charged that the city becomes virtually a character in the novel. From his opening paean in the Prologue to the closing pages of the book, Charleston, in all its charm and beauty, but also in all its darker, even sinister, aspects is constantly in the foreground. The epigraph from Baudelaire emphasizes the uglier aspects of the city, but its opening phrase is "with heart at rest":

> With heart at rest I climbed the citadel's steep height, and saw the city as from a tower, hospital, brothel, prison, and such hells, where evil comes up softly like a flower. (vii)

At the end of the novel Will McLean will have climbed "the citadel's steep height" (Conroy cannot have been unaware of the play on words here), and though his heart is scarcely at rest, he has achieved catharsis in his winning struggle with evil in the city itself and at the Institute inside it.

From almost the first words in *The Lords of Discipline* Will speaks of his ambivalent feelings about Charleston:

> The city of Charleston, in the green feathery modesty of its palms, in the certitude of its style, in the economy and stringency of its lines, and the serenity of its mansions South of Broad Street, is a feast for the human eye.... The city of Charleston burns like a flame of purest memory. It is a city distorted by its own self-worship. (1–3)

Throughout the novel Will speaks of the decadence, snobbishness, inbreeding, and corruption of Charleston (especially in the section South of Broad). In contrast, again throughout the novel, there are passages in which Will rhapsodizes about its beauty, elegance, and allure.

Part of Will's ambivalence comes, of course, from its being the home of the Institute. While there is a stark contrast between the outward severity of the Institute's architecture and discipline and Charleston's luxuriant, southern refinement, there is actually a curious symbiosis between them. As Will walks through the city on the night before graduation, he muses on the ways in which the Institute and Charleston, both

separately and together, have made him a man. The beauties and betrayals of Charleston, the tests of love and loyalty in spite of the horrors
of the Institute, have made him the poised, mature man of strength he
has become.

THEMATIC ISSUES

James Dickey has said, "*The Lords of Discipline* is a novel about virtues
we neglect to our diminishment: courage, brotherhood, and victory over
the difficult obstacles to authentic manhood." This is an apt introduction
to the broader thematic issues of the novel. Although Will McLean's
coming-of-age is at the center of *The Lords of Discipline*, just as Ben Meecham's was in *The Great Santini*, the later novel is so much richer in the
texture of its plot and structure that Will's rites of passage are an integral
part of the overall thematic statement of the book rather than the nearly
single focus that Ben's were in the earlier novel. Will's sexual initiation
with Annie Kate is set apart from the world of the Institute, and his
discovery of the hypocrisy and false values of Charleston society is, in
part, independent of his relationship with Tradd St. Croix, but almost
all of the rest of the tests of manhood that Will undergoes are in the
context of his four years at the Institute. They include the physical and
psychological torture he survives in his plebe year; later the maintaining
of his integrity and intellectual honesty amid the enormous pressures for
conformity and uncritical acceptance of the military mentality; and, finally, the courage to act, even at serious risk to himself, in the service
of what he knows to be right. Perhaps most important of all, he at last
overcomes the urge to please, to be a "do-gooder," that has plagued the
Conroy alter ego in *The Water Is Wide*, *The Great Santini*, and the first
three-fourths of *The Lords of Discipline*. Will's reaction to Pig's ordeal and
death finally pushes him beyond that weakness of character (and hin-
drance to good writing) that Will has so lamented in himself. "I have
eyes that give people what they want, eyes that whore in order to please,
commiserate, endorse, affirm" (30). As Lamar York says: "He comes to
the truth of the artist, that only the individual is ever too holy to violate"
(45). He is now ready to speak the truth, whatever the consequences of
that may be.

Tied closely to these aspects of Will McLean's coming to manhood is
Conroy's severe indictment of the military ethos, particularly at the Institute, which encourages all of the abuses, corruptions, and hypocrisies

that are developed through the plot and characters. If Will has, as he frequently says, a love/hate relationship with the college, the love side of the equation is in spite of its policies and tactics under the direction of Bentley Durrell. Will's mixed emotions are reflected by contrasting characters: if Durrell is a villain, Berrineau is a hero; if Fox is a sadist, John Kennell is a decent human being; if Tradd St. Croix is a traitor, Mark Santaro is a giant of loyalty. Thus, Conroy's comment on the Institute and all it stands for is ambivalent, though his positive feelings and memories seem to have developed quite aside from the system rather than because of it.

Male bonding, in both its positive and negative aspects, is a major component of the novel's themes. The extraordinary loyalty and supportiveness of the four roommates (until Tradd betrays them) is one of the most obvious benefits of this bonding. Born in part of mutual need, but strengthened by growing affection and respect, this brotherhood is so strong and unusual that it inspires the awe and bewilderment of most of the roommates' peers. Hence, Tradd's betrayal is made to seem all the more heinous.

On the negative side of the male bonding theme, Conroy has much more to say and a great deal of harsh criticism. Obviously, in the military, order and effectiveness depend on the instinctive and unquestioning loyalty of one individual to another. Thus, any military institution, whether at the officers' or enlisted men's level, emphasizes this in many ways. That emphasis, however, when so obsessive and misdirected as Conroy shows it at the Institute, leads to any number of abuses and actual violations of the very values it purports to establish.

"The system," designed to create the Institute "man," has become, at least under General Durrell's tenure, a vicious cycle of sadism. It brings out the worst, most barbaric aspects of human nature, where a kind of competitiveness develops in which one cadet tries to outdo the next in the degree of his brutality. Many of the plebes who survive this nearly yearlong assault then repeat the insidious ritual when they become seniors, determined to make the next class of plebes suffer what they did. It is a system, says Conroy, that fosters bestial behavior and thinking even in its routine forms. Taken to an even more intense level, as it is with the Ten, it then becomes a Ku-Klux-Klan monstrosity of "cleansing" that knows virtually no limits in its tactics.

It is hardly surprising that in this all-male environment, there should be a strong undercurrent of homosexual innuendo and harassment, but at the same time a degree of eroticism. Conroy said in a *Washington Post* interview with Christine Williams, "There is no homosexuality under these conditions. If you smile, they'll kill you. You can imagine what would happen to a homosexual" (D11). On the one hand, Conroy seems naive; on the other, an openly gay student could hardly have survived at the Institute in the mid-1960s, nor would he have a much easier time in the 1990s. But Susan Faludi's article includes a long and thoughtful section on the substantial number of gay cadets who have relationships in the Charleston homosexual community. Indeed, she says The Citadel is often called "the Closet" because of the size of its repressed gay student population (80). Doubtless in the more permissive nineties there are more gay cadets who are willing to risk exposure than there were in the sixties, but Conroy's denial of any homosexuality is unconvincing.

Of course, in the macho society the cadets work so fiercely to portray, derogatory remarks about "faggot" and "fairies" are common. Tradd St. Croix's "Honey Prince" is an unusually gentle example. There are dozens of such disparaging remarks and jokes about homosexuality in the novel, in fact, so many that it is an indication that it is a subject never very far from the consciousness of the cadet corps.

What Conroy, himself, may not have been aware of is that there is a running theme of homophilic behavior in the novel. This moves from the totally non-sexual love of the four roommates and their frequent kissing of each other and long embraces in moments of particular tenderness to the more overtly erotic, as in Fox's sadistic attack on Will in the shower room:

> His lips touched my ear in a malignant parody of a kiss. The pleasure of discipline to Fox, I realized as I felt his tongue close to my ear, was related to a ruthless sexuality. There was something nightmarishly erotic in his brutality. (148)

Bo Maybank's giving Will a massage in the locker room is innocent of any overt erotic intent, but there is a distinctly sensual feeling imparted (322). There is the implied voyeurism of the cadre on Hell Night (138). And there is the far more innocent, but nevertheless obvious male bonding of athletes: "Athletes have a strange but genuine compulsion to touch each other's asses" (310).

Finally, in the climactic scene of the novel, Will says to Abigail that he "wouldn't let Tradd unzip my fly" (494). That he chooses this trope to declare his abhorrence of what Tradd has done is remarkable in that it indicates that although Tradd may not be literally homosexual, he has degraded himself so completely that in Will's mind he is morally perverted. Probably Will, alone, as a liberal among the majority of knee-jerk homophobes in the novel, would have had no trouble in accepting the fact that Tradd was, indeed, gay, but he is so appalled by Tradd's betrayal that he lashes out by saying that Tradd is not an honorable man, gay or otherwise.

In addition to the many levels of the themes in the novel dealing with the military in general and the Institute in particular, perhaps the next most prominent issue is the xenophobic snobbery and false values of Charleston society. These are embodied chiefly in the St. Croix family and the pathetic Annie Kate Gervais and her mother. These and the other families that constitute the aristocracy believe in a caste system they attempt to impose as rigidly as if they were members of nineteenth-century European nobility and almost as rigidly as "the system" is imposed at the Institute. Although cultured and genteel, their values depend largely on appearances, and their judgments of people begin with questions about their ancestry and where they were born. Will is immediately conscious of this arrogance, but he is also captivated, first by Abigail and then by Annie Kate, so that he tends to repress his innate dislike of such pretensions. At the end, betrayal on all sides makes him fully aware of, and fully disgusted by, the deceptions and shallow characters of these pompous mandarins.

As in all of Conroy's work, the issue of racism is prominent here. In *The Great Santini* it is largely rural rednecks who make up the bigoted segment of the population. In *The Lords of Discipline* it is the alumni, faculty, and students of a college who are determined to keep the "nigger" from graduating. It is all the more appalling, says Conroy, to find such attitudes among the presumably educated leaders of the military and civilian societies. The effort, at all levels, to destroy Tom Pearce is a disgrace and a parallel to lynch-mob psychology, only worse, because in its most virulent form, it hypocritically pretends not to exist.

STYLE AND LITERARY DEVICES

If Conroy's style in *The Great Santini* is a workmanlike, serviceable, largely undecorated one, the opposite is true of *The Lords of Discipline*. From the very first page of the novel the reader is struck by Conroy's richly, almost self-consciously, literary prose. The vocabulary is varied and esoteric; there are dozens of lengthy poetic descriptions (particularly of Charleston, but of many other things as well) filled with similes and metaphors:

> I tried to join the flow. . . . But the guerrilla within asserted his presence if not his primacy from the very beginning, and a small bloodless war, without strategies or anthems, began to rage for the control of my interior. (152)

There are many extended metaphors like this: for example, Will uses geography to analyze his personality during the dark days after Poteete's suicide (211–12). There are allegories such as Will's identification with whales which exhaust themselves looking for mates (54). There are interior monologues such as the one that begins Part II (127–28), and there are set pieces such as the description of Will's final basketball game (316–25). In fact, it is probably this highly embellished style, albeit for the most part appropriate and controlled, that gave Conroy his first push toward comparisons with other southern authors like Thomas Wolfe. (It would not be until the publication of the more gothic *The Prince of Tides* that this comparison would become commonplace.)

At the other end of the stylistic spectrum, Conroy is capable of writing lean, suspenseful prose that gives the novel its tension-filled moments, especially in the final one-third. As Pearce and Will become convinced that the Ten do exist and are determined to drive a black man out of the Institute (329 ff.); on the night that Will leaves the barracks after taps in order to find out what the Ten are doing to Pearce (382 ff.); in the actual discovery and aftermath of that spying (390 ff.); during the scene when the Bear and Will confront General Durrell (Chapter Forty-seven)—these and many other scenes show Conroy's ability to switch gears and write action-driven prose that leaves imagery and metaphors aside and moves forward with page-turning intensity.

Thus, Conroy has, by the time of *The Lords of Discipline*, become an accomplished stylist, able to create a variety of moods and a richly textured novel of literary merit. What is more, he has become equally adept with a variety of figures of speech, symbols, and allusions. Conroy does not depend heavily on symbols, but there are many in *The Lords of Discipline*, some of them obvious and pervasive, some subtle and used in isolation. Among the continuously-used and self-defining ones is, of course, the ring. Far more than a simple college class ring, the Institute ring supposedly announces to the world that its wearer has achieved not only the vaunted "manhood" promoted by the Institute's publicity, but values of loyalty, pride, and integrity that go beyond even those of other military institutions like West Point. There is an elaborate, almost religious ritual in the awarding of the rings (Chapter Twenty-six), and there are continued references throughout the novel to the significance of "wearing the ring." Indeed, Part III is subtitled, "The Wearing of the Ring." That so many wearers of the ring turn out to be villainous betrayers of those very virtues it purports to convey makes it a mockery on one level, but, on another, it continues to carry its awesome power. When Colonel Berrineau gives Will his ring as an earnest of his loyalty to the cause of exposing the Ten, this is an act of ultimate commitment, and when Pig begs to be allowed to keep his ring, even though cadets who have been discharged for honor violations are required to return them, it is a poignant reinforcement of the great symbolic value placed on the ring by the cadets and graduates.

Other less pervasive, but nonetheless powerful symbols occur. Some of the more notable are the delivery of Annie Kate's baby, dead because its "umbilical cord [was] wrapped three times around its throat. It was as if the child was hung from a tree and strangled a little bit at a time" (346). The strangling, inbred, false values of Charleston society could scarcely be more vividly presented. The sand dollars, fragile and filled with religious symbolism, so lovingly collected by Will and Annie Kate during her pregnancy, come back to Will in a box from California (with no return address), most of them shattered in the transit. The lion in the park, "old and humiliated . . . [but] at night there was some dignity and sense of dread in his roar" (210) and the 11:42 train are symbols of stability and constancy for Will in his troubled moments (for eleven days after the suicide of Poteete he is so stunned and puzzled that he doesn't hear them). It is also the 11:42 train before which Dante Pignetti throws himself, a collision of two indomitable forces.

There is a striking use of allusion in the Prologue when Will speaks of himself, in spite of his love of Charleston, as always feeling like a visitor even though he has spent four years there. Will then compares himself to Edgar Allan Poe, who wrote "The Gold Bug" while he was stationed at Fort Moultrie and was also a "misplaced soldier" (1). From Poe he turns to Osceola, the Seminole chieftain, who was held prisoner at Fort Moultrie, and says that, like Osceola, he has spent time in a Charleston "prison." Later in the novel there is the anecdote of the whale that mistakenly swam into the Charleston harbor, was butchered, and whose skeleton now hangs in the museum, like a symbol of Charleston's rejection of outsiders. (264). Thus, through a series of historical allusions and symbols like the whale and the mournful lion in the park, Conroy constructs a motif having to do with Charleston's exclusivity.

An even more pervasive motif is created by Conroy's repeated references to nine-month periods. From the first pages of the novel, Will speaks of the nine months until he will graduate (11), often of the nine long months of Hell that were his plebe year (170, 184); and although Annie Kate is already pregnant when Will meets her, she frequently speaks of her nine-month ordeal and, in her more neurotic moments, of the nine months of her life that have not existed (235). These are by no means the only references to nine months, and they fit into another pattern of birth as in, of course, Annie Kate's baby, but also repeatedly to the making of the Institute man. This pattern of related phrases and images is a constant reminder that the real, albeit metaphorical, birth of the novel is that of Will McLean. He speaks again and again of the boy who walked through the Gates of Legrand in September 1963, of his innocence, of his naiveté, of his lack of self-confidence. The man who walks out of the Gates of Legrand in June 1967 has long since lost those qualities and replaced them with courage, self-confidence, and integrity:

> I had come to Charleston as a young boy, a lonely visitor . . . who grew fluent in his devotion and appreciation of that city's inestimable charm. . . . The boy was dying and I wanted to leave him in the silent lanes South of Broad. I would leave him with no regrets except that I had not stopped to honor his passing. I had not thanked him for his capacity for astonishment, for curiosity, and for survival. . . . He had challenged me to become a gentle, harmless man. For so long, I had felt like the last boy in America and now, at last, it was time to leave him. Now it was the man. (496)

A MARXIST READING

Marxist literary criticism has a much larger scope of interest than a narrow reading of the name might imply. Obviously it has its roots in the theories of Karl Marx (1818–1883) and his collaborator, Friedrich Engels, whose *The Communist Manifesto* (1848), contains as clear an outline of their ideas as is to be found anywhere. Fundamentally, Marx believed that the prevailing economic system in any historical period produced the social and political organization of that period. This theory leads him next to the premise that all of history is one struggle between the exploiting (ruling, wealthy) and the exploited (oppressed, poor) classes. His conclusion was that the time (mid-nineteenth century) was ripe for revolution in which the working classes would rebel against and overpower the bourgeois, capitalist elite and create a classless society. Marx and Engels did not live to see their predictions come to pass, nor did the revolution happen where they thought it most likely that it would—western Europe—and, when it did in Russia, certainly not in the Utopian way they envisioned.

While Marx himself and his immediate followers may have looked at literature primarily as a text in which attention to the class struggle was the preeminent indicator of its value, even they, as Raman Selden says, "look[ed] for 'progressive' aspects of bourgeois writing rather than merely to damn all pre-socialist culture as reactionary" (158). This first generation of Marxist critics "would not—indeed could not—think of aesthetic matters as being distinct and independent from such things as politics, economics, and history. Not surprisingly, they viewed the alienation of the worker in an industrialized, capitalist society as having grave consequences for the arts" (Murfin "Marxist" 334). Thus, at the heart of Marxist literary criticism from its beginnings has been a primary interest in content rather than form. Although this approach to literature has undergone a number of evolutionary stages, this concern with content, especially as it has to do with social, political, and economic issues, has remained at its center.

The next "generation" of Marxist literary critics broadened their interests to the extent that they believed literature could have an important role in social reform. Wilfred Guerin and his colleagues put it this way:

> [T]here was considerable stress on the uses of literature in the proletarian revolt and on seeing literature as a projection of the movement of social history. Some believed that dialectical materialism could provide a sufficiently large frame of reference, a worldview, within which literature would have a practical, even a polemical role. (273)

This generation of Marxist critics (roughly those writing in the 1920s through the early 1940s) had little sympathy with authors who did not direct their attention to working-class problems and share working-class ideals. These Marxist critics fell into disrepute among other critics almost from their earliest pronouncements. The opponents' claim was that such criticism was reductionist, seeing art as didactic.

In part because of the discrediting of the Marxist critics of the pre-World War II variety by newer schools of thought about literature, in part because of the hostility to communism in the years of the "cold war" and its recent collapse in Europe, and in part because of the influence of other theories of literary criticism (especially psychological and deconstructive), a third generation of Marxist critics has developed in the last twenty-five years. They are often divided among themselves about the aims and methods they should endorse, but they are agreed that there is still a valid place for a Marxist approach to literature. In a seminal article, Richard Wasson claims that because Marxist criticism examines the work of literature in relation to its historical and social background, it transcends what he calls the "mystifications and sterilities" of other critical schools such as reader-response and formalism (171). A leader of this new breed of Marxist critics (or neo-Marxists as they are often called) is Frederick Jameson, who has attempted to develop what he calls "dialectal criticism," which is really a blend of the old-style Marxist criticism with a broader spectrum of approaches, the result being a methodology that examines a work in its thematic and technical aspects as well as its social context. In "Questions Marxists Ask About Literature," Ira Shor lists in concise form (two pages) the primary concerns of today's Marxist critics. While all of his questions are pertinent, a few of the major ones are particularly relevant to a study of a work like *The Lords of Discipline*:

> What are the work's conflicting forces? . . . What threatens order? . . . Who wins in the end? . . . In terms of characterization . . . are characters from all social levels equally well-sketched? . . . What are the values of one class to another and how are they expressed? . . . What do characters (or classes of characters) worry about? . . . What considerations override basic impulses toward love, justice, solidarity, generosity, etc.? . . . Which values allow effective action? . . . Does the protagonist defend or defect from the dominant values of the society? . . . What controls (sanctions or procedures or protocol) exist within each group of characters to control behavior? (178–79)

The aristocracy of Charleston in *The Lords of Discipline* would prove as obvious and vulnerable a target for Marxist critics as Bull Meecham does for feminist critics in *The Great Santini*. From Conroy's opening description of Charleston South of Broad, its attitudes and values, its inbreeding and insularity, to the last pages of the novel when Annie Kate explains why Abigail St. Croix would never have allowed Tradd to marry her, the indictment of this class is unremitting:

> Observers have described Charlestonians as vainglorious, obstinate, mercurial, verbose, xenophobic, and congenitally gracious. . . . Aristocrats in Charleston, like aristocrats the world over, had proven the dangers of sipping from the genetic cup without a sense of recklessness or a gambler's eye for the proper stranger. Too many blue-eyed men had married too many blue-eyed third cousins, and it was not uncommon to find husbands and wives who looked like brother and sister. (16–17)

Examples of these qualities abound. Many come, of course, from the St. Croix family—its inherited wealth and social position, its over-insistence on a kind of artificial formality, the hypocrisy and snobbery of Commerce in his symbolic, locked-room study. As for the St. Croix mansion, even its garden is too well manicured, and Tradd, long before his betrayal, remains aloof from his best friend with a kind of formality that is a manifestation of the St. Croix's attitude that any physical contact is demeaning to people of their station. Tradd's effeteness; Abigail's over-refined hands; Commerce's sinister, secret journals; and dozens of other examples would be for the Marxist critic the strongest possible evidence of the decadence and potential for evil of a class so rigidly bound to its social position, wealth, and power.

While the St. Croix are to the manner born and have at least the outward resources, both financial and cultural, to maintain their way of life, Annie Kate Gervais and her mother are pathetic in their attempt to make themselves and others believe that they are still members of the aristocracy. A perfect symbol of their decline is their garden, which is wildly overgrown and untended in comparison to the St. Croix's too-artificially groomed grounds. Although it is true that "blood" is more important than money for being considered a part of this social elite, Mrs. Gervais calls Will "a callow-faced merchant's brat" (295), wallows in self-pity about her situation, and yet boasts about her aristocratic heritage. Her class consciousness is almost more arrogant, because less secure, than that of the St. Croix. Mrs. Gervais's alcoholism, her constant complaint about what Annie Kate has done to *her* as opposed to concern about her daughter's needs, and all her false values, a Marxist critic would abhor and would see as the vile fruits of a totally decadent class structure.

If Annie Kate's attitudes are slightly more flexible than her mother's, they are only marginally so, and she is equally snobbish and shallow. She denies the existence of the baby, and she tells Will never to mention the subject to her again. She claims that after these "nonexistent" nine months are over, she will return to Charleston society as if nothing had happened (292). When Will asks her what she plans "to do with this phantom child who's going to be feeding at your breast" (291), Annie Kate replies that she would never consider breast-feeding a child because she thinks it spoils women's breasts. And, when he asks her if she might ever have come to love him had she not been in trouble, she says that she has been "programmed" to marry someone who is her social equal (290). Annie Kate comes to have some affection for Will and to depend on him as her only companion, but she never once questions her feeling that he is her inferior. Thus, she is cruel to the one person who has supported her. She does come to the realization that perhaps she will never be able to go to the debutante ball, but that is about as far as she gets toward a recognition of reality. Even in her final letter to Will (which she asks him not to answer) she is back at playing her role. She tells everyone in California that she is from an old, aristocratic southern family and plays the part of southern belle for its maximum effect. To a Marxist critic (or, in fact, to any other type) this behavior is prima facie evidence of the ways in which a class system such as Charleston's viciously distorts ordinary human decency, to say nothing of its judgments about what is of true value.

While society South of Broad would be the chief object of Marxist critics' attention in *The Lords of Discipline*, the Institute, with its brutal treatment of the plebes, its hypocritical use of excess discipline to harass a cadet who is deemed unfit, its driving students to disgrace and even suicide on trumped-up charges, and its crypto-fascist "cleansing" through the Ten would come in for a large share of opprobrium. These abuses are so excessive that a Marxist critic (or, again, almost any other kind) would immediately recognize Conroy's interest in addressing many of the "Questions" Shor poses. In particular, when Shor asks about justice and the protagonist's reaction to the dominant values of the society, it seems almost as if he was writing with a novel like *The Lords of Discipline* in mind. In an examination of the Institute, there are several "conflicting forces," the chief of which are those having to do with power rather than social class. As in any military organization, there is, and has to be, a hierarchy of command and authority; but at the Institute, on both the cadet and administrative levels, that authority is exercised in an obscene parody of what might be judged necessary for good order and training.

The cruel behavior of the cadets is bad enough, but that of the administration is even worse. In the first place, under Bentley Durrell's leadership, instead of curbing the worst atrocities of the Taming, he has actually encouraged more severe physical and psychological torment. In response, then, to Shor's question about controls of unacceptable behavior, the answer is that at the Institute there are virtually none. Finally, of course, the very existence of the Ten and their activities—condoned and abetted by men like Durrell, Commerce St. Croix, and Tradd—are an ugly blot of the most offensive kind on any standard of humane behavior. Any Marxist critic, neo- or otherwise, would find the Ten, and Tradd's betrayal of those he claims to love, ultimate examples of the dehumanizing effects that can result when the ruled have insufficient resources to resist the malignant motives of rulers who have near-total power. Will McLean is a hero by the criteria of any critic, but he would be of particular interest to a Marxist: first, because of his betrayal by, and final rejection of, the decadent Charleston aristocracy; and, second, because of his relentless determination to expose the abominations of the Ten, among which are the attempt to destroy any chance of a minority student's graduation and the driving of a naive young man to suicide by virtue of their insidious endeavor to preserve, at whatever cost, their secret sources of power.

NOTE

1. In *The Lords of Discipline*, one of Pat Conroy's major plot threads, with reverberations on several others, involves the Institute's formerly overt and now covert attempts to prevent the first black's being allowed to survive his "knob" year (a cadet's first—called "plebe" in the book) at the college and thence to graduate.

VMI (Virginia Military Institute) and The Citadel are the last two military colleges in the United States that receive public funds yet have refused to accept female cadets. Both institutions have argued vigorously that the inclusion of women would so radically alter the very nature of the indoctrination and training they provide to create "the whole man" that it would virtually destroy their programs. In 1995 VMI reached a tenuous compromise by creating a facsimile program at nearby Mary Baldwin College (an arrangement challenged by the U. S. Justice Department), and The Citadel, under a Federal District Court order to admit Faulkner or provide an alternate program by the beginning of the 1995–1996 academic year, has established an ROTC-type curriculum at Converse, a private women's college in the area. Twenty-two women have been accepted and began their training there on August 31, 1995, but Faulkner and her lawyers flatly rejected the Converse arrangement as an acceptable alternative.

In early August 1995, The Citadel made last minute appeals to Justices Rehnquist and Scalia of the U. S. Supreme Court to stay the lower court's ruling; both refused. Thus, on August 14, 1995, Shannon Faulkner became the first female cadet in The Citadel's history. But, having won her legal battle, Faulkner resigned after her first week as a cadet, citing the enormous emotional toll her struggle had taken. Immediately, a second woman, Nancy Mellette, sought through legal intervention to be admitted to The Citadel in the fall of 1996, and at least two hundred other women have inquired about admission under the court ruling that allowed Faulkner her few days as a full-fledged cadet. Now that the Converse program is in place, The Citadel will doubtless argue strenuously to have it declared a satisfactory alternative when a Federal judge rules on the matter. If the ruling is against The Citadel, it will certainly appeal again as far as the Supreme Court; if the ruling is in favor of the Converse alternative, then the Justice Department will challenge the single-sex education there as it is doing with VMI and Mary Baldwin. The ultimate outcome may be several years in the making, but the final ruling seems inevitable—separate cannot be equal. In any case, the controversy provides an interesting gloss on many of Conroy's observations about the attitudes and rearguard actions of The Citadel's administration and alumni of a quarter century ago.

The Prince of Tides
(1986)

With the success of *The Great Santini* and *The Lords of Discipline*, helped along by their popular movie versions, Pat Conroy became a name that commanded attention in the field of popular fiction. It was not, however, until *The Prince of Tides* was published in 1986 that he attained mega-star status. In its original hardcover edition it stayed on the best-seller list for almost a year, only to be displaced by the paperback version, which stayed on that best-seller list for almost another year (Max 84). When the movie was released, sales once again soared for both the hardbound and paperback versions of the book. Max reports that Conroy wrote to Streisand complimenting her on the film, and that, extraordinary as it is for an author to be pleased with the film version of his novel, even more extraordinary was the fact that, even in blasé New York, moviegoers turned to each other recommending the book as the credits came on the screen (Max 84). "During President-elect Bill Clinton's campaign, he said his two favorite books were *One Hundred Years of Solitude* and *The Prince of Tides*. That got Pat Conroy's vote" (Hopper C1).

Although reviewers were less unanimous in their enthusiasm, many of them, like Gail Godwin, praised its power and invention. Others went further:

> Pat Conroy has fashioned a brilliant novel that ultimately affirms life, hope and the belief that one's future need not be contaminated by a monstrous past. (Bass 3)

But what almost every reviewer said, including those who were generally well disposed to the novel, was that it was overlong and overwritten:

> Inside this fat book, a thin book is struggling to get out. It never does, but from time to time, we glimpse an elegant ankle, a sinewy wrist and the flash of eyes alive with wit and compassion. (Eder 3)

Others found too many scenes that stretch credibility and are not strictly germane to the plot. Weeks said that the profusion of grotesquerie in the novel is sometimes almost overwhelming ("Pat Conroy . . ." 14). Only one or two reviews were almost entirely negative: "It's Confederate prose like this that gave Southern writing a bad name" (Geeslin 8).

Conroy reacted to the success of *The Prince of Tides* with understandable pride and with remarkable restraint about some of the negative reviews. He told Abrams that reviewers in New York and Los Angeles probably wanted him to restrict the focus of the novel to the romance between the coach and the psychiatrist and thought he was exaggerating when he included a Bengal tiger and a criminal who was a giant, but that these were facts of life in South Carolina (1). Thus, *The Prince of Tides* received its share of critical praise and censure. This has not seemed to interfere at all with its continuing popularity and success in what Conroy set out to do—to write a southern family saga in the tradition of William Faulkner and Thomas Wolfe. He has said repeatedly that he knows he is not a writer of the same caliber as they, but that it is to their kind of writing he aspires. *The Prince of Tides* is a southern gothic novel (see definition in Chapter Two) in the subgenre that Conroy has chosen. *The Prince of Tides* belongs with William Styron's *Lie Down in Darkness*, Reynolds Price's *The Surface of Earth*, the novels and stories in Carson McCullers's *The Ballad of the Sad Café*, and the somewhat less ambitious novels of authors like Elizabeth Rivers Siddons among many others who write in the tradition established by Faulkner and continued by Flannery O'Connor, Tennessee Williams, and Robert Penn Warren. *The Prince of Tides* is a novel that might be called overblown, but it is, at the same time, a novel filled with wonderful chapters of storytelling, sometimes humorous, sometimes adventurous, and sometimes threateningly violent, with plot-related relevance; there are other chapters that, if only tangentially related to the plot, involve matters that concern the development and the destinies of the major characters.

It seems that Conroy might have responded to his critics by saying, "It isn't *The Prince of Tides* that you find overwritten, but the school of southern gothic fiction that you dislike." That might be a legitimate critical position, but neither Conroy nor the critics really have emphasized it. What seems almost irrelevant to that critical debate is that the public has continued to this day to love *The Prince of Tides*, the critics notwithstanding. There are flaws in the novel that even its most ardent admirers will admit, but there are strengths that so outweigh its weaknesses that there are few who would deny it a preeminent place in the field of popular fiction.

NARRATIVE POINT OF VIEW

One of the things critics and some readers have difficulty dealing with is Conroy's handling of narrative point of view. The novel is told in the first person by Tom Wingo, but this is complicated by at least several levels of storytelling. In the Prologue Tom speaks in both the past and the present tenses, giving us something of his family's history, briefly going back several generations, but seeming to indicate that he is going to tell us the story of his eccentric relatives:

> The Wingos were a family that fate tested a thousand times and left defenseless, humiliated, and dishonored. But my family also carried some strengths into the fray, and these strengths let almost all of us survive the descent of the Furies. Unless you believe Savannah; it is her claim that no Wingo survived.
> I will tell you my story.
> Nothing is missing.
> I promise you. (8)

Then in Chapter One, his mother, Lila, arrives announcing Savannah's most recent suicide attempt and sending Tom off to New York to find out what her situation is. Once there, Tom gives us a chapter dealing with the time, nine years before, when he and Luke came to New York for Savannah's first poetry reading. From then on until the Epilogue, there are chapters about the Wingo past that are ostensibly intended to help Savannah's psychiatrist, Susan Lowenstein, get to the roots of her patient's problems, but it becomes almost immediately apparent that these stories of his and his family's past are told in an appeal to help him regain control of his own life. Lowenstein has taped what seems like gibberish that Savannah speaks when she first regains consciousness after her third suicide attempt, and she asks Tom whether any of it means anything to him. His reply is that it does and that it is essentially Savannah's autobiography:

> "Her autobiography? Will you stay in New York and tell me all you know?"
> "From the beginning to the end, Doctor. For as long as you need me. . . . I've got some terrible things to tell you."
> "Thank you for wanting to help Savannah, Tom," she said.
> "No," I replied. And, almost strangling, I said, "Help *me*. Help *me*." (58)

For nearly five hundred pages we have a mix of chapters dealing with the stories that Tom and Susan think are of importance in direct relation to Savannah's current collapse. Sometimes these are introduced by "I told Lowenstein" devices, and at other times they conclude by his saying, "Lowenstein told me that what I had told her helped her enormously in understanding Savannah." Other chapters are written as if Conroy were reverting to Tom-speaking-to-the-reader narration, but it seems that we are to believe these are also tales told to Lowenstein even when her name doesn't appear in the chapter at all.

Interspersed through these stories about the Wingo family are episodes, or parts of chapters, having to do with the developing relationship between Susan and Tom, his coaching of her son in football, and the whole plot line having to do with Susan's unhappy marriage and Tom's role in that imbroglio, which have almost nothing to do with Savannah's problems but which have everything to do with Tom's unofficial therapy.

There is an enormously rich mix of chapters about the Wingos' past, going back to his grandparents' marriage and separation; the horrific night on which Tom and Savannah were born in the midst of a hurricane; Henry Wingo's harrowing escape from Germany into Switzerland during World War II; and other stories that Tom can have learned only through the repetition of family legends. Some are comic, some violent, and some heroic, all told, presumably even when there are not clear signals, to Lowenstein. Then there are the chapters with Susan; her husband, Herbert Woodruff; and their son Bernard—a dysfunctional family in whose lives Tom comes to play an important role. The counterpoint of these plot lines, all told by Tom, is part of what gives the novel its richly textured dimensions. This is also, doubtless, part of what makes it seem, at times, too big, although the parallel dysfunction of the Wingo family and that of the Lowenstein-Woodruff family offers an interesting contrast, in that they come from such totally different geographic and socio-economic milieus. There is almost too much going on, but Conroy succeeds, at least on first reading, in making the reader ignore these problems because, as author, he is so expert in making the tangential stories fascinating in their own right.

Then, quite amazingly, in the Epilogue, Conroy achieves closure of all this adverse personal history and trauma. Tom doesn't fool himself into thinking that everything is solved for Savannah, Susan, or himself, but there is a glorious epiphany in the closing pages of the book. Tom is back in Charleston and at peace with himself and his family, but there is still a part of him that loves Susan Lowenstein and is grateful for what she has done. Each evening, as he is driving home from coaching:

> [A]s I reach the top of [the] bridge I say it in a whisper, I say it as a prayer, as regret, and as praise. I can't tell you why I do it or what it means, but each night when I drive toward my southern home and my southern life, I whisper these words: "Lowenstein, Lowenstein." (567)

PLOT DEVELOPMENT

It would be possible, perhaps, to unscramble the totally unchronological presentation of events in *The Prince of Tides* and chart several sequential plot lines with beginnings, middles, and ends. To do so, however, would destroy the richness of one of the novel's greatest appeals. On what might be considered the major plot level of the book, Tom Wingo is telling Susan Lowenstein stories about the family history, and especially those involving Savannah, in order to help the psychiatrist in understanding her patient's illness. These stories come in no particular order save that Tom recognizes many references in what he calls "Savannah's autobiography," and he attempts to explain these references, which often become the triggers that set him off on a particular anecdote or shocking episode. But even these are certainly not given in the order in which they occur on Lowenstein's tape.

Simultaneously, as Tom is telling Lowenstein these stories of the Wingo children's past, he is undergoing an unofficial therapy of his own. From the first chapter of the book, we realize that Tom is going through a midlife crisis. Not as melodramatic as Savannah's, Tom's nervous breakdown, caused in large part by the death of his beloved brother, Luke, has cost him his job and is in grave danger of costing him his marriage. He speaks constantly of his mediocrity and his need "to turn his life around." Unlike Savannah or Luke, Tom is not a person given to grand gestures (in this sense he makes the perfect narrator-protagonist because as readers we can identify with him in ways that we could not with Savannah or Luke). But one of the most important plot threads in the book is Tom's attempts to set his own life in order.

Ironically, another major plot thread, closely interwoven with the first two, is the development of the love affair between Tom Wingo and Susan Lowenstein. While on the surface, Lowenstein is a cold professional, her personal life is a disaster; and the growing respect between a fairly rough-hewn, southern "boy" and a sophisticated, New York, Jewish psychiatrist that eventually blossoms into a passionate, though brief, affair is one of the most interesting plot developments in the novel. It is one that proves healing for them both. As a subplot in this strand of the narrative, Tom's coaching of Bernard and the growing surrogate father-son relationship between them is another healing element for both the man and the boy.

Perhaps it seems incidental when viewed in the order of plot developments discussed above, but what is really the overreaching plot element in the novel is the history of the Wingo family in all its eccentricity, ferocious battles, and traumatic experiences. Among these are episodes that become subplots on their own, such as the Atomic Energy Commission's decision to take over Colleton County, evacuate all of its citizens, and construct a facility to manufacture weapons or fuels for nuclear power plants. Luke's one-man guerrilla operation to obstruct this project takes up the whole of one long chapter and part of another. If it seems as if Tom is telling Lowenstein about his childhood, his parents' near-constant warfare, and his brother's heroic stature in order to help her understand Savannah and himself, that is, at least to some extent, a literary device to allow Conroy to report the saga of this extraordinary clan.

In addition to these plots and subplots, Conroy includes a rich collection of anecdotes, yarns, and family stories that have nothing to do with moving the action forward but which contribute greatly to our knowledge of the Wingo family. Chapter Eight, for example, provides a wonderful bit of comic relief, set as it is between others having to do with Savannah's problems and Lila's social ambitions. Tolitha, having returned to Amos (Tom's grandparents) after years of marriage to another man and several years of world travel, decides to choose her coffin. The entire chapter, including busybody Mrs. Blankenship's hysterics as Tolitha sits up in the coffin and Tolitha's being so overcome with amusement that she has to squat behind a shrub to relieve herself, is a set piece of comic delight.

Similarly, Chapter Sixteen, having to do with the white dolphin, Snow, comes abruptly between a chapter involving Tom and Lowenstein in New York and one concerning Tom and Savannah's reaction to the arrival of the first black student at Colleton High School. It is another set piece, in this case a bit more relevant to the character development of the Wingo children, especially Luke, but actually a delightful adventure that could stand apart as a short story in its own right. The audacity of the Wingos' "rescue" of Snow from a Florida aquarium in order to return her to the South Carolina waters that are her home is the kind of anecdotal digression that gives *The Prince of Tides* some of its wonderful variety.

There are parts of other chapters that serve much the same purposes. When Amos's driver's license is revoked because he has run over Mr. Fruit (a Colleton "town character"), and Patrolman Sasser says that he is a danger on the road, Amos (at this point in his late seventies or early eighties), in outrage at being called infirm, announces that he will water-ski the forty miles between Savannah and Colleton. And he does! Again, this episode is a set piece of description that has almost nothing to do with the main plot development of the novel, but it shows the tenacity and eccentricity that are hallmarks of the Wingo family. Similar stories include the depositing of a decomposing turtle in Reese and Isabel Newbury's bed and Amos's carrying a cross through town on Good Friday. Although the children's feeding of Papa John Stanopoulos's black widow spiders and Henry Wingo's improbable acquisition of Caesar, a Bengal tiger, seem at first to be further digressions of the same kind, they turn out to have plot bearing when both are involved in the contests with "Callanwolde," the giant who is to become the ugliest villain in the book.

The telling of these tales completely out of chronological order is precisely the way family stories are passed down. Grandmother does not sit down one day and give us a year-by-year account of what has happened to the family since its beginnings. We learn family history as one event in the present reminds us of a particular event or story of long ago. We look in retrospect to find the roots of an act that seems unexpected at the time it occurs but then find that there were foreshadowings years before that we had overlooked or failed to recognize as significant. Thus, in presenting the history of the Wingos in what seems at times almost chaotic disorder, Conroy achieves verisimilitude as we, the readers, learn about them, just as we have learned the histories of our own, perhaps less colorful, parents and grandparents. This big, somewhat excessive novel with its cornucopia of tales, anecdotes, and terrifying episodes is a magnificent rendering of an unusual family in precisely the right way—not chronologically, but in the haphazard way in which legends are created.

CHARACTER DEVELOPMENT

Tom Wingo is both the narrator and protagonist (chief character, "hero") of *The Prince of Tides*, and he is at the present time of the novel in a crisis of self-doubt and despair. Although the immediate catalyst for his condition seems to have been the death of Luke, his older brother whom he has idolized, as Tom tells the story of his youth and early manhood it becomes obvious that he has emotional problems that stem from much deeper and longer-standing sources. In the first place, all three Wingo children have suffered irreparable damage by growing up in the household of a violent father and a mother who desperately aspires to social status denied to her by a lack of money and by being married to a shrimp-boat captain.

Not only does Henry Wingo physically abuse his wife and children (reminiscent of Bull Meecham in *The Great Santini*), he creates an atmosphere of constant fear and unpredictability in the household. Lila acts as best she can to buffer the children from their father's violence (again, similar, to the role Lillian plays in *The Great Santini*), but she has ambitions of her own, and these often cause the children confusion and embarrassment. Tom feels that neither he nor his siblings will ever fully recover from the damaged childhood they suffered at the hands of Henry's violence and Lila's insistence on "family loyalty." All three children suffer from their parents' never-ending conflict, but they suffer in somewhat different ways. Luke becomes a stoic loner and Savannah becomes psychotic. (There are many other things, of course, which contribute to the development of the children's characters, but this dysfunctional family is certainly a major one.) Tom, like Ben Meecham (*The Great Santini*) and Will McLean (*The Lords of Discipline*) grows up as a child eager to please and do well, the normal, courteous, well-behaved son who seeks and receives approval.

As he grows older, Tom, who is obsessed by what he calls his mediocrity, attributes much of it to this childhood effort to please. He also acknowledges that his older brother Luke's powerful integrity, on the one hand, and Savannah's neurotic brilliance, on the other, made him feel "ordinary." This inferiority complex continues to plague him in college, where it turns out that, at least at first, he is only a very average football player and where he is rejected by every fraternity to which he applies because he is perceived as such a "hayseed." He even meets the girl, Sallie, who will later become his wife, because she too has been rejected by the sororities. Although later, when he has become a football hero, the fraternities beg him to pledge, his pride is too great to countenance this about-face. He takes some satisfaction in the reversal of roles, but damage has been done to his ego that really cannot be undone.

In spite of his love of literature (it is significant that, like Conroy, Tom especially admires Faulkner) and his delight in coaching, even before his breakdown and being fired, he has come to find his job less challenging than he at first expected it to be. Although he claims that it does not bother him that Sallie, as an M. D., makes far more money than he did when he was working, and now that he is without a job, is the sole support of the family, it clearly does wound his ego and contributes to his self-pity and despondency.

Furthermore, at the very moment Lila is sending him off to New York to see what can be done for Savannah, Sallie tells him that she is having an affair. Ever since Luke's death, Tom and Sallie's relationship has deteriorated. She claims, and he admits, that he has become morose and withdrawn. He acknowledges that he has become too introspective and unable to express his feelings. This is really only a part of a larger problem Tom has with women and love—one that he talks about at length with Lowenstein. He tends to lay the major blame for this failure in his emotional maturity on Lila, yet he knows also that it stems in large part from his own insecurity and inability to be open about his feelings. These two causes are intimately related, since Lila as mother has had a great deal to do with the personality of the son. Like many people with damaged psyches, Tom has a tendency to make cynical jokes when conversation touches raw nerves, and Tom's nerves are very raw on a number of subjects. This is only an outward manifestation of a deeper neurosis that runs through the Wingo family—repression. It has its roots in Lila's "family loyalty" refusal to let the public know of anything untoward in the family's history. In its psychotic form it is at the heart of Savannah's illness. Even Henry, late in the novel, denies that he ever abused the children, and Luke, who seems the most stable of them all, simply tries to ignore the past although this blocking out contributes to his isolation.

This habit of repression has become for Tom a defense mechanism, yet it lies at the heart of his own emotional problems. When Savannah asks him why the past has not harmed him as it has her, he replies that he tries not to think about it. This is not strictly true, but until he begins telling Lowenstein the stories of his past, he has, for the most part, tried to forget the past rather than face up to its implications, and nowhere has this been more damaging than in his continuing obedience to Lila's order that the savage rape never occurred. Though a man as scarred as Tom Wingo at age thirty-six can probably never turn his life completely around, his revelations to Lowenstein, which amount to admissions to himself about what happened in the past, and his affair with her, do marvels in helping him regain a degree of self-esteem. He can return to Sallie in an effort to make a new beginning in their marriage, and though he does not say it directly, it seems that he has his old teaching-coaching job again. The novel ends with him bittersweetly content with his life as it is at the moment, and that is certainly an enormous change from the situation in which we meet him in the early pages.

In addition to the help from Lowenstein, Tom has some inner strengths that have helped in reaching this catharsis. He has maintained, since childhood, his love of the southern landscape and has a real sense of roots, which he repeatedly talks about as sustaining:

> To describe our growing up in the lowcountry of South Carolina, I would have to take you to the marsh on a spring day, flush the great blue heron from its silent occupation, scatter marsh hens as we sink our knees in mud, open you an oyster with a pocketknife and feed it to you from the shell and say, "There. That taste. That's the taste of my childhood." I would say, "Breathe deeply," and you would breathe and remember that smell for the rest of your life, the bold, fecund aroma of the tidal marsh, exquisite and sensual, the smell of the South in heat, a smell like new milk, semen, and spilled wine, all perfumed with seawater. My soul grazes like a lamb on the beauty of indrawn tides. (5)

He has a resiliency that he temporarily forgets, and he has the temperament of a true teacher, as we see in the near miracle he works with the sullen Bernard Woodruff. Tom Wingo is a flawed hero, who has gone through rites of passage, both of the coming-of-age type like Ben's and Will's, but, even more difficult, those of the adult type in career, marriage, and self-assessment. At the end of the novel, Savannah, at least temporarily in control of herself, asks Tom if he thinks they are survivors. He replies that he feels fairly certain about himself but not so sure about her, yet he says the family gave her a greater gift than survival—genius.

Tom Wingo as survivor is an enormously sympathetic character; his twin Savannah as genius is a more problematic case. First of all, it is difficult for us as "normal" readers to identify with a psychopath. Secondly, her hatred of her family and the South seem extreme. She says, even as a teenager, that she hates the South and wants to escape at the first possible opportunity. The negative feelings are understandable, but the intensity of them is not. This is a case of unhealthy repression, just as is Tom's saying that he tries never to think of his childhood, but Savannah's is more fierce. Among the many things that Savannah is trying to repress, perhaps the single most important one is the rape that Lila claims never took place. (It was almost immediately after this that Savannah made her first suicide attempt.) But Savannah's problems go much farther back than that. She, unlike Luke and Tom (but somewhat like Mary Anne of *The Great Santini*), knows that what Henry and Lila have done to the children is something more serious than just making their lives miserable. She knows that there is emotional and psychological damage that may be more serious and long-lasting than the physical.

One of the earliest examples of Savannah's serious problems occurs when she holds one of Lila's stillborn babies (which had been put in the freezer until it could be buried the next day) in her arms all night and sees it as a symbol of the evil in the house. What is even more troubling than this bizarre behavior is that, the next day, Savannah doesn't remember anything about the episode, and only when she finds a wet spot in her bed from where the frozen baby had begun to thaw, does she admit to Tom that what he has told her is true. Her early denial of this incident and many others like it, prefigures her larger denials of reality that are to come later in the novel. Unlike Lila's denials, which are fully conscious and deliberate, Savannah's are involuntary—at least at first—and are, therefore, revelatory of a deep-seated psychosis.

The most dramatic of these is, of course, her attempt to assume the identity of Renata Halpern, a lesbian friend who nursed Savannah through one of her severe psychotic episodes and then, for reasons we are not told about except that she was also a suicidal personality, threw herself in front of a train. In this ultimate rejection of her past, Savannah begins to write poems under the name of Renata Halpern. She writes a children's fairy story that totally disguises and turns the events of the real rape into a fable with a happy ending. While one may try to understand a character, even feel sorry for one who has attempted suicide three times and has attempted to change her identity, it is very difficult to find her sympathetic. When she smears herself with her own excrement, when she becomes catatonic, we can understand why, but it is hard for the layman to accept the extreme depths of this self-loathing.

Indeed, were it not for the continuing love of Luke and Tom and were it not for some charming moments of her childhood and teenage years that we learn about, it would be hard to view Savannah as anything but a textbook psychotic. From her earliest days Savannah is a hypersensitive, intelligent person. She is impish and adventurous, always seeking a new challenge, taunting her brothers about their too-easy acceptance of life as it is. Very early she begins keeping a journal (which Lila burns because Savannah has recorded, word-for-word, one of her parents' vicious quarrels). She initiates, and then forces Tom to join her in, the welcoming of Benji Washington, the first black to be enrolled at Colleton High School. She is a cheerleader and the valedictorian of her class, and she is as bound to nature as are Tom and Luke, although this would seem to be something that she sacrifices in her total rejection of her past. But even behind these seemingly carefree episodes lies her need to escape. She says that, when she goes to New York, she will write poetry and live as wild an existence as she can socially, sexually, and emotionally.

Indeed, when she reaches the city, she does many of these things. She becomes a bisexual, radical feminist, a Vietnam War protester (while Luke is fighting there), and, most of all, a successful poet. It is, then, with delightful scenes from childhood and stories about her being "wild" in New York, that Conroy makes Savannah a character we find interesting and complex, even if we cannot fully sympathize with her. At the end of the novel, when there has been a reconciliation with Henry, and Savannah comes to visit Tom and Sallie, she says:

> "I'm going to make it, Tom," she said. Then, looking at the sun and the moon again, she added "Wholeness, Tom. It all comes back. It all comes full circle."

> She turned around, and facing the moon, which was higher now and silvering, she lifted herself on her toes, raised her arms into the air, and cried out in a brittle yet defiant voice, "Oh, Mama, do it again!" (566)

With these words Conroy makes the novel come full circle, since one of the opening scenes in the Prologue was of Lila's taking the children down to the river to point out the nearly simultaneous setting of the sun and rising of the moon: "Savannah, though only three, cried aloud to our mother, to Luke and me, to the river and the moon, 'Oh, Mama, do it again!' " (5) That Savannah has recovered enough to remember—and accept!—that moment in her past is Conroy's attempt to suggest that, although nothing with Savannah can ever be certain, there is a chance for her to regain stability, and in doing so he gives her a character we can respond to with affection and hope.

Of the three Wingo children, Luke may be the most enigmatic. In an early analysis, Tom sums up one side of Luke's personality very well. He says that Luke, as the oldest and the least intellectual of the children, became fixated on justice and constancy and became the protector of his younger siblings. Luke was "the hurt shepherd who drove the flock to safety" (44), as, by himself, he faces Henry's wrath. Tom tells Lowenstein that Luke's injuries were internal and that, because he was a man of action rather than of words, the others never knew exactly the extent of his hurt. He was the linchpin of the family because of his down-to-earth solidity.

And it is Luke, after all, who is the Prince of Tides! We don't know this until the end of the novel, when, as Tom and Savannah are burying him at sea, she reads her elegiac poem, "The Prince of Tides." There is a foreshadowing very early in the book as Tom reads and chokes up at the dedication to Savannah's second volume of poems, titled *The Prince of Tides*:

> Man wonders but God decides
> When to kill the Prince of Tides. (47)

We have no idea then, of course, that Tom is brought close to tears because it reminds him of Luke and his death. Nor do we yet know why Savannah chose that term to describe Luke or why Conroy chose Luke, at least on one level, as the title character of the novel. On another level, just as we have thought from the beginning, Tom is also a Prince of Tides. Although Luke is clearly not the hero (protagonist), he becomes a hero in an almost mythological sense. That he is a prince in every way (except in the strict, genealogical one) and a man with a passionate love of the sea, the estuaries, and the marsh lands become abundantly clear as the novel develops. Thus, while Tom, Savannah, and Susan Lowenstein may be more important on the plot level, it is Luke who embodies all the qualities of compassion, loyalty, commitment, and integrity that Conroy wants to celebrate as healing virtues in this book so full of characters in need of Luke's type of strength and honesty.

Throughout their childhood, Luke is thought of as not very bright and even told so by his parents. Actually, Savannah finds out by snooping through school records that Luke has the highest I. Q. of the three. A man of enormous physical strength, Luke is just far more interested in hunting and fishing than he is in matters of the intellect. On one level, he sees simplistic solutions to complex problems (e. g., if Savannah would simply get out of New York and stop writing poems about what has hurt her, her psychosis would disappear). He is totally unsophisticated and hates New York even more than Tom does. On the other hand, he is almost Christ-like as he tries to help every drunken bum or drug addict he meets on the streets. From his earliest days he fearlessly defends Tom and Savannah from Henry's attacks. Indeed, he is fearless in any situation, from his attack on Callanwolde to his eloquent endorsement of Benji Washington. He is the leader in the campaign to divert and discomfit the team sent from Miami to capture Snow, and it is his inventiveness and instinctive courage that makes her rescue a success. And if he is Christ-like in many situations, he is a modern St. Francis of Assisi in his affection for Caesar, the tiger Henry has bought as the mascot for his filling station. Tom and Savannah spy on Luke's training of the tiger to obey commands, including jumping through a burning circle and returning to his cage at a given signal:

> "He's crazy," I whispered to Savannah.
> "No," she said, "that's your brother Luke. And he's magnificent." (265)

Although he says that all he wants from life is to be a good shrimper and to be steady, there are far deeper aspects of Luke's character than those that are apparent in his pose and description of himself as a southern redneck (he is adamant, however, in his opposition to the racial attitudes usually associated with the type). He is clever and decisive as he unleashes Caesar on the rapists; he is persistent and prescient in keeping

Amos going in the waterskiing episode. In Vietnam he injects a lethal dose of morphine that puts his friend out of his misery; and in an incredible act of strength and valor, with increasing danger to himself, he brings the body of another friend back to the American base. Through it all, in spite of Bronze and Silver Stars, Luke retains his modesty and his honest desire for nothing more than a quiet life as a shrimper in Colleton County.

But, of course, this is precisely what he is denied. Through a bit of chicanery in Lila's divorce settlement, Reese Newbury gains, by his later marriage to Lila, ownership of Melrose Island, the Wingo family homestead. Added to his other large landholdings in the county, this gives him virtually a free hand in dealing with the Atomic Energy Commission in its plan to take over all of Colleton County and turn it into an atomic materials base. Shrimping is banned in the waters off the coast and the population of the town and the offshore islands is evacuated. Luke is so outraged by this wholesale devastation of the land and waters he has loved, that he vows to wage a one-man guerrilla war against the project. In his obsession with this battle, Luke shows enormous cunning and succeeds in some serious destruction of the government's vehicles and supplies. Unfortunately, in blowing up several bridges, he kills four men on a train that he had not expected to be crossing one of them on that particular night. Thus, he becomes the object of a search by the FBI as well as the government agents in charge of building the atomic facility. In this long contest, that Luke himself knows he cannot ultimately win, he shows some of the Wingo "madness." His tenacity becomes a kind of mania; his battle becomes an unrealistic crusade.

Tom and Savannah work out a bargain with an FBI agent named Covington, who promises that if they can find Luke and get him to surrender, he will guarantee a minimum sentence. Though Luke knows that it is only a matter of time until he will be captured in any case, he finds it hard to give up. Finally, Tom and Savannah persuade him to accept the terms Covington has offered, but in a last, sentimental journey back to Melrose Island before he surrenders, he is shot by one of the troops organized to hunt him down.

Luke Wingo is a figure larger than life. He is not only a physically powerful man, but he is incapable of compromise on moral issues. In one of the few times he ever turns on Tom, he calls him a coward for refusing to join in the battle against the government. When Lila sends a check to each of the children and to Henry as a kind of propitiation for her having let Melrose Island go, an act she realizes they despise, Luke

burns his. Luke's integrity is unshakable, even when it becomes misguided. He dies thinking that he has done nothing wrong (although he
deeply regrets the deaths of the four trainmen). Combining the qualities
of Christ and Don Quixote, Luke is the kind of hero around whom legends grow.

While Luke may have inherited some of his quiet virtues and fierce
integrity from his grandfather, Amos, those qualities skipped a generation as they bypassed his father, Henry. A violent, mean-spirited man,
Henry is primarily responsible for the misery that is the Wingo children's
life. Lila, in more subtle ways, must bear some responsibility for this
dysfunctional family's near-constant turmoil, but it is Henry, who,
sometimes in drunken rages, and often without any apparent provoca-
tion, lashes out verbally and physically at Lila and the children: "Without equivocation, I will tell you that he was a terrible and destructive
father" (242). Almost worse than Henry's actual physical abuse is the
total unpredictability of his moods and behavior.

Henry Wingo is a man with a permanent chip on his shoulder and a
cruel streak in his nature that borders on barbarity. He delights in telling
stories about napalming North Koreans when he has been recalled to
duty during that war. When Savannah says she wants to say hello to
her stillborn sister, Henry's reply is cruelly inhumane: "Rose Aster isn't
nothin' but dead meat. There's nothing there. Do you hear me? She's
like five pounds of dead shrimp" (144). He is a rabid sexist: "I don't
take shit from women, Lila," he said turning to her. "You're a woman
and nothing but a goddamn woman." (99). Only late in the novel does
he admit any remorse for having strangled a pregnant German woman
during his escape to Switzerland.

Part of Henry's rage, no doubt, comes from his feeling of being abandoned when Tolitha left Amos during the Depression and Amos's itinerant salesman's life set Henry adrift with distant relatives and servants.
Another part of it is fueled by his frustration at not being able to make
a success of any of his forays into the world of commerce. In the shrimping season, Henry is at his best; he is good at his job and he has an
affinity for the waters around Colleton that all the Wingo children in-
herit. But in the off-season, partly because he wants to please Lila by
making money and partly to prove to the world that he is a man of
ingenuity and business acumen, he becomes involved in a series of ventures that invariably end in disaster. These range from the gas station to
a taco stand operated by a Mexican who does not know how to make
tacos to trying to sell Christmas and Easter cards in which all the figures

are black. Savannah calls his the Sadim touch (Midas spelled backwards). Henry Wingo seems to learn nothing from his commercial failures; indeed, he rationalizes to such an extent that he thinks each new failure presages an extraordinary bit of luck in his next venture. So avid and insensitive is he in the pursuit of money that he writes the "anonymous" letter (and receives $1000 for his Judas-like betrayal) to the Miami Seaquarium about Snow that helps Captain Blair in her capture. Luke accuses him of committing a sin that not even God will forgive.

There are very few redeeming features in Conroy's portrait of this harsh, angry, and foolish man. There are small evidences that, in spite of his treatment of them, he really loves his children—such as the way he behaves with them when they go with him on the shrimp boat. He tries desperately to please Lila and earn her respect, often with his absurd business schemes, and in this he is a total failure. Only rarely as in the early description of Henry, when he has been shot down in Germany during World War II and is hidden by a priest, is there a glimpse of a man who is capable of gratitude and compassion. Finally, when he is released from prison (where he has served a term for drug running, the most disastrous of his get-rich-quick schemes), Henry Wingo seems at last to have come to some self-knowledge and regret for the wreck he has made of his life. As the novel ends, Henry is preparing to return to his shrimping, with a boat that Lila, in a gesture of peacemaking, has bought for him. Thus, even Henry can be welcomed back into the family, all of whom have suffered, but all of whom, at least for now, seem tentatively healed.

Not so Lila. In her decision to divorce Henry and marry the despicable Reese Newbury, she has cast her lot where she has always wanted it—with the rich and socially prominent. She would not be a welcome participant in the family reunion at the end, even if she wished to be. In his autobiographical sketch for *Book-of-the-Month Club News*, Conroy says that he promised his dying mother that he would make her beautiful in his new novel but that she might not like his depiction of her (5). Conroy clearly must know that his mother would not like his portrait of her as Lila since she is one of the most unsympathetic characters in the novel. In some ways, her behavior, although softer and more subtle than Henry's, may be even more damaging to the family than is his. This is evident in a number of ways. When the children are small she is nurturing and sensitive in teaching them to love nature and in protecting them from Henry's violent temper, but there are signs, early in the novel, of her selfish, manipulative personality. In terms of chronology, Chapter

One occurs in the present time of the novel so we are seeing Lila after she has married Reese and alienated her children by her part in the destruction of Colleton County, but as the novel goes on, the traits she displays there are shown to have their roots in the far distant past. When Tom asks her if she plans to go to New York to see Savannah, she uses the lame excuse that she can't go because she is having a dinner party that has been planned for months. She reverts to the age-old, self-pitying ploy of claiming that Savannah's suicide attempt is an effort to hurt *her* [Lila] and that all of her children hate her. Before she leaves she manages to lay guilt on Tom for being out of a job, to show her anti-Semitism in talking about Lowenstein, and to try to deny that heredity and environment have anything to do with psychosis (in an attempt, obviously, to deny that she might have had any part in creating Savannah's illness).

In fact, Lila has had a large role in making her children unhappy and emotionally disturbed. Even in her nurturing role there has been an element of hypocrisy. On the one hand, she seemed to overwhelm the children with love and care; on the other, there was a hidden part of Lila's character that almost resented them for having been born. At one point she calls Luke a fanatic, Savannah a lunatic, and Tom a mediocrity. One of the things that puzzles the children is that they can see or hear Lila being abused by Henry at night and then see her, the next morning, kiss him passionately. Another is her obsession with being accepted by the women of Colleton society, who often quite openly and cruelly humiliate her. At one point, because she so desperately wants to curry favor with the Newburys, she makes Tom apologize to Todd Newbury even though Todd has been outrageously rude and insulting. At another, having been blackballed for membership in the Colleton League, she attempts to gain entry by submitting an original recipe for their cookbook, an effort that Isabel Newbury denigrates by suggesting that Lila has copied it from another cookbook.

In this nearly neurotic effort to ''have what she can't get'' (228), she lies so long and so often about her family's background that she has almost come to believe that she is the daughter of a prominent banker in Georgia and a socially privileged mother, when in fact she is the daughter of blue-collar parents, her father an abusive alcoholic and her mother a nearly illiterate textile-mill worker. These lies about her background and her desire to better herself are not only at the heart of her contempt for Henry as a shrimper, but contribute significantly to the children's confusion, when on the one hand she praises them individually and on the other berates them for being vulgarians.

Damaging to the children's sense of identity and self-confidence as are Lila's attempts at social climbing, putting on appearances, and telling outright lies, a far more serious impediment to their emotional stability is a form of denial Lila calls "family loyalty." This refusal to admit reality reaches proportions of neurosis in Lila and causes, if only in part, Savannah's terrible illness and much of the distress that Tom and Luke suffer in their youth. Whenever Henry abuses her or the children, she denies that it has happened and forbids them ever to mention it publicly. Lila takes this position of disguising the truth about every unpleasantness she suffers. She refuses to tell even Amos and Tolitha of their desperate financial straits in the year after a cold winter has devastated the shrimp crop. Lila's reasoning is that it is a matter of family pride to present a unified, untroubled face to the world, lest people look down on them for their internal troubles and discords.

This "family loyalty" reaches its apex in Lila's denial of the rape of Savannah, Tom, and herself by Callanwolde and the other two escaped convicts. In an incredible feat of physical and emotional will, she manages to have Tom and Luke bury the rapists (who have been killed by Caesar, Savannah's gun, and Tom's wielding of the Infant of Prague statue) and to clean the house of all the blood and gore that have been generated by the rape and its aftermath before Henry returns in the evening! She makes the children swear, even when they need medical attention and Caesar is dying from the wounds he has received, that nothing has happened and that they will never mention the event to a living soul. This ultimate denial Lila claims is necessary if she is to maintain the family's honor and Savannah's ability to marry well. At this point her denial has reached psychotic proportions, and it has the immediate result of Savannah's attempting suicide three days later and the long-lasting effect of her suffering for the rest of her life from the repression of this traumatic event.

In this instance Luke makes one of his rare miscalculations about what is "right" and essentially sides with Lila, though his words are of "forgetting" rather than "denial." What, however, Luke can never forgive Lila for is her perfidy in giving Reese Newbury control over Melrose Island. In a cynical move to insinuate herself with the Newburys, Lila takes on, almost single-handedly, the nursing of Isabel through her terminal cancer. This is the woman who has repeatedly insulted and humiliated Lila for years, but Lila swallows her pride in order to be "available" as Reese's second wife once Isabel dies. She divorces Henry and marries Reese, finally achieving her long-standing desire to be a member of Colleton society (she is almost immediately inducted into the Colleton League) and its monied class. Lila has achieved what she has always wanted and glories in the perquisites of being married to Colleton's leading citizen, but she has done so at a terrible cost: her sons' abhorrence at what she has done; a knowledge of, and sense of guilt about, her children's hatred of her new husband; and, worst of all, her own integrity.

Although they are certainly secondary characters, no history of the Wingo family would be complete without including Amos and Tolitha. Conroy uses these two eccentrics for comic relief, but he also uses them to fill out his portrait of this southern gothic family. Not incidentally, he uses them to illustrate a kind of honesty and forthrightness, a kind of guileless probity in even their most outrageous behavior that is both a contrast in some ways and in others a legacy to the next generations. As alternately a barber and a traveling Bible salesman, Amos is a figure of amusement and admiration:

> Saints make wonderful grandfathers but lousy husbands. Years later, my grandmother revealed that when Amos made love to her he kept moaning, "Thank you, Jesus. Thank you, Jesus," as he writhed within her. She claimed it took her mind off what she was doing when he invited Jesus between the sheets. (129)

With the help of the midwife, Sarah Jenkins, Amos behaves heroically on the night of the twins' birth during a ferocious hurricane, saving the lives of Lila and the babies by moving them from the house, under life-threatening conditions, to the higher ground of the barn. On the other hand, his annual carrying of a ninety-pound cross through the streets of Colleton on Good Friday makes him saintly in the eyes of some and a total fool in the eyes of others. When, at sixty, he finds the cross too heavy for him to drag for the three-hour walk, he adds a wheel, and the event becomes even more a kind of sideshow. Tom, as a teenager, is vaguely embarrassed by the spectacle; Luke thinks it is magnificent; and Savannah commemorates the occasion in her poems as if it were a re-enactment of the "shy Oberammergau of the itinerant barber" (282).

It seems eminently fitting that after his wild, but successful, forty-mile waterskiing exploit, Amos should drop dead in the grocery store a year later. Town character and man of absolute, childlike faith, Amos Wingo is one of the most winning figures in the novel. Colleton may have laughed at him, but Colleton knows that his kind will never come again and that "it had lost something exquisite and irreplaceable" (477–78).

If Luke inherits some of his saintly integrity from Amos, Savannah surely inherits some of her wildness from Tolitha. Eccentric in her own way, which is nearly the opposite of Amos's, Tolitha is another delightful character that Conroy creates for comic purposes but also as a figure of individuality, who cares not a bit about public opinion (in stark contrast to Lila), and who, in her own way, has an integrity that matches her husband's. Having left Amos during the Depression because they were penniless (Amos, in one of his typically erratic decisions, has quit his job as a barber in order to preach the Lord's word because he thinks the Depression is a sign that the world is coming to an end), Tolitha moves to Atlanta. Within a few weeks of her divorce from Amos, she marries Papa John Stanopoulos—a man she has met when he gets lost in the lingerie department of the store in which she has taken a job. She insists that the children call her Cousin Tolitha because she has told Papa John that she has never been married. This kind of irregularity bothers Tolitha not at all, and she has only contempt for Lila's conventionality.

After Papa John's death, with the money he has left her, Tolitha sets out on a three-times-around-the-world journey that is epic in the sites she visits and the experiences she has. It is in the reports of what she has done on these travels that we see Tolitha's wonderful, fearless curiosity and her awesome, adventurous character. Tolitha sees the places she has chosen to visit, not by packaged tours through the famous cities of Europe and Asia (although she does visit them as well), but by a loner's intrepid taking advantage of whatever new experience that offers itself. She brags about having had diarrhea in twenty-one different countries and sees this as a symbol of her willingness to explore the less well-traveled roads.

When she returns to Colleton and moves in with Amos as if nothing had happened in the intervening twenty years, everyone in Colleton, including the younger Wingos, is stunned. " 'Even a sea bird's got to rest sometime' was the only thing she offered as explanation to anyone" (127). Although her return might seem to signal a diminishment of her eccentricity, that is by no means so. She continues to do exactly what she wants and say whatever she thinks. The scene in which she tries out her coffin and takes such delight in sending Mrs. Blankenship into hysterics is typical. On Good Friday, when Amos takes to the streets with his cross, Tolitha shows her disapproval by retreating to her bedroom with a full bottle of Beefeater gin:

On Sunday morning, sickened by her debauch but having
made her annual point, my grandmother, as she put it "rose
from the goddamn dead" in time to accompany my grandfather to Easter Sunday services. (267)

It is sad that she ends in senile dementia in a nursing home. Tom feels
guilty in not being able to care for her at home since he recognizes that
she is a remarkable woman and that he loves her deeply. Tolitha, like
Amos, is one of the most charming characters in the book, and Conroy
uses her for many of the same purposes. Her iconoclastic attitudes and
behavior make her, to some extent, an even more amusing figure, though
that in no way detracts from Amos's unique stature.

In addition to Tom and the Wingo clan, Susan Lowenstein is clearly
the other major figure in *The Prince of Tides*. Her role is a complex one,
since she functions on several different levels of the plot, and as a psychiatrist, she has the difficult obligation of trying to keep her private and
professional lives separate. When he first meets her, Tom is put off
by her seemingly cold impersonality and by what he takes to be her
contempt for the South. This phase passes quickly, and after several
meetings in which he tries to help her understand Savannah, both Tom
and Susan realize that his sessions with her are really a kind of unofficial
therapy for him in addition to whatever help he can provide for Savannah.

Gradually, as their relationship develops over the summer, the line
between patient and friend begins to blur. Susan tells him of her own
marital difficulties and her sense of failure as a mother. In spite of her
impenetrable composure in the office, Tom senses immediately when he
sees her in her apartment that she is a sad, unfulfilled woman. When
she asks Tom to coach her son, Bernard, she is doing something that she
knows her husband will abhor, and therefore perhaps not consciously,
but nonetheless actively, brings Tom into a marital triangle. At this point
the triangle has gone no farther than Lowenstein's defiance of her husband by creating a semi-businesslike arrangement with Tom. But this
phase also passes quickly, if not immediately into outright love, to a
friendship that goes far beyond that of doctor and patient. Conroy does
a splendid job in plotting the development of this relationship from original hostility to a passionate love affair during the course of Tom's stay
in New York by showing how, almost against their wills and their nearly
opposite backgrounds, Tom and Susan are drawn to each other. Each is

involved in a failed marriage and each offers the other a kind of appreciation and ego-boosting they both desperately need.

The scene in which Herbert Woodruff has invited Tom to dinner with the express intention of insulting him and thereby humiliating Susan is one of the most dramatic in the novel. Conroy renders it in an extremely effective way, as he builds from its very beginning by showing Herbert's increasing sarcasm and rudeness. Susan is so outraged that she turns on Herbert's lover, Monique, and Tom rises to confront Herbert's insults, threatening to drop his Stradivarius violin from the balcony unless he apologizes to all concerned. Herbert's behavior toward Susan has been as ugly as it has been to Tom. She follows Tom as he leaves the apartment:

> 'Have you ever made love to a psychiatrist?" she asked.
> "No. Have you ever made love to a football coach?" I asked.
> "No," she said, "but I plan to have a different answer tomorrow morning." (437)

Their affair is brief but intense. It is a healing experience for them both; indeed, it probably does as much or more to restore Tom's self-confidence than does his time with her in her office. Susan has been made to feel neglected and unwanted by Herbert's stiff, arrogant attitude toward her and by his having an affair with Monique. Tom is Herbert's complete opposite in that he is totally unaffected and open in his obvious appreciation of her physical and personal charms. Susan gives Tom a feeling of worth that almost all the other women in his life at this moment have denied him. One of the most affecting, poignant scenes in the novel comes with their parting. When Sallie calls and asks Tom to come home, he says that he must return and try to make something good of the wreckage of their marriage. He knows that, in spite of his love for Lowenstein, the South is where he belongs and that if he can restore his life as husband and father, it is what he must do. Even Susan knows that this is his true character and one of the things she loves about him. She pleads with him to stay, and their last bittersweet night together shows her as more vulnerable and therefore more engaging than we have ever guessed that she might be. As he kisses her goodbye at the airport, she says:

> "Tom, remember the dream I had about you and me dancing in the snow storm?"

"I'll never forget it," I said.

Now Susan was crying and leaving her was a killing thing again when she said, "Promise me this, Coach. When you get back to South Carolina, dream one for me. Dream one for Lowenstein." (562)

And of course he does. Even though at the end of the novel, his reunion with Sallie and their daughters and his return to teaching-coaching seem to be successful, he knows that, in large part, it is Lowenstein who has made it possible, and he evokes her repeatedly in thanks and love. Heartbroken at Tom's departure, she is also a survivor and, apparently having rejected Herbert's appeal for forgiveness, is dating a lawyer. Susan Lowenstein is a remarkable character in many ways, and Conroy has done a remarkable thing in conveying her complexity so well.

Of the remaining characters, Herbert and Bernard have important, if small, roles to play. Herbert, an internationally famous violinist, is a cold, egocentric man, who makes both his wife and his son miserable by his dictatorial manner and his total commitment to his profession at the expense of his family. He refuses to allow Bernard to play football lest he injure his hands and take time away from his studying the violin. He treats Susan abominably by flaunting his mistress in front of her and insulting all of her friends. It is, in part, his character that makes Susan turn to his complete opposite in Tom. When Tom first agrees to coach Bernard, he encounters a surly, unhappy boy. It is through Bernard and his gradual warming to Tom that we see how good a teacher and coach Tom really is. He is hard on Bernard, but he knows that this hardness will go a long way in making the boy a better player—and, not incidentally, a better man. Turning from initial hostility to something close to love, Bernard comes to see Tom as the father figure Herbert has never been. One of the most touching scenes in the novel comes in the middle of Grand Central station as Bernard is leaving for music camp and Tom asks him to play the Bach Chaconne, which he does, whereupon Tom gives him a new football.

There are dozens of cameo roles in *The Prince of Tides*, many of which, like those of Reese and Isabel Newbury, have importance on the plot level. Reese is a self-important and devious businessman, whose land dealings have made him the most powerful person in Colleton County. Isabel is a snob of the most insufferable sort, and it is Lila's involvement with them, after their despicable treatment of her and the Wingo family, that so outrages Luke and Tom. More sympathetic and eccentric figures abound. Three, in particular, are worth mentioning in that they show Conroy's skill with tiny roles as well as with major ones. Mr. Fruit is the comical, self-appointed director of traffic in Colleton; he relies on intuition rather than the color of the light to steer people through the intersection he has adopted as his own. Not only does Mr. Fruit direct traffic, he is also, again self-appointed, the parade marshal for all of Colleton's public affairs, including Amos's Good Friday cross-carrying march. After Colleton has been evacuated at the end of the novel, Luke finds Mr. Fruit wandering through its deserted streets, the last, disoriented, and gloriously eccentric reminder of the city that used to be. Luke tries to explain that Mr. Fruit's appearance is symbolic of Colleton's will to survive, but people will not listen, because they have no sense of the enormity of the devastation that is being visited on them.

Two other extremely minor characters are nevertheless important in the parallel heroic roles they play in spite of their being very ordinary, unheroic people. In Chapter Four, in one of his most inventive narrative devices, Conroy crosscuts again and again between the birth of the twins in the hurricane in South Carolina and the hiding of Henry Wingo after his having been shot down in Germany during World War II. Sarah Jenkins, an eighty-five-year-old, black, former slave, midwife delivers the twins and literally gives her life in helping to bring them to safety in the barn as the waters rise to threaten the house.

> "You aren't afraid?"
> "Gotta die of somethin'," she said.
> "It was good of you to come, Sarah."
> "I like bein' with my daughters when their time comes.
> Black or white, it no matter. They all my daughters then. I got
> a thousand children walkin' round these islands." (65)

Meanwhile, Günter Kraus, a man who has been in the past anything but heroic, hides Henry Wingo in his church and helps him arrange an escape to Switzerland. He is later hanged by the Nazis for having helped Henry to get away. Thus, the parallel is inescapable: two very ordinary people are capable of rising to heroic levels of action. Every year, on the twins' birthday, Lila takes the children to the Negro cemetery where Sarah Jenkins is buried, and, on the same day, Henry has roses placed on the grave of Günter Kraus. Conroy's point with these minor characters is that obviously "little" people can achieve a place of importance in the large world of moral integrity.

If Sarah Jenkins and Günter Kraus are heroic, Callanwolde is the ultimate villain. He has stalked Lila since the year that the family lived in Atlanta while Henry was in Korea, and he wreaks his revenge on her rejection in the horrific rape scene in Chapter Twenty-two. Papa John Stanopoulos has no importance on the plot level of the novel, but he is yet another delightful eccentric. It is in great measure with characters like these that Conroy fills out the book and gives credence to the claim that this is a novel of distinction in the southern gothic tradition.

THEMATIC ISSUES

In addition to his analysis of a southern family in all its idiosyncrasy and violence, Conroy addresses a number of other themes. One of the most obvious is the contrast between the values of a land-grabbing developer like Reese Newbury and the older, bucolic, land-loving qualities of characters like Luke Wingo. Conroy speaks repeatedly of all the Wingos' feeling of identity with the land and sea about them. They relate to nature in an almost symbiotic way. From the first page of the novel, when Tom tells of being punished by Henry for having killed an eagle, to the very last page, when the family is reunited and is cruising at sunset on the waters they love so much, the Wingos, including Lila in the sections of the novel that deal with the children's upbringing, are constantly in touch with nature. In contrast, Reese and Isabel Newbury are identified by their elegant mansion in town, and it is a clear symbol of Lila's betrayal that when Tom comes to speak to her on Henry's behalf, she is so impressed by the museum-quality antiques in the Newburys' drawing room that she barely hears his parting words. Reese Newbury represents the new order and Luke Wingo the old. If Luke's world was not quite Edenic, it was at least one in which man and nature were in harmony. In Newbury's world, nature is bulldozed in the name of economic "progress."

A related issue is the contrast between southern culture and New York sophistication. Luke and Tom dislike New York for its impersonality, its frenzied pace, and its snobbish contempt for all that is not New York. Savannah's early realization of her hatred of all that the South represents comes in large part from her unhappy childhood, but her equally early decision that New York is the place where she belongs is puzzling to her brothers. For Savannah New York provides the intellectual stimulation and anonymity that she claims she needs for her creativity. For Luke it represents chaos and rootlessness.

Susan Lowenstein is the quintessential upper-class New Yorker: chic, with a taste in clothes and furnishings that her wealth allows her to indulge; known by the headwaiters of all the best restaurants in the city; and, at least initially, brittle and condescending to Tom's somewhat exaggerated southern, old-boy pose. That she and Tom should fall in love and that Tom can come to see some of the excitement that New York offers is another of the many instances in which we see Tom as the mean between Savannah on the one hand and Luke on the other. Tom, like Luke, belongs in the South, but his distaste for New York is less extreme after his affair with Lowenstein. In one sense Savannah betrays her heritage by rejecting the past, and in another sense Lila betrays it by turning over to Reese Newbury the deed to Melrose Island. In his futile battle with the government, Luke finally gives his life in homage to that past, and Tom, as usual, admires Luke's brave stand but does not have the obsessive drive to follow him in his crusade. Thus, whether it be in contrast to New York or in the depiction of the characters' relationship to their southern background, Conroy uses the southerner's relationship to the land and to the past as a prominent theme.

As in all of Conroy's books southern racism is another important theme. In *The Prince of Tides* it comes up most powerfully when Benji Washington integrates Colleton High School. Most of the white students are openly hostile to him and make remarks that are unforgivable in their crude ugliness. Savannah decides immediately to befriend Benji and, somewhat against his will, Tom takes up the challenge of fighting Oscar Woodhead (certainly not an accidentally assigned surname) when he insults Savannah by calling her a "nigger-loving bitch" (321). The use of the despicable term, "nigger," is commonplace in the South of the 1960s, and even Tom is guilty of using it, despite the fact that Lila has forbidden it and Savannah takes him to task for it: "It's a nasty, disgusting word," she said, "and it makes you sound mean when you use it. . . . You don't say that word around me, Tom" (279). Although Tom bristles at Savannah's rebuke, he never uses the word again, and he becomes one of Benji's champions when they are friendly competitors and teammates on the football field. Although Conroy is certainly not suggesting that the larger problem can be so easily overcome, Benji's prowess as an athlete and his modest manner make the senior class give him a standing ovation on graduation day. Tom realizes that history is being made as Benji and others like him have forever changed the contradictory southern ethos of hating "the nigger" and loving Jesus.

But the overarching theme of *The Prince of Tides* has to do with anger, guilt, repression, denial, confession, and redemption. It is a complex issue, and all the major characters in the novel reflect some aspect of it. Lila, with her creed of "family loyalty," is perhaps the chief architect of the Wingo family's struggles with repression and denial. She commands that they never talk about family problems, even among themselves, and, of course, her handling of the rape episode is only the most dramatic of her rejections of reality. Such denials breed anger and guilt, and there can be no release from this destructive frame of mind without confession, acceptance, and forgiveness. Savannah is, perhaps, the chief victim of this unhealthy attitude of repression, although there are suggestions of her emotional instability that are only tangentially related to that main cause. Her first suicide attempt comes shortly after the rape, and though it is foolish to speculate about the "might have been," there is certainly the possibility that, had she been able to talk about the shame she felt, the degradation, and the pain, she might have been able to recover from the horror in a more constructive way. The causes of her continued psychotic behavior are no doubt complicated by her confusion about her sexuality and by her total rejection of her family, the good as well as the bad. It is obvious, however, that the denial insisted on by Lila is at the root of Savannah's problems as evidenced by her attempt to take on the personality of Renata Halpern and her fairy story, which completely rewrites the rape episode.

But Savannah is not the only character who bears lasting scars from the family's history of denial. Tom's depression and self-doubt, though directly the result of Luke's death, go much farther back to his feelings of inadequacy spawned by Lila's pretensions to social status that the Wingos simply could not achieve. Even Henry convinces himself that he never abused Lila and the children. Luke might seem to have escaped the damaging psychological effects of this syndrome, but actually his war against the government is a form of denial of reality. He does not end in an asylum as does Savannah, nor does he have to have electric shock treatments as does Tom, but there is a form of self-destructive "madness" in his battle that cannot be won.

Clearly, although it is by no means simple or easy, the solution to the problem lies in confession and acceptance of things as they are. Tom's "confession" to Lowenstein sets Tom and Savannah free:

she from her amnesia and suicidal rages, he from his depression and bitter cynicism. His confession allows them both to achieve an integration that shame fought at all costs. (McCormick 35)

Conroy is too good a novelist and student of human nature to leave the reader feeling that all is healed for Tom and Savannah and that their demons may have been banished forever. There is, however, a sense of newfound peace for them both. Savannah is calm and assured; Tom has come to a reconciliation with his situation as an ordinary human being. But, as David Toolan puts it, Tom may seem to have come to terms with himself, yet he is a man who knows that "he dwells in a fearfully *un*safe world" (131).

Anger and guilt, denial and repression, confession and forgiveness—these are the things, in spite of the sprawling family saga that occupies the central plot focus of the novel, that *The Prince of Tides* is all about. It is an enormously powerful theme, and Conroy explores it in depth and in many of its various manifestations. Unlike *The Great Santini* and *The Lords of Discipline*, *The Prince of Tides* does not end with a sense of final closure, and that is one of the many things that makes it a more challenging book than its predecessors. A tentative peace has been achieved: "But the black sounds, the black sounds, Lord. When they toll within me, I am seized with a capacity for homage and wonder" (566).

STYLE AND LITERARY DEVICES

No one could read *The Prince of Tides* without reacting to its ornate style. Some find it the glory of the novel; others find it bloated and excessive. Even Conroy's staunchest defenders will admit that there are spots in which the novel is overwritten. Conroy seems to get carried away by his own voice. It is surprising that, after the plain, unornamented style of *The Great Santini* in 1976, Conroy could have developed in ten years into a stylist who it seems would have benefited from the restraining hand that editor Max Perkins exercised on Thomas Wolfe.

There are long, often lyric descriptive passages such as that of Lowenstein's waiting room (46), of Tolitha's world travels (126–27), of the extremely cold winter that downed trees and killed shrimp (229), or of Tom's triumphant touchdown run (337–38). There are countless other passages in which the verbiage is luxuriant. Conroy's vocabulary is rich throughout the book, but it occasionally becomes esoteric: "scintillant" (126), "gneiss" (161), "enfilading" (229). Similes and metaphors abound:

> As I listened to her read her final poem, I thought of a dream I used to have of Savannah and me in the womb, floating side by side in our mother's inland sea—hearts forming together, fingers moving, the patient blue coloring of four sightless eyes in darkness, the blond hair flowing like underwater grass, the half-formed brains sensing the presence of the other, gathering comfort from that nameless communion which sprang up between us before we were born. In the life before life, in the breathless womb and wordless safety of bloodstreams, I dreamed that something special happened to us. (33)

Poetic imagery and tropes such as these occur on nearly every page; often extended metaphors are developed throughout long paragraphs. A number of Savannah's poems are quoted in full, as well as the complete fairy story she has written under the name of Renata Halpern, "The Southern Way." Luke's eloquent speech at the hearing about the Atomic Energy Commission's plans for Colleton shows that, when the occasion demands, this usually taciturn man is capable of the same verbal power that his siblings have. *The Prince of Tides* is so rich in its linguistic virtuosity that it does have some resonances of Faulkner and Thomas Wolfe; a slightly tighter control of these linguistic outpourings might have brought it even closer to the works of Conroy's acknowledged literary heroes.

One might expect so highly textured a book to depend heavily on symbols. Actually, if one uses a narrow definition of the term, Conroy doesn't use very many. The white dolphin, Snow, is seen as a symbol of good luck in Colleton, which makes Henry's betrayal all the more heinous and the younger Wingos' rescue all the more heroic. Savannah creates symbols out of things like seals and tigers, and the lost ring that she hid too well becomes a symbol for her of what only the poet can find. In the naming of boats there is a symbolic implication. While Savannah keeps extensive journals, those that she sends Tom for Christmas each year remain blank, clearly a symbol of his sense of mediocrity and inferiority. Callanwolde, the red giant who stalks Lila and is the leader of the rapists, becomes the embodiment of evil.

Defined more broadly, *The Prince of Tides* is full of symbols. The age-old healing, cleansing quality of water is used repeatedly. Tom recalls the underwater bonding of the three children as they swam together after being hurt by their parents' punishment or anger (380); Luke spends six and a half hours in the water as he brings home the body of his friend, Lieutenant Blackstock; the final scene of the novel occurs on the water at sunset with the Wingo family reunited and at least temporarily at peace. On a somewhat different level, episodes like Amos's famous waterskiing venture are symbolic. Flamboyance, and nothing could illustrate this more clearly, has long been a hallmark of the Wingo family and Amos's grand gesture in water is a perfect example.

Taken in this way, one could almost say that much of the action of the book is symbolic. Savannah's suicide attempts and smearing herself with her own excrement are symbols of her psychotic self-hatred. Luke's burning of Lila's check is a symbol of his refusal to compromise his integrity. Even Henry's saying that the only thing he ever did right was being a good convict is a symbolic confession of the ruin he has made of his life and the pain he has caused his family. Tom's breakdown after Luke's death is a symbol of just how deeply he loved his brother and how bereft he feels without him as a moral stalwart. This may be stretching the term "symbol" rather far, but it is a testimony to Conroy's careful use of action to define character and illuminate theme.

A FREUDIAN READING

A novel that features a psychiatrist, a psychotic, and at least one neurotic (if not several) as major characters, *The Prince of Tides* would seem to be fertile ground for the Freudian or psychological critic. And indeed it is. Any critic, of whatever persuasion, must deal with the issue of repression and its effects on the major characters in the book. The Freudian critic would simply pursue these lines of inquiry and others with psychological implications farther than would the average close reader. Savannah's illness, Luke's intransigence, and Tom's depression would, at the very least, stir a Freudian critic to an examination of causes that might go beyond those that the general critic might pursue.

Although in recent years, the term Freudian, to describe a particular kind of criticism, has often been broadened to the more generic "psychological" (so as to include other schools of psychological analysis such as those of Alfred Adler [1870–1937] and Carl Jung [1875–1961]), in the twentieth century it has been the theories of Sigmund Freud (1856–1939) that have dominated this approach. His was the first systematic attempt to analyze characters in literature from a psychological point of view. It is primarily Freud's concern with the unconscious mind, starting with his seminal book, *The Interpretation of Dreams* (1900), and continuing in many other publications, that lies at the heart of psychological criticism. His emphasis on repressed wishes and fears, sexual desires, and the conflicts these often subconscious feelings create, has led to a vast amount of critical literature that attempts to understand both the creative minds of authors and the behavior of their characters through an analysis of their psyches.

Freud postulated that the human mind is tripartite: it consists of the *ego* or the "I" of rational, orderly, conscious activity; the *id* or the irrational, passionate, unconscious part; and the *superego*, which serves either directly or in conjunction with the *ego* to repress the drives of the *id* in order to maintain what society considers acceptable behavior. When these three parts of the mind are operating in proper balance, the individual might be said to be healthy. But to one degree or another in almost every human there are elements of repression that manifest themselves "in disguised forms: in dreams, in language (so-called Freudian slips), in creative activity that may produce art (including literature), and in neurotic behavior" (Murfin "Psychological" 243).

Among these repressions, none was to Freud more significant than those of sexual desire, which he says can be traced to infancy. One of the most commonly encountered of these unconscious sexual desires is what he named the Oedipus complex:

> According to Freud, the child reaches "genital primacy" around the age of five years, at which time the Oedipus complex manifests itself. In simple terms, the Oedipus complex derives from the boy's unconscious rivalry with his father for the love of his mother. Freud borrowed the term from the classic Sophoclean tragedy in which the hero unwittingly murders the father and marries his mother. (Guerin et al. 130)

In girls the parallel repression is called the Electra complex, named after the character in several Greek plays who aids or abets her brother Orestes in murdering their mother. If the child develops in a healthy manner, she or he outgrows this nearly universal phase of maturation and it never really becomes a neurosis. In other individuals it can become a serious, long-lasting problem that is never fully resolved and may well interfere with a smooth transition to heterosexual love.

Since Savannah's latest suicide attempt and subsequent catatonia lie at the heart of the plot, the psychological critic would probably be most immediately interested in her. Some years before her present collapse, Savannah has had frequent hallucinations that would cause a Freudian to pronounce her paranoid and probably schizophrenic: lynched angels hanging from lampposts, screaming and dripping blood from their genitalia; a tiger (reminiscent of Caesar?); black Dobermans whom Savannah is sure are determined to hurt her.

That critic would see immediately, of course, that repression, especially of the rape, is a major factor in her psychosis. The fairy tale she writes under the name Renata Halpern would be a major point of interest in that the Freudian critic would see in its details many things revelatory of Savannah's condition. She speaks, for example, of the mother's silence after her husband's supposed death and the way this disturbs her daughters. A psychological reading here is that Savannah is referring to Lila's refusal to speak about any of the abuses that Henry has inflicted on them or any other family troubles. The daughters, unable to communicate with their mother, develop remarkable powers of communication with animals and insects, and when the three villains threaten to rape the mother and abuse the daughters, all of nature seems to unite in coming to their rescue. This might be a subconscious memory of Caesar's attack on the rapists and the fact that spiders play a part may be Savannah's recall of Papa John's collection of black widows, which once helped to repulse Callanwolde. More important, it is Savannah's fanciful attempt to show that nature was offended by what the rapists did, and in fiction, if not in reality, nature is able to prevent the disaster. Furthermore, there is a happy ending when the father returns alive and the family is reunited in peace and harmony (certainly not something Savannah ever experienced in the Wingo household, which she likens, in talking with Tom, to Nagasaki and Auschwitz).

Going beyond this and other obvious manifestations of the effects of repression on Savannah, the Freudian critic would be especially interested in other aspects of her childhood that might figure in causing her psychosis. Not only in her insistence on silence was Lila sometimes what a psychologist might call a bad mother, but her mercurial attitudes toward the children certainly contributed to their emotional instability (Luke might seem to be an exception here, but he has problems of a different sort). For example, she tells each of the three on separate occasions that he or she is her favorite. Freud would say that, not only does this lay a tremendous burden on the child in wanting not to disappoint the mother, but when they later learn that she has done the same thing with all three, it makes them cynical and distrustful of anything she says or does. At times she seems to dote on them as the only good thing to come of her marriage to Henry and at others to make them feel as if they have ruined her life by being born. She burns Savannah's journals and has no sympathy with her desire to be something more than a conventional wife and mother. In addition, Lila's and Henry's constant warfare is enough to make a sensitive child like Savannah come to hate her family and all that is associated with it.

While Conroy does not offer specific clues to Savannah's early problems with memory loss and emotional instability, the Freudian critic might speculate that they too come from being a hypersensitive child in this chaotic, destructive family. But her violent hatred of her family and the South seem excessive, and in her New York experiences she seems to drift into groups who are also angry (the radical feminist lesbians, for example) and unstable. Although Tom and Luke distrust psychiatry, it is obvious that Savannah has needed help for a long time. As her hallucinations have become more violent and her control of her life more precarious, she has changed frequently from one therapist to another and that, too, might be a contributing factor in her unsteady grip on herself and reality, since none before Lowenstein has had the invaluable information that Tom provides. While at the end of the novel Savannah seems to have a better chance of escaping her demons than she has had for a long time, a history such as hers would seem to a Freudian critic a bad omen for the future.

Although less dramatic than Savannah's suicide attempts and psychosis in the present time of the novel, Tom's emotional problems and their sources would be of equal interest to the Freudian critic. To begin with, his Oedipus complex is an almost classic case that makes Ben Meecham's (*The Great Santini*) look like an adolescent's brief problem of adjustment. Bull Meecham is in fact killed, though obviously not by Ben, when the boy is eighteen. Thus the overt problem, if not all of its lasting effects, is ended. At nearly thirty-seven, Tom Wingo is prepared to forgive his still-living father for much of what he used to hate, but Henry is a constant reminder of the childhood conflict, and so is Lila, who is now in the reversed role of being the despised mother whom he once adored.

Conroy is not subtle in his development of this aspect of Tom's character. While Henry is away in Korea, Tom prays that Henry will be killed. These are not nightmares, but prayers that he may escape the agony of living in his father's house. Later Tom realizes that his problem in finding satisfactory relationships with women stems from his early idolization of his mother:

> Once inside a woman, to my horror, I heard my mother's voice, and though my lover would be calling out "yes yes yes," it was not as powerful a cry as my mother's cold "no." I took my mother to bed with me every night of my life and I could not help it.
>
> These thoughts came unannounced, unbidden. Sex, I thought . . . the central issue of my conflicted, unsuccessful manhood. (294)

At least a large part of Tom's current hostility to Lila comes from this recognition that the difficulties in his relationships with women is a result of his excessive love for her when he was a child. Another contributing factor to Tom's anger with Lila at the moment is her guilt-laying about his attitude toward her and his joblessness. But there are also the same factors that give Savannah and Luke problems with their mother: her betrayal in marrying Reese Newbury, her repression of the truth, and her social-climbing pretensions.

A Freudian critic would also be particularly interested in Tom's feelings of mediocrity. Savannah is merciless in telling him that he is wasting his life with his lack of ambition and lack of interest in anything beyond remaining in a safe environment of the known and unchallenging. His admiration of Luke is a constant reminder that he is not made of the same moral fiber as is his brother. He is caught in a kind of Catch-22 (a no-win situation); because of his doubts about his self-worth, he turns inward, which only increases his alienation and causes further doubts about his strength of character. It is his "confession" to Lowenstein about his past that helps him to accept the present, and it is his love affair with her that reaffirms Tom's sense of his masculinity and his realization that his life with Sallie and as a teacher-coach is not the travesty that Savannah has claimed. It may not be all that he was capable of, but it is a life that he can see as fulfilling and ultimately, if not as dramatic as Luke's, one of integrity.

The Freudian critic would be interested, of course, in the psyches of all the major and many of the minor characters: Luke's near megalomania in his war with the government, Dr. Lowenstein's inability to heal the wounds in her personal life, Herbert Woodruff's egomaniacal cruelty, Lila Wingo's obsession with social status and public opinion, Bernard Woodruff's sullen rebellion against both parents, and Henry Wingo's violent, abusive temper. In each case Conroy provides enough background information for the psychological critic to speculate about the sources of these personality traits, even though he may not develop them at the same length as he does with Savannah and Tom.

In addition to the analysis of characters, the Freudian critic of *The Prince of Tides* would be especially alert to actions and attitudes that have psychological implications. For example, Herbert Woodruff's refusal to let Bernard play football is almost certain to create hostility and an even greater desire on Bernard's part to be an athlete than if Herbert simply let the matter pass. His insistence that Bernard be a violinist like himself is even more potentially dangerous, in that if the boy does not match his father's preeminence he could be psychologically damaged in several ways. Henry Wingo's ideas about raising his sons are equally misguided, though in a totally different way. He insists that they be fighters, not "lovers," and he urges them to beat up every boy in Atlanta while he is away.

On nearly every page of the novel there is some insight or comment that would be of particular interest to the Freudian critic, or for that matter to the more general critic, since the book is so heavily weighted with psychological discussion. Although Lowenstein is the licensed psychiatrist, Tom is capable of some fairly astute analysis of his own. He says that girls frequently choose husbands like their fathers (a manifestation of the Electra complex), especially if they have been daughters, like Lila, of violent men. They tend, he claims, to associate love and pain and therefore seek out men who will repeat the love-pain syndrome. He has parallel theories about the way sons tend to turn every woman they love into images of their mothers (86), and the way his father's cruelty made him despise his own masculinity. Chiefly, then, because of Conroy's primary focus on the psychological makeup of his characters, his exploration of the repressions and other factors that have made them what they are, the Freudian critic would find *The Prince of Tides* a fascinating work. The action of the novel, especially that part involving Tom's sessions with Lowenstein, might almost be excerpted as a therapist's case study. In addition, even when it is not directly related to plot or character, Conroy fills the book with material that is of psychological interest to every reader, Freudian critic or otherwise.

Beach Music
(1995)

Beach Music is a family saga on an even larger scale than *The Prince of Tides*. In addition, some of its most important plot and thematic elements have to do with its central character's (Jack McCall) childhood friends and their careers since their high school and college years. Supplement all this with the material having to do with the persecution of the Jews in Europe and other extended narratives, which may be plot related but are almost capable of standing alone, and one has an enormously varied and richly textured novel that at times seems unable to contain all of its parts. But it is this bounty that is one of Conroy's hallmarks and a cause for his immense popularity.

The novel was published on June 28, 1995, and on July 16 (the first week for which sales figures were available) it was number one on *The New York Times* best-seller list. Its 750,000-copy first printing was sold out before its official publication date. So great were the popularity and success of *The Prince of Tides* that *Beach Music* was almost certain to make the list and stay there for a long time. That it should leap in at the top is a testimony to just how big a name Pat Conroy has become in the field of popular literature.

No doubt the nine-year hiatus between *The Prince of Tides* and the new novel created a great deal of anticipation and a rush to bookstores to find out whether Conroy had lost his touch or whether he could outdo himself. The latter proved to be the case, but since his publisher and his agent had been tight-lipped in the months before publication, very little was known about *Beach Music* until it appeared. Surely, the lack of pre-publication publicity was deliberate in order to create the curiosity it did, but it was also the result of the urgency with which Doubleday pushed to get the book in print. After so many previously announced publishing dates had come and gone, several customary stages in the normal course of a book's being published were skipped or compressed. Thus, there were far fewer advance copies and they came to reviewers much later than is usual.

As much as several years before publication, jockeying for film rights began. The successful bidder turned out to be Paramount ($5.1 million). Assuming a good screenplay (which Conroy is scheduled to write) and good direction and casting, the movie version could easily equal or out-strip the success of Barbra Streisand's *The Prince of Tides*. There are meaty roles for at least a dozen actors and there are many more for the sup-porting cast. The camera will caress Rome, Venice, and the South Car-olina low country, and there is enough plot action to fill three movies. The trick will be to shape all this material into a manageable, cohesive, esthetically satisfying package. That will not be an easy task.

While the book sales may set records and the movie version may win awards, many of the professional reviewers have been considerably less than well-disposed to *Beach Music*. They have made many of the same comments they did about *The Prince of Tides*, but several of them have been even more critical of Conroy's ornate style, his cramming the book with a great deal of material that hardly seems to fit, and a straining of credibility in a number of incidents.

One of the most severe of these reviews is that by Mark Harris in *Entertainment Weekly*: "To say that Conroy is trying to do too much doesn't begin to convey how overloaded *Beach Music* is" (93). Harris, like others, is especially hard on Conroy's elaborate prose. Tom Shone in *The New York Times Book Review* spends much of the space in his review lambasting Conroy's style, and in *Time*, R. Z. Sheppard claims Conroy's "Attempts to relate the madness of Vietnam to Hitler's evil are loopy" ("First-Person" 77). Not all of the reviews were so negative. Mi-chael Harris says in the *Los Angeles Times*:

"Beach Music" is blockbuster writing at its best. . . . Conroy's main asset is his emotional range. He's a warm and decent man who expresses love and nostalgia without embarrass-ment. (1)

And Brigitte Weeks says: "The range of passions and subjects that brings life to every passage of this story is almost endless" (*The Washington Post Book World* "Where . . ." 5)

Whatever its faults, *Beach Music* is another of Conroy's big novels that aspires to achieve the fictional power of Thomas Wolfe. With this novel it becomes clear that it is Wolfe more than Faulkner who is Conroy's master. Conroy took obvious pride and delight in mentioning at his Smithsonian lecture late in June 1995 that he had that very day signed a contract to write the screenplay for *Look Homeward, Angel*. That, in conjunction with the extensive post-publication talks and book-signings of *Beach Music* and Conroy's involvement in writing the screenplay for the movie version of the novel, may well cause another long delay before his next book appears. His ardent fans certainly hope it will not be another nine years.

NARRATIVE POINT OF VIEW AND STRUCTURE

Like Tom Wingo of *The Prince of Tides*, Jack McCall is the first-person narrator-protagonist of *Beach Music*. He, too, is a man in his mid-thirties whose life is, if not in turmoil, certainly not in harmonious balance—in this case because of his wife Shyla's suicide, his mother Lucy's leukemia, and his alienation from his family and his South Carolina roots. Although he has attempted to escape the demons of his past by becoming an expatriate in Rome, a number of things occur that intrude on this effort at isolation from his former friends and his family. He is drawn back, against his will, but ultimately to his enormous emotional benefit, into the web of interrelated people and events that he had sought to put behind him.

In *Beach Music* Jack speaks directly to the reader, thus avoiding the sometimes awkward "I told Lowenstein" devices of *The Prince of Tides*. It is interesting that Conroy and his editor at Doubleday, Nan Talese, at one point thought the narrative point of view should be third person to avoid its being too similar to the voice of Tom Wingo (since both are such highly autobiographically-based characters). For nearly five years Conroy wrote the novel in the third person. Then he and Talese agreed that, after all, the first person was the right point of view, and together they transposed the 2,100 pages that Conroy had written (in longhand on yellow legal pads). Berendt says that Conroy feels the exercise was worth the effort since what emerged is clearly a different voice from that of Tom Wingo (140).

The structure of *Beach Music* is similar to that of *The Prince of Tides* in many respects: the novel's main action takes place in the "present," in this case, of 1985–1986; there are many flashbacks having to do with Jack's childhood, youth, and college days; there are a number of histories about his family and other people in Waterford going back in time to before he was born; there are set pieces of storytelling such as that of his mother Lucy's true background and that of the fishing expedition that involves the giant manta ray. What is different about *Beach Music*, however, is the inclusion of long digressions told to Jack by several of the secondary characters: Max Rusoff tells of his escape from a pogrom in czarist Russia; Ruth Fox describes her flight from Poland during the Holocaust; George Fox laments his early collaboration with the Gestapo and his degradation in the concentration camps of Auschwitz and Dachau. Conroy has thematic reasons for including these long stories of the horrors inflicted on the Jews of Europe, but on the surface level, they interrupt the narrative flow of the novel.

Although *Beach Music* is divided into six discrete sections with Prologue and Epilogue, the narrative voice of Jack McCall remains constant throughout. While Tom Wingo sought the help of Susan Lowenstein in setting his life in order, Jack, in part by the accident of events, in part by the urging of his family and friends, and in part by deliberate decisions of his own, achieves much the same kind of healing and reconciliation independently. Part I is set in Rome, where Jack has been living with his young daughter, Leah, in self-imposed exile. His voice here is one of outward satisfaction with the routines of the life he has chosen and his love of Rome and the other cities to which he journeys as a professional food and travel writer. There is, though, more than a hint that something is missing beneath the surface of this smooth existence; it seems as if Jack is trying to convince himself that his life is as fulfilling as he wants it to be. When the past intrudes in the form of a visit from his sister-in-law, the arrival of two friends from his childhood, and the news that his mother is dying of cancer, his protective shell is broken.

Part II is set in Waterford, South Carolina, the place of Jack's birth and of the trauma of his youth in yet another of Conroy's dysfunctional families. As he is forced into a renewal of contact with his family while they watch by Lucy's bedside, his mood and his voice are at first irritable and hostile because he has had to break his vow of never returning to his past. Then, as his stay lengthens and his bond with his brothers is re-

awakened, he comes to realize that he can never renounce his heritage
and that he has been wrong in denying Leah hers:

> I had taken her away from what we both were. I had given
> her everything except the South. I had stolen her calling card.
> ... I found myself in love with my own story all over again.
> (206)

Part III takes place back in Rome, where Lucy, in remission from cancer, comes for a Christmas visit and, although Jack is seriously wounded
in a terrorist attack at the airport as he and Leah are preparing to accompany Lucy home and for Leah to meet the family she has never
known, there is a growing sense of his being more at ease with himself,
his family and his friends, and the world in general than he has been
even long before Shyla's suicide. Ledare Ansley, his high school sweet-
heart, flies to Rome immediately to be at his bedside and Jordan Elliott,
the best friend of his youth, risks his cover of anonymity to rush to the
hospital. In parts IV, V, and VI, all of which take place in Waterford and
its environs, the action shifts back and forth between present and past,
going back to Jack's childhood and his teenage bonding with Jordan,
and his other boyhood friends, Mike Hess and Capers Middleton. There
are bitter memories from their college years during the Vietnam War,
and there are long chapters involving Mike Hess's attempt, once and for
all, to get at the facts of Jordan's behavior during the war protests and
thereafter. Throughout all of this part of the novel, Jack's tone becomes
more and more one of accommodation. He even becomes, at least formally, reconciled with his parents-in-law, who had sued to gain custody
of Leah after Shyla's death and who were the foremost of all the people
Jack swore never to see again.

Then, in the Epilogue, Rome and Waterford are brought together at
Jack and Ledare's wedding. Although it takes place in Rome, almost all
of the Waterford community comes for the feasting and celebrating. Conroy uses this scene, which contains so many traditional symbols of harmony and reunion, to bring the novel to a close with the "rebirth" of
Jack McCall after years of alienation and bitterness: "I touched the new
ring and it felt very much like new life" (627). Conroy also uses the
Epilogue to bring closure to other plot-and character-related threads. For
example, Shyla's coin necklace and her letter to Jack before her suicide,
both of which are mentioned in the Prologue, are only fully explained
in the Epilogue. Thus, the Prologue and Epilogue serve as framing ele-

ments to give the novel a well-defined structure that reinforces the sense of wholeness and completion symbolized by Jack's wedding ring.

R. Z. Sheppard calls Conroy's narrative point of view "first-person portentous," suggesting that like several other Conroy narrator-protagonists, Jack McCall's story is told in prodigious detail with credibility-straining events. While there is some justice in the charge, Sheppard goes on to say that when Conroy's first-person narrator is on firm ground, as in his descriptions of the South Carolina low country, and is using somewhat less embellished prose than in some of the more ornate passages in the novel, "there are flashes of a gifted novelist" ("First-Person" 77). Conroy's use of first-person narration in *Beach Music* is a tour de force in scope but also one of the major ways in which he portrays Jack's progress from rejection and cold impersonality to integration and a measure of equanimity. The tone of the narrative is carefully, almost imperceptibly, modulated over the six-hundred-plus pages; the voice of the man who speaks in the Epilogue is in an entirely different key from that of the man in the Prologue, who in honest but bitter self-criticism claims that he has deliberately run away from his past.

PLOT DEVELOPMENT

Beach Music is another family saga in the southern literary tradition. As a part of that saga, one of the most important elements is Jack McCall's rites of passage that echo those of all of Conroy's protagonists. Though superficially more stable than Tom Wingo, Jack makes a now familiar journey from bitter rejection to harmonious reunion through the effects of full admission of the truth, compassion, and love. Indeed, Conroy makes his healing almost too complete to be entirely convincing. Tom Wingo, at the end of *The Prince of Tides*, has been healed too, but both he and the reader know that it is a tenuous balance he has achieved. Jack McCall seems to have banished his demons more permanently, and the only thing that keeps his recovery from being almost sentimentally too neat is his realization that, although marriage to Ledare is right for them both at the moment, it will never displace the love he still feels for Shyla nor fill the emptiness caused by her loss. In spite of all the real and symbolic elements of reunion and reintegration in the Epilogue, Jack's words that end the novel are of recommitment to Shyla.

Another important strand in the fabric of the McCall family story is that of Lucy's illness and death. It is the news of her being in a coma that initially brings Jack back from Rome, and during the long hours of waiting outside the intensive care unit, he and his brothers are thrown together in a tense, claustrophobic situation. Their alternating moments of impatience with each other and rebonding are actually the result of Lucy's critical condition. To the immense relief of them all, Lucy emerges from the coma and enters a period of remission. It is during this period that we come to see her in all of her charm and some of her more irritating moods. On the whole, however, this interlude before the end is full of delightful episodes that reveal the complex woman she is. Then, in some of the most poignant moments in the novel, the brothers gather outside her hospital room again, very near the end of the book, to await the inevitable moment when she dies. Thus, in one sense, her illness and death provide the beginning and the conclusion of the McCall family's struggle toward reconciliation and reunion.

One might say that the story of Leah's growth is another subplot of its own under the umbrella of the McCall family saga. We hear a great deal about how she has been brought up by Jack since he brought her to Rome when she was almost three years old. His cautious, watchful care has made her a child sophisticated beyond her years before they return to South Carolina when she is almost nine. It is here that we see her introduction to a family and a culture totally different from anything she has known before—and she embraces them eagerly. In everything from being taught the shag by her uncles and waterskiing by Ledare to the resetting of loggerhead turtle eggs with Lucy, she is an apt and enthusiastic student. She is also instrumental in bringing about the reconciliation between Jack and the Foxes since Jack is forced to meet with them in dealing with Leah's visits. At times Leah seems precocious to the point of becoming too precious, but on the whole, the story of her "education" is a charming one that complements Jack's gradual return to the bosom of his family and at least several of his old friends and acquaintances.

As in *The Prince of Tides*, chapters telling the history of the McCalls come in what seems to be no particular order. Lucy's real childhood and life before she met Johnson Hagood McCall, for example, are not revealed until Chapter Twenty-seven, over halfway through the novel; Jordan Elliott's arrival in Waterford and his becoming Jack's closest friend, in Twenty-one, long after we have come to know at least part of his history and life as a Trappist monk in Rome; Jack's high school and college years aren't described in detail until very near the end of the book. This is a deliberate ordering on Conroy's part, as it was in *The Prince of Tides*, to give verisimilitude in the novel to the way family histories unfold. It is also a means of creating suspense. We know, for example, from the instinctive reaction of Ginny Penn (Lucy's mother-in-law) and from other evidence of her lack of sophistication and her illiteracy that Lucy's story of coming from a distinguished Atlanta family is counterfeit, but we don't learn just how counterfeit and what the true horrors of her background were until one hundred pages later.

Stories of Jack's youthful adventures, like that of the nearly fatal fishing expedition (which, like the dolphin episode in *The Prince of Tides*, is virtually a short story that could stand by itself) come two-thirds of the way through the novel. Why Jack's dislike of Capers Middleton is so violent and absolute is not explained in full detail until we learn in Chapter Thirty-seven of his betrayal of his friends. Other family episodes, past and present, make *Beach Music* another treasure-trove of tales. Some are comic, such as Ginny Penn's "escape" in her wheelchair from a nursing home; some are lavishly detailed, such as the party to celebrate Lucy's remission (although, in fact, the cancer has returned); some have elements of lyric beauty, such as the one in which Jack and three of his brothers swim together after John Hardin (their youngest brother) has forced them at gunpoint to strip naked in public and jump off a bridge; some are idyllic, such as the episode in which Jack and his three friends spend two weeks at his grandparents' fishing camp; and some are totally imaginary, such as The Great Dog Chippie stories Jack makes up for Leah's amusement. It seems as if Conroy has almost endless inventive powers as he creates story after story, all of which have a center of interest of their own, but all of which contribute to the overall depiction of Jack and the McCall clan. The brothers, themselves, are adept in the art:

> They were Southern boys and they knew how to make a story sizzle when it hit the fat. Their voices bloomed around me and I loved the sound of my native tongue as it came out of Southern mouths. (206)

Conroy even speculates about the origin and art of storytelling: "Stories don't have to be true. They just have to help" (247). In the specific instance Jack means that a story in which evil is punished, if only by the mythological Great Dog Chippie in the Rome terrorist attack, is a way of coming to terms with the random and senseless harm done to totally innocent people. Somewhere, in the large scheme of things, there will be redress. But stories help in a fuller sense in that they aid us in understanding ourselves and our pasts, the torments that we and others have suffered. They may be grim or humorous, enlightening or explanatory, confessional or historically informative. They define us. And Conroy, perhaps above all his other achievements as a novelist, is a master storyteller.

If the McCall family story, with Jack's rites of passage, Lucy's illness, and Leah's growth in it, is the major plot line of *Beach Music*, there are numerous tangentially related subplots, some introduced to extend the depiction of Jack and his relatives, some introduced largely for thematic purposes, and some to create suspenseful action. Several, such as those involving Jack's friends, incorporate all three. Mike Hess, who has become a Hollywood mogul, has decided to produce a television miniseries based on the lives of the close-knit group that included Jack, Capers Middleton, Jordan Elliott, and himself plus Ledare Ansley and Shyla Fox, who were intimately involved with them in several ways. This decision makes him seek out Jack, whom he wants to hire with Ledare to write the screenplay. It also makes him determined to find out whether or not Jordan Elliott is really dead, as everyone except Jack and Jordan's mother has believed, or is in hiding and living in disguise. Capers, in his political ambition, also wants to find Jordan in order to smooth over his betrayal of his friends during the Vietnam War protests. Equally determined to find out Jordan's whereabouts is his father, General Rembert Elliott, who, in what is almost a parody of Marine Corps loyalty and patriotism, wants his son prosecuted and imprisoned for what he did during those protests.

With different motives these three characters set in motion what is perhaps the most suspenseful subplot in the novel—the pursuit of Jordan in a cloak-and-dagger style chase that lasts, on and off, through the whole book. It comes to a conclusion in the climactic, if somewhat improbable, mock trial that Mike arranges in Part VI. This "trial," which takes up four substantial chapters, brings together most of the major characters, includes Johnson Hagood sitting as "judge," and serves not only to bring Mike's movie and the Jordan subplot to closure, but also to bring *Beach Music* itself to a dramatic high point. The subplot involving Jordan is one of real suspense, and it also highlights one of Conroy's major thematic concerns—the effect of the Vietnam War on the spiritual fabric of American society.

Coming at this thematic element from an entirely different perspective,

Conroy introduces an episodic subplot, consisting mainly of the histories
of three Jews who have arrived in Waterford by different routes, but all
of whom have endured unspeakable atrocities at the hands of their op-
pressors in Europe. Max Rusoff is a minor character, George and Ruth
Fox secondary ones, but the lengthy tales of their escapes to the United
States from the horrors they have witnessed and experienced form what
Conroy is attempting to set up as a parallel between the effects of the
Holocaust on its victims and the effects of the Vietnam War on American
values. Jack says that he hated that war intensely, not only for the military intervention itself, but for its far-reaching effects:

> I had blamed it for the great unraveling it had brought to
> America, the self-doubt, the breakdown of courtesy, the death
> of form, and the falling apart of all the old truths and the
> integrity of both law and institutions. . . . Nothing survived
> the cut. (578)

Shyla goes so far as to see parallels between the Vietnamese with the
Jews of Europe and the Americans as Nazi invaders. This radical stretching of logic is reinforced in her view when National Guardsmen kill
student protesters at Kent State University. This subplot having to do
with the Vietnam War also involves Capers, who becomes a leader of
the movement at the University of South Carolina, when, in fact, he has
infiltrated it as an agent of SLED (South Carolina Law Enforcement Division) and as state's witness turns against his friends at their trial. And
it is Jordan's protest in the blowing up of an airplane, inadvertently
killing a young couple who were clandestinely making love in it, that
sets in motion his flight and exile in Rome.

Beach Music, like *The Prince of Tides*, is so rich in its complex, interrelated plot threads, developed largely through anecdote and dramatic incident, that at times it seems to overflow its own structure. But as
Sheppard says: "Conroy's expansive storytelling style tends to disarm
criticism" ("First-Person" 77). It is a big novel in several senses, and if
all the parts don't fit comfortably in the whole, those parts are nevertheless, almost without exception, fascinating and compelling in their
own right.

CHARACTER DEVELOPMENT

As the narrator-protagonist of *Beach Music* Jack McCall (christened
Johnson Varnadoe Cotesworth McCall (the Varnadoe and Cotesworth

names being given him by Lucy to curry favor with the reclusive but socially prominent Harriet Cotesworth) is the novel's focal character. Not only is he its center, but nearly all the other characters are important in large part because of their relation to him. Our interest in some, like Lucy and Jordan Elliott, develops to some extent independently of Jack, but they are, nonetheless, intimately bound to him. Conroy uses Jack not only as his protagonist, but almost as a magnet who holds together some other very disparate characters and their stories.

When we meet Jack McCall in the Prologue and Part I, he is an outwardly poised, secure food and travel writer living almost smugly in Rome with his young daughter. He takes great satisfaction in being accepted with affection by the Italian vendors of the Piazza Farnese and the waiter at his favorite restaurant and in the fawning attention given Leah by the nuns at the school she attends. He delights in the sights, art and architecture, and sensuous atmosphere of the city. It is almost immediately apparent, however, that this assimilation is a protective shield that Jack has built to block out memories and people from his past. The more he says that he hates the South and that he never wants to see any of his family or friends again, the more apparent it is that his Roman life is a fragile facade that will almost certainly be shattered in one way or another.

There are several reasons for Jack's flight to Europe. The most immediate are his wife's suicide, which he is unable to explain to himself, and the ensuing court battle with her parents over the custody of Leah. He feels that he must be responsible, at least in part, for his wife's despair since he wasn't even aware of how severe it had become. On the other hand, he knows that her emotional instability had been of long standing and that there was little that her therapists or he had been able to do to alleviate it. A second cause of Jack's rejection of his past is the tumultuousness of his ever-explosive family. His father has been an unregenerate alcoholic for as long as Jack can remember, and his mother, now divorced and remarried, is another in the list of Conroy mothers who are manipulative, self-centered, and interfering. Of his four brothers, one is a paranoid schizophrenic, who is a constant threat to himself and the peace of the whole community. The other three are quarrelsome and volatile.

Although it is an event that took place a number of years before, Jack has never forgotten nor forgiven Capers Middleton for his betrayal of his friends during the Vietnam War protests, and he tends to see Capers's behavior as symbolic of what he dislikes about southern values. Jack has lost his religious faith along with his belief in the essential goodness of people. Thus, it is as a bitter cynic beneath the cosmopolitan veneer that we encounter Jack at the beginning of the novel.

It is a mark of his alienation that soon after moving to Italy he is in Venice to write about the revelry of Carnevale and becomes so swept up in the "open-ended immoderation" (52) that he is drawn into an anonymous but steamy, sexual encounter. In all of Conroy's work this is his only use of an explicitly detailed description of sex, and so startling is it that the reader realizes that Conroy is using it in part to show the depth of Jack's loneliness and detachment. It is the first time he has made love since Shyla's death (two years before), and he reflects afterward that it is the first time since then that he has really felt "alive." That he never even sees the woman's face clearly and never learns her name underline how far Jack has moved in his breaking of emotional ties (except, of course, with Leah) and the coldness which has become the hallmark of his personality.

It is when he returns to South Carolina in Part II, and to an even greater extent in later sections, that he begins to realize that however manipulative Lucy may be, he nonetheless does love her; that however fractious and difficult his brothers are, there is a bond between them that is stronger and more important than his irritations with them; that his ties to the land and waters of his youth are indelible. Gradually he comes to understand that one cannot escape one's past and damages oneself in attempting to do so.

In retrospective chapters we see that Jack was, before the events that made him so bitter, an open, sensitive, idealistic boy and young man. As the eldest of five brothers he has accepted responsibility without complaint. Jordan and Capers are most often the leaders in the adventures of the four boyhood friends, but it is frequently Jack who is the mediator in their minor disagreements. He is hurt by the breakup of his high school relationship with Ledare, but he reacts with equanimity. Almost at the same time, Shyla dares him to fall in love with her though that does not occur until their senior year in college. If not often the leader, Jack has a romantic, daredevil streak that occasionally shows itself, as in the night that he and Shyla continue to dance, to the music of "Save the Last Dance for Me," in a house that is breaking up in a hurricane while Ledare, Capers, and the others scream from the shore that they must abandon the disintegrating building. In college during the Vietnam War he and Jordan are at first not so radical as Shyla (and Capers as he pretends to be), but they are sincere in their opposition to the war and remain firm even when they know they have crossed a legal line as they participate in a break-in at the Selective Service Office.

Jack McCall is low-keyed but steady and principled. He takes firm stands against his drunken father, the sadistic General Elliott, and a rowdy teenager who is about to kill a loggerhead. His revulsion at what Capers has done to his friends is unalterable until the very end of the novel. His devotion to Leah is almost too intense, but he is determined to spare her the scars of an unhappy childhood (during their time in Rome he tells her stories only of the beauty and good times he had in Waterford). He is practical and level-headed whereas Shyla and several of his brothers are temperamental and irrational. Thus, unlike Tom Wingo, whose problems are obvious, Jack's are internalized. As he looks out the window of his apartment in Rome on the bustling crowds in the Piazza below, he sees himself reflected in the glass:

> I had just turned thirty-seven . . . but the slouching figure I saw squinting back at me . . . had felt inanimate and periph- eral to the main flow of action for too long now. . . . I longed for engagement, intrusion, a little more Mardi Gras than Lent in my life. . . . I realized that I had satisfied myself with ob- server status in the human race for too long. (227–28)

With this resolve, Jack sets about remaking himself. He has already agreed to work with Mike and Ledare on the film project, and after his recovery from the injuries he suffers at the airport, he and Leah go back to South Carolina and he wholeheartedly undertakes her, and thereby his, reintegration into the McCall family. Although his reconciliation with the Foxes is more guarded, the healing of that breach is a vital step in his healing of the old wounds that have tortured him for so long. Meanwhile, Ledare is not very subtle in her efforts to reawaken a ro- mantic interest from their past. Although he finds working with her com- fortable and companionable, at first he resists her overtures even though he knows that he is beginning to fall in love with her. He still feels that there is a cold emptiness in himself that would be damaging to anyone with whom he attempted intimacy:

> I had failed to live fully because I had not come to terms with the alliances and fates of this imbalanced gathering of souls [the people gathered for Mike Hess's mock trial]. (578).

Jack's reconciliation with family and friends—including even Capers Middleton and the Foxes—are all necessary steps for rejoining the human community, but it is his marriage to Ledare that both actually and symbolically completes the process.

The friends of Jack's youth all have major roles in the plot of *Beach Music*, and several serve functions in developing thematic issues. Shyla Fox, whose family's house backed that of the McCalls, has been a friend of Jack's since childhood; she and Jack have grown up crawling over the limbs of an oak tree to talk to and comfort each other. Seeking release from the strict, grim atmosphere of her parents' house, she is a frequent visitor with the more open, rambunctious McCalls. From as early as ten Shyla has shown signs of emotional instability. She becomes withdrawn, has hallucinations, and finally has to be committed to a mental asylum. Part of her neurosis comes certainly from her mother's paranoia and horrific stories about the Holocaust. Shyla takes these so personally that she tries to imitate Ruth's suffering by refusing food and water; at one point she buries all of her dolls in a mass grave. Part, too, comes from George Fox's cruel pushing her at the piano, knowing that she does not have the talent to become a great virtuoso (as he has been) but insisting that she try ever more challenging works until she breaks under his pressure.

What finally triggers her collapse is a hallucination involving the Virgin Mary (set off, we later learn, by the central importance of a statue of the Virgin, who in Ruth's story of her escape from Poland is called the lady of the coins). After six months in the mental hospital and electric shock treatments, Shyla returns, seemingly "cured." Meanwhile Jordan Elliott has arrived in Waterford, and his immediate attention to her and his appreciation of her beauty give her a new beginning. Through high school and the early years of college Shyla seems to be a normal, intelligent, active girl of her age. She is popular with the men she meets, succeeds in both academics and extra curricular activities, and remains loyal to Jack and Jordan when the others of their childhood group drift off to other pursuits. Nothing would seem to have been an omen that in her senior year she would become one of the fiercest of the anti-war demonstrators.

She becomes politically radicalized when she meets "Radical Bob" Merrill, ostensibly sent to organize the protesters at the University of South Carolina in a chapter of SDS (Students for a Democratic Society). When Capers pretends to be a leader of the movement and is effective in his role, Shyla becomes his lover and his second-in-command. They are soon to become the most famous students in the state (aside from athletes) as a result of their arrests and their increasingly provocative actions that culminate in their break-in and arson at the Selective Service Office, a federal crime. It is hardly surprising that her idealism and her psyche receive severe blows when it turns out that not only Radical Bob, but also Capers, have been infiltrators for the FBI and SLED. It is in the aftermath of the trial that results from this event that Jack and Shyla are drawn together as the victims of their friend's treachery, and Jack knows that this humiliating, disillusioning experience is a factor in her suicide several years later. He says that she could have accepted the consequences of her own actions but could not accept the shame she felt in being made to seem a fool in her naive idealism: "So she turned to me and I turned to her, neither of us knowing that we were both keeping a ruthless appointment with a bridge in Charleston" (565).

On a camping trip that Shyla and Jack have arranged to help Jordan escape to Canada, they consummate their love, and Jack thinks that their marriage and the birth of Leah have, if not healed, at least mitigated Shyla's wounds. Not so! In a curious twisting of logic, she seems to have felt that by committing suicide she can join and thereby honor the Jews who were victims of the Holocaust. Just before she jumps from the bridge, she has had her father's Auschwitz number tattooed on her forearm, and though Conroy tries to make this illogic of Shyla's understandable in the letter that she leaves for Jack, he is only partly successful. Yet, in this poignant document Shyla's torment is made clear as she describes a reappearance of the lady of the coins in a hallucination that is this time accusatory because Shyla is a Jew. This disturbed woman and her suicide are central to several plot elements in the novel and to Jack's withdrawal from the world in the years immediately thereafter. Even though she is dead before the novel begins, her role is critical in the cast of major characters.

Although Jack is the protagonist, Jordan Elliott is, without question *Beach Music's* most charismatic character. From the moment he arrives in Waterford as a long-haired teenager from California until they part company in their college years, he is clearly the leader of the four inseparable friends. Capers protests his loss of the leadership role, but he has no chance against Jordan's derring-do and capability. It is Jordan who, early on, defies the town bully; it is Jordan who is the superb athlete in three sports; and it is Jordan whose survival training gets them through the fifteen-day ordeal of their ill-advised fishing expedition.

Jordan, as the battered and humiliated child of another of Conroy's sadistic Marine Corps officers is rebellious and sullen, but his bonding with Jack, Capers, and Mike seems to take some of the edge off his anger.

He and Jack immediately recognize that they are soul mates as the result of being sons of abusive fathers. Jordan, even as early as his boyhood in California, has acknowledged a deep religious faith (in part as a defense against his father's brutality), and it surfaces again when he claims that the Virgin Mary has been responsible for their survival in the fishing escapade.

The heroic side of his character is evident when he swims toward a shark in an effort to divert its attention long enough for Jack and Mike to get Capers back aboard the boat during that episode. The daredevil side is beautifully illustrated by his complicated scheme to get himself expelled from The Citadel (where his father has insisted that he go). The cunning side is shown by his rigging an apparent suicide scene to mask his escape to Canada after the arrests in the Vietnam War protests and by his becoming a Trappist monk in Rome. There is no question that his vows to the church are sincere, but they also provide him what he hopes will be a nearly impenetrable disguise and shelter from his past.

Inevitably, however, that shelter becomes harder and harder to maintain. From a wildly coincidental meeting in which his high school speech teacher confesses to him in Rome and recognizes his voice, there is a growing belief that he is not in fact dead, but living incognito. While Jordan continues to elude those who want to find him, he also has an increasing need to have a final resolution of the guilt he feels about the couple who were killed (when he blew up an air force plane during the protests) and some kind of accommodation with his father. All this comes about in Mike Hess's staged "trial" in Part VI although Jordan has already turned himself in before the "trial" begins. In a somewhat improbable reconciliation, Jordan and his father strike up a firm friendship after a lifetime of war between them, and Jordan finds his incarceration no hardship after his years as a Trappist monk. He becomes pastor to the many of his fellow inmates in need of spiritual guidance and teaches courses in theology and philosophy.

Jordan Elliott is a remarkable character. Only a writer of Conroy's skill keeps him from "stealing" the novel from Jack McCall. Jordan is active, aggressive, wily, and saintly. If not passive, Jack is a much more conventional man. From the moment Jordan makes his entrance maneuvering a skateboard through Waterford's downtown traffic and we see him arranging Shyla's hair and recognizing George Fox's playing of Beethoven, we know that he is a complex character. He is embarrassed at being singled out by one of his teachers as the scion of a distinguished southern family (while Capers basks in such attention), but he has no hesitation in challenging the local policeman's authority by eating the ticket he has been issued over the skateboard incident. Jordan is both sensitive and fearless, a combination that makes him the most dynamic character in the novel.

Capers Middleton is a much less attractive figure because he is nearly a stereotype of southern aristocratic pretentiousness and a self-centered prig. From as early as the ninth grade he brags about his ancestry and shows the manipulativeness that will be a central facet of his personality throughout the novel. He recognizes immediately that Jordan Elliott is a potential rival for leadership and befriends him in order to preclude that rivalry from developing in ways that he cannot control. Jack observes later that even as early as their youthful, seemingly carefree days, Capers was already mapping his future: "Self-doubt was unknown to him. He always knew exactly where he was going." (294). He certainly does not know where he is going when, in an act of foolish bravado (which he later "forgets"), he harpoons the giant manta ray that nearly destroys their boat and brings them close to death. This is, of course, not quite what Jack means when he says that Capers "knows where he is going," but it reveals his desire to appear manly and decisive after he has suffered the disappointment and embarrassment of losing a huge marlin that he had temporarily hooked.

When the novel opens we learn that Capers is running for governor of South Carolina as a stepping-stone for his ultimate political goal of the presidency. We also learn from Ledare and Jack that he had talked of just that when he was in the first and second grades. He is an unprincipled politician in that he will do or say whatever is expedient; Ledare says that, if one were to put Capers next to a chameleon, it would be Capers who would change colors. He is not above using unethical means to obtain what he wants. For example, for political purposes he wants a reconciliation with Jack, and with Jordan if possible, lest his betrayal of them during the Vietnam War protests should become a campaign issue. When Jack refuses, Capers threatens to use Jack's love for Jordan as a weapon that he can wield to get Jack's cooperation.

Meanwhile, Capers has divorced Ledare in order to marry a younger woman (who was Miss South Carolina) presumably in large part because she will be an asset to his political ambition. Mike Hess, who has agreed to work for Capers's election, brings Jack, Ledare, Capers, and the new wife, Betsy, together in an ill-advised effort to smooth over the bitterness that might erupt and mar the campaign. A furious confrontation ensues. The reason for Ledare's outrage at being tricked into this meeting is obvious. Not only has she been rejected by Capers, but he has custody of their children. The reason for Jack's adamant, hostile denunciation is not really clear until late in the novel when we learn in detail of Capers's Judas-like betrayal of his friends in the war protest movement. But though we don't know the extent of his treachery, his behavior in this scene is enough to show his pompous, self-righteous exploitation of any bit of evidence he can use for promoting his image. Like Rembert Elliott, Capers claims to put loyalty to country before loyalty to the individual, but he does not have the general's rectitude, and so there seems something hollow and self-serving in his stand.

That Ledare and Jack can be brought to forgive him and resume a semblance of friendship with Capers is almost as remarkable as Jordan's reunion with his father. At the mock trial, almost for the first time since their youthful camaraderie, Capers seems genuine when he apologizes to Jordan and Jack. He acknowledges that he behaved badly and that he would do everything differently now. Given the character Capers has always shown and his political ambitions, Jack remains skeptical, but he participates in the healing recreation of a moment from their past when the four boys clung to a surfboard in the waters of the Atlantic. In a tender scene the four seem to regain, not their innocence of course, but the unself-conscious fondness they once had for each other. When Capers makes good on his promise to use his political influence to obtain a substantial reduction of Jordan's sentence, we are left with the impression that even Capers has learned something from the mistakes he has made and something about the values of compassion and love.

Of the four friends it is really Mike Hess who has changed the most since the days of their boyhood. From a wisecracking teenager Mike has gone on in college to become a member of the most prestigious Jewish fraternity, a business major, and a fanatic about movies. He is never without a camera, and he takes every available course having to do with film. We don't learn much about how Mike moved from the University of South Carolina to become the enormously rich and powerful Hollywood producer that he is in the present. We do learn, however, a great deal about the way he has become another somewhat stereotypical character—the Hollywood vulgarian. At their high school reunion some years before, he arrived bedecked in gold chains; he has been married four times and has spent five years in psychiatric therapy; he lives in a pretentious mansion; and he blusters ostentatiously in restaurants.

He has the insensitivity to trick Jack and Ledare into the bitter meeting with Capers, and his idea about the movie of their lives is as much stimulated by his desire to make an important film as it is by nostalgia. He is as eager to flush Jordan out of hiding as Capers is and for equally selfish reasons. Mike claims that the movie cannot be "honest" unless he has Jordan's participation. Behind the vulgarity and the self-importance, however, there are remnants of the old, playful, generous Mike Hess. He hosts the extravagant party for Lucy, and he swears that he is working for Capers's election because he is genuinely convinced that Capers will be a true reformer.

Perhaps his greatest coup is the arranging of Jordan's mock trial. How he persuades all the warring participants to come together and allow themselves to be filmed stretches credibility, but it is a brilliant climax both for Mike's movie and Conroy's novel. Mike acts as the director and, while there is no script for this scene, he manages it masterfully. His sense of the dramatic may have inspired him to create this charade, but as the various members of the "cast" testify, it brings all the old animosities into the open and, therefore, helps to make possible the several reconciliations that ensue. We are never sure just how much of this Mike foresaw and planned, but he is too clever and worldly-wise not to have known that this "acting out" would bring some degree of catharsis.

What is most redeeming about Mike, in the end, is his self-knowledge. He recognizes his own shallowness. For money and power he has made a succession of second-rate adventure movies, guided almost entirely by box-office success. He knows that he has made too much money too fast, and that he has been uncouth in making sure everyone, both in Hollywood and in Waterford, is aware of what he has achieved. He confesses to Jack that he abhors what he has become and that even his mother is embarrassed by his transformation. Now, partly in penance and partly in an effort to change the direction of his life, he wants to make a film of stature that simultaneously pays tribute to his family and his past. Whereas at the end of the novel the destinies of all the other major characters seem certain at least in the short term, Mike's is left open-ended. Jack says at one point that Mike was not afflicted by the Southerner's preoccupation with "looking back" (573). But his movie is a looking back in a major way. Whether it provides the same kind of purging for him that it does for the others we never learn. What does seem clear is that his recognition of his fall from the "nice" person he was is a positive step in the direction of his regeneration.

Of the childhood friends, Ledare Ansley is the least colorful, and in college she is as superficial and tradition-bound as Capers. She has dropped Jack as her steady boyfriend because her family thinks his social status is not adequate for her position as a debutante. She quickly joins a popular sorority and remains aloof from the turmoil of the war protests. It is only after her disastrous marriage to Capers that she comes to a realization of how false her values have been and how they have led her into a loveless marriage and a bitter divorce.

Ledare's awareness of Capers's treacherous character comes long after that of Shyla, Jack, and Jordan and from different causes, but when it comes, it is just as clear as theirs. He has divorced her, he says, because her screen-writing career has become more important to her than being a wife and mother. The truth is that she has failed to lose the weight quickly that she gained during her last pregnancy, and Capers wants a dazzlingly beautiful woman at his side for photo opportunities during his political campaigns. She loses custody of the children because Capers has hired a private detective to take pictures of her in compromising situations with several men, one of them black. That one picture alone would have been enough to convince a South Carolina judge of the time that Ledare was an unfit mother.

After several years of emotional drifting, Ledare has come to a self-reliance that, if not an ideal state, is at least one with which she can live in dignity and stability. She signs on with Mike for the movie in part because she wants to find out where she went wrong in her decisions as a young woman, and she enthusiastically urges Jack to join her. It soon becomes apparent that this urging comes as much from a hope of renewing their earlier relationship as it does from a need for his professional help. Although she is quite open about her hopes for a romance with Jack, she is far too wise to push too hard and too quickly, for she realizes that Jack is not sufficiently recovered from Shyla's death and his other wounds to make a commitment. When the right moment comes for Jack to ask the question, at the party the night before Jordan leaves for prison, he finds that Ledare and Leah have already picked out the wedding dress and made up the guest list. Ledare, and even Leah, have known that Jack would eventually propose; it was only a matter of when. Her thought of asking Ruth and George Fox to be the attendants at the wedding is a mark of Ledare's instinctive graciousness and her realization that, in doing so, she and Jack are ratifying the reconciliation that has taken place.

That Jack and Ledare are well-suited for each other they have found by working closely together on the movie. They have both suffered and they have both learned from their experiences. These are omens for a good marriage, though both of them know it will be a very different kind from Jack's to Shyla and certainly from Ledare's to Capers. On the night before the wedding Jack asks Ledare to read Shyla's last letter, in which among many other things she tells Jack to remarry, but to "save the last dance for me" (620). Ledare, wise and generous woman that she has become, replies that she hopes she and Jack will have a wonderful life and "love each other as well as we can. But Shyla can have the last dance. She earned it" (621).

Aside from the childhood friends, Lucy O'Neill McCall Pitts is the other major character in *Beach Music*. She is a remarkable figure in many ways. Although we don't learn this until long after we have seen her as a gracious hostess, telling the story of the romance between Elizabeth Cotesworth and General William Tecumseh Sherman to groups on the annual house tours of Waterford, she has come from a childhood of almost unbelievable atrocities. (The chapter in which this story is told, Twenty-seven, is southern gothic writing—see the definition in Chapter Two of this book—in its most authentic form.) It involves a drunken, abusive father and, among other horrors, murder, arson, and rape. At age thirteen, after a harrowing journey from her birthplace, Lucy lands on the streets of Atlanta as an illiterate girl with no family or friends. Lucy's resourcefulness, however, makes her a survivor. It involves some very unattractive means, but she uses what little she has to make a living. When a drunken Johnson Hagood McCall meets her in a burlesque club and does not realize that she is a striptease dancer off duty rather than the daughter of a distinguished Atlanta family as she claims, Lucy seizes on this opportunity to escape the tawdry life she has been living for three years. She is four months pregnant when she and Johnson get married, and she suffers the withering scorn of Johnson Hagood's mother, Ginny Penn, who immediately spots the impossibility of Lucy's coming from anything but "trash."

Ginny Penn, to her credit, undertakes to teach Lucy some of the basics of taste and deportment, and Lucy, to her credit, swallows her pride and gratefully accepts her mother-in-law's training. She has the tact to accede to Ginny Penn's advice, but she has the cunning to play up to her father-in-law, Silas, in showing off her skills in hunting and fishing. Lucy's education is advanced further when she ingratiates herself with her land-lady, Harriet Cotesworth, and eventually inherits Harriet's house and its magnificent antiques. It isn't, however, until Jack goes to school and reads to her that she becomes fully literate.

From the earliest days of her marriage, there is a fierce struggle for control. Johnson Hagood is an alcoholic who realizes too late that Lucy is not what she appeared to be, and that she is manipulative and socially ambitious. Their quarrels are almost constant and of epic proportions. Into this turmoil five sons are born (Lucy has prayed for at least one daughter) and all of them, but especially the younger ones, suffer from Lucy's "boredom" with motherhood. She is more interested in her social milieu and the compliments she receives from admiring men than she is in the role of nurturing mother. Like all of Conroy's mother figures she is simultaneously maddening and charming, devious and loving. She is infamous for saying that she is dying in order to gain sympathy or whatever else it is that she wants at the moment. She also, like Conroy's own mother and Lila of *The Prince of Tides*, after some thirty years of stormy marriage, divorces Johnson Hagood and remarries.

Lucy's decision seems a valid one since Dr. Pitts is devoted to her and relieves her of the tension and abuse of Johnson Hagood's drunken churlishness. Unfortunately, hardly has this improvement in her life begun than she is stricken with leukemia. It is in the months between her first, near fatal, coma and the final days of her struggle that we see the most attractive of Lucy's many sides. In remission Lucy becomes the mother and grandmother that redeems her earlier failures and lies. She is magnificent as she undertakes Leah's introduction to the natural wonders of the low country, not the least of which is the rescue of loggerhead turtle eggs from the ravages inflicted by beach erosion and overdevelopment. She is at one of her finest hours when she not only defies, but wins over, Jane Hartley, the South Carolina Wildlife Department's agent who has objected to Lucy's interference with the natural rhythms of the turtles' breeding habits. In a different vein, she comes to Rome for a Christmas visit and is like a child in her wonder at the many churches she visits and the midnight mass at St. Peter's.

Like other Conroy mothers she is guilty of repression when she claims that John Hardin is merely sensitive, not truly disturbed. But she is unlike other Conroy mothers in her recognition that it is best for all concerned that she finally reveal the truth of her background. In one of the poignant scenes before she succumbs, she is gallant at the party in her honor even when she knows that cancer has returned. She dances with Johnson Hagood, who, remarkably, has stayed sober for the affair, and gives no hint of her recognition of the irony in the celebration. She dies with a dignity that she never quite achieved in life. She tells her sons that she is aware of her failures as a mother and asks their blessing. Whatever feelings of animosity Jack and his brothers have felt toward

Lucy over the years melt away as she slips from them quietly and grace-fully.

The rest of the McCall clan are minor characters on the plot level of the novel, but they are major players on the larger family-saga level. Leah is present in many scenes, but as a child of nine, she has a small role in the affairs of the adults. It is because of the bitter custody fight that Jack has such venomous feelings about the Foxes, and the first in-truder on his exile is Martha Fox, begging him to let her parents see Leah either in Rome or in Waterford if Jack will bring her there for a visit. Jack's attention to Leah is almost obsessive, and she becomes a great favorite with her uncles and grandmother when Jack does bring her to South Carolina. She is an extraordinarily pretty child, whose re-semblance to her mother is remarked on by everyone who sees her. Her beauty is matched by her intelligence and lively personality. If she sometimes seems a bit too mature for her years, that is doubtless ex-plained by her having been raised in Europe by a cosmopolitan father who dotes on her and does not condescend. He has not told her the full story of Shyla's death (though it turns out she has discovered it on her own), and he has romanticized the stories he has told her of Waterford, but in almost every other regard Jack treats her as an equal rather than a child. He realizes that this may have robbed her of some of an average child's innocence, but on the whole, he does not regret the decision. Leah and Ledare immediately like each other so it would seem the future is bright for this engaging child and her newly-established family.

Her grandfather's past, present, and future do not seem bright at all. Judge Johnson Hagood McCall is not as physically abusive as are Bull Meecham and Henry Wingo, but his alcoholism frequently causes scenes so unpleasant that Lucy takes the children to the refuge of the abbey where her brother is a monk. What is almost more disquieting than his at-home behavior is the Judge's public displays of addiction—falling down drunk in gutters, vomiting in bathrooms, passing out in hospital corridors—and, in spite of numerous vows to renounce liquor, to the very end of the novel, he has failed to conquer his problem. His was a brilliant legal mind, and his basic values are admirable, as we see in his rulings on racial issues (which of course make him unpopular in the South of the 1950s), but his weakness makes him a pathetic character rather than the admirable one he might have been.

Johnson Hagood recognizes, soon after his marriage to Lucy, that he has made a mistake (as usual, under the influence of alcohol) in marrying this woman from a totally different social background, and this, on his part, is the beginning of the never-ending conflict between them. It also, no doubt, contributes to his worsening problem with alcohol. When he has been drinking, which is most of the time, he is alternately testy, sanctimonious, maudlin, threatening, and self-pitying. He confronts Lucy and Dr. Pitts on their return from their honeymoon with a gun that he is too drunk to use; on the other hand, he is abstemious during the party for Lucy's return from the hospital, and he plays his role as "judge" in Mike Hess's "trial" of Jordan Elliott with impartiality and probity. His letter to Jack and Ledare, saying that he won't come to Rome with the rest of the McCall clan lest he spoil the festivities of their marriage by getting drunk is a final and poignant testimony to his recognition of the disaster he has made of his own life and an apology for the damage he has done to those he has loved well but unwisely:

> "I can't make it, Jack and Ledare, and there's no excuse for it. I just can't. My wedding present to you is that I won't embarrass either of you at your wedding. It's the best I can do." (624)

Not the least of those he has hurt is, of course, Lucy. Over the years, after his initial regret about the marriage, it seems as if he has come to rely on her for stability. Although there is a large degree of self-pity in his emotional outbursts of love after the divorce, there is also a recognition that without her he no longer has an anchor. There is a remarkable scene during Lucy's final party, when, as they dance together once again, both of them knowing it is for the last time, Johnson Hagood recognizes that his failure of self-discipline is the primary cause of his loss.

Conroy uses Jack's four brothers, along with Lucy and Johnson Hagood, to convey the remarkable volatility and diversity of this dynamically charged family. Although none except John Hardin plays a significant role on the action level, each contributes a part to the incredible, almost explosive, atmosphere that is created by the McCalls when they are in the same room. Dupree, the second son, is a pragmatist. He is a social worker in a mental hospital, and he, more than all the other brothers, has sympathy and love for John Hardin, the paranoid schizophrenic brother. He tries to be a negotiator in the family feuds, and he tries to protect John Hardin from the consequences of his irrational behavior. That he seldom succeeds but nonetheless goes on trying marks

Dupree as one who knows the values of love and compassion which several of the other members of the family have yet to grasp.

Dallas, the third brother, is a conventional lawyer. He has joined his self-destructive father in a law practice that is constantly declining as a result of the Judge's atrocious behavior. Dallas is forever fearful (with some justification) that each event that exposes the McCall family to ridicule will cost the firm more clients. On the other hand, when Jack suggests that he go out on his own, Dallas replies with the somewhat lame excuse that his father needs him. However loyal this response may be, it reveals Dallas's lack of initiative. He is, of all the brothers, the least imaginative and the least adventuresome, but he is nonetheless important because, more than any of the others, he stands as the person who is content being a Southerner and aspires to nothing more than peace in his life.

Tee (Tecumseh) is the most emotional of the brothers. He has been embarrassed all his life by Lucy's whimsical naming him after General Sherman, but at the same time, he has longed for her attention and her love. As a teacher of autistic children, he lives on the edge of emotional trauma day-to-day, but as a younger brother he has been painfully aware of Lucy's disaffection with motherhood. Thus, it is he who reacts with the most overt distress at her illness, is capable of tears when none of the other brothers is, and who keeps the emotional tension at fever pitch as they await word from the intensive care unit. It is he who is most enthusiastic about Lucy's recovery party, and it is he who is most open in his grief. Of all the brothers, Tee is the most readily readable on the surface; this does not make him superficial, but it does mark him as a character who, coming late in his parents' marriage, suffers from his mother's loss of interest in child rearing, and who, therefore, craves her love even more than do his older brothers.

John Hardin is a special case. As a paranoid schizophrenic and the youngest of the five brothers, he has always been treated by his parents as a hypersensitive "child" (even as he nears thirty), who needs special attention and love. He is an expert carpenter and craftsman who has built an elaborate tree house on the family's property on the Isle of Orion. He arrives at the party celebrating Lucy's remission with a beautifully made coffin that he has designed for her. Despite the inappropriateness of its timing, Lucy gallantly diffuses the tension and embarrassment the guests feel by telling John Hardin that it is precisely the gift she wanted and is eager to try it on. Then in an eloquent speech

John Hardin explains why he has made the coffin, picks it up, and drives
away:

> "Upstaged by a schizophrenic," Dallas said. "The story of
> my life."
> "No," I [Jack] said. "What we just saw was more. The party
> just had a perfect ending." (493)

  For his brothers John Hardin is a constant problem since no one can
predict what will be the next bizarre manifestation of his illness. The
largest burden falls on Dupree as a professional in the field of mental
disorders, and ironically, though John Hardin seems to dislike all his
brothers, it is Dupree for whom he harbors a positive hate. Apparently
John Hardin's behavior can be kept under control if he receives a periodic "shot" (presumably of Thorazine), but he frequently fails to get that
shot, and then he is capable of almost any kind of antisocial act. Along
with his near-constant anger at his brothers and the world in general, he
especially deplores the development of the offshore islands, and in protest, he holds the drawbridge over the Waterford River open, blocking
traffic on both sides and keeping the sheriff and the McCall brothers at
bay with a gun. Dupree is finally able to negotiate with John Hardin to
throw away the gun and close the bridge, but at the cost of the brothers
jumping naked from the bridge. Later, when Lucy's leukemia has
reached its final stage, John Hardin, who has maintained from the beginning that it is not cancer but the doctors who are killing her, steals
her from the hospital and again holds the brothers off at gunpoint. Only
through Dupree's calm behavior and Jack's impetuous decision to call
John Hardin's bluff are they able to get their mother back to the hospital.
  In spite of their temperamental differences and their fiery personalities
the McCall brothers have a bond that Jack realizes he cannot forget or
deny in spite of his vow to do so. Conroy has said that it was only after
his own mother's death that he came to appreciate how much he loved
his brothers and sisters (ABC Interview), and much that same thing happens with the McCalls. We see them quarrel, but we see their joyous
camaraderie and humor in scenes such as the one in which Ginny Penn
returns from the nursing home. John Hardin has built a ramp to accom-
modate her wheelchair, Tee clowns as he teases her, and Dupree joshes
her for not even thanking them for building the ramp and being there
to welcome her back. This bonding of the brothers is one of the chief
elements that makes the family-saga level of *Beach Music* so engaging.

Ginny Penn and Silas McCall are not as colorful, nor do they have as large parts, as Tolitha and Amos Wingo in *The Prince of Tides*, but Ginny Penn is a feisty and snobbish grandmother while Silas in his solidity and integrity is a legend in Waterford. Among the other minor characters of importance are Ruth and George Fox. It is largely through their individual stories of the horrors they have suffered in the Holocaust that we come to understand the forbidding atmosphere that haunts their house during Shyla's childhood, and for different reasons both come to realize that they have been largely responsible for her emotional instability and ultimate suicide. From an uneducated, peasant background Ruth is by nature superstitious and paranoic (although her experience is terrifying enough to engender those reactions in anyone). George comes from a totally different class of European Jew. His was a rich, cultured family, and until the advent of the Nazis, one esteemed by the German and Polish societies in which they were elite, prominent, and complacent. Thus, George is even more stunned than Ruth by the changes that occur in the 1930s and early 1940s.

If Ruth is an awkward and fearful member of the Waterford community (she, for example, gives a disastrous Jewish birthday party for Shyla's Christian friends that is salvaged only by Lucy's diplomacy), George is a bitter, angry man. His role as a member of the Judenrat (Jews who cooperated with the Gestapo in order to save themselves at the expense of other Jews) continues to plague him with guilt and shame. His sneering contempt for Jews and Gentiles alike who fail to appreciate culture, especially music, makes him a cold, forbidding figure. He makes no effort to embrace his new life in Waterford, and he tells Jack that his devotion to his first wife and their children (killed at Auschwitz) remains so intense that he has never loved Ruth, Shyla, and Martha. George Fox is the quintessential example of a man who has resisted, and therefore failed to benefit from, the healing qualities of compassion and love that so many of the other characters come to experience.

There are dozens of cameo roles in *Beach Music*, some of which make a comment on thematic levels, others of which have parts on the edge of the McCall family saga, and still others of which exist for local color. Max Rusoff, Mike Hess's grandfather, the Great Jew, is used as a contrast to the Foxes. A Jew, who has his own story of horrors suffered in Russia during the revolution, he has come to Waterford with a totally different attitude from theirs and, with the help of Silas McCall, has become a prominent and beloved citizen of the community and for a time its mayor.

Dr. Pitts, Lucy's second husband, is everything that Johnson Hagood is not—sensitive, gentle, devoted to her well-being. One of his most important contributions comes, however, when, in an angry attack on the McCall brothers' emotionalism, he puts his finger on what makes the family so tempestuous:

> All of you need to learn to be part of a room without filling
> it up. You need to learn to be in a scene without being the
> whole scene. . . . there's too much commotion around you
> boys. I demand that you quit turning every single thing into
> an event. . . . Why must every day seem like a home movie
> from the Apocalypse? (479)

More important on the plot level is Rembert Elliott, the Marine Corps father who treats his son so violently and contemptibly that he almost makes Bull Meecham of *The Great Santini* look like a mild-mannered man. His physical and psychological abuse are so extreme that it is surprising that Jordan survives with a personality as much intact as it is. In a wonderful scene of retribution, his wife Celestine leaves him stranded in Rome without passport, money, or credit cards (he has never carried a wallet because he has thought the bulge in his pants pocket detracted from his military bearing) after he has attempted to betray Jordan.

Also making a contribution to the theme of betrayal is "Radical Bob" Merrill, the SDS organizer who is really an agent of the FBI. Tony Calabrese's remarks about integration bring about a Ku-Klux-Klan–style retribution on both him and Johnson Hagood for having ruled in his favor in the court suit in which he tries to regain his teaching position. Father Jude, the ascetic monk, whom the McCall brothers think at one time is Lucy's lover, turns out to be her brother and has shared in her trauma following their mother's flight and suicide. These and many more fill the large cast that populates *Beach Music*. Conroy even includes some real figures: novelist Gore Vidal is his sharp-tongued self at a Christmas party in Rome; Senator Strom Thurmond tries to kiss every woman's hand at Lucy's party; and Senator Ernest Hollings strives mightily to be in every photograph taken at that affair.

THEMATIC ISSUES

Like *The Prince of Tides*, with its focus on family relationships, *Beach Music* is a novel that explores a great variety of emotions, resentments, and angers, as well as the love and loyalty, that exist in a southern family in the second half of the twentieth century. At the beginning of the book Jack feels alienated from his alcoholic father, his manipulative mother, and his contentious brothers. With the news of his mother's leukemia and imminent death, he feels a renewal of love for her, which turns out to be a healing value for himself, and he comes to an equally restorative relationship with his father and brothers.

Simultaneously, by returning to Waterford with Leah, he is willy-nilly brought into a restoration of a cool, but at least cordial, accommodation with Shyla's parents. And thanks to Mike Hess's passionate commitment to a movie about their youth, Jack is also able to come to terms with Capers's betrayal, and even, to some extent, with Shyla's suicide. Thus, the major theme of *Beach Music* has to do with the healing values of forgiveness, confession, compassion, and love.

At the same time Conroy probes, as he has in previous novels, the relationships between mothers and children, husbands and wives, fathers and sons. Lucy's marriage to Johnson Hagood, Ledare's to Capers, Celestine's to Rembert Elliott, and to some extent Ruth's to George Fox are used as examples of unfortunate matchings. In all of these cases it is the husband who is abusive or self-serving, but, except for Ledare, the wives tolerate their situations for twenty-five years or more. Almost without exception the children of these marriages are disturbed, unhappy, and rebellious. Jordan's case is an especially painful one in that his father's twisted sense of "manhood" is constantly used to make the boy miserable. Jack McCall and his brothers suffer as well from their father's surly, unpredictable drunkenness. Though he comes to a renewal of his love for his mother, Jack says that mothers tend to make their sons dangerous to the women in their lives by teaching them all the tricks that can be used in the conflict of the sexes. One of Conroy's chief themes in *Beach Music*, then, involves the chemistry of dysfunctional families.

He touches on related matters such as the dangers of repressing the truth, men's inability to express their emotions, and sexual stereotyping. As usual Conroy lashes out at the narrowness of Roman Catholic doctrine, but his portrayal of an evangelical religion employing snakes is positively chilling. And, again, he attacks the extremity of the military mind-set as it is embodied in Rembert Elliott and encountered at The Citadel. He decries the overdevelopment of the offshore islands, not only in John Hardin's diatribes, but in his description of the damage done to the land and its wildlife.

Along with these themes come associated ones such as southern fam-

ilies' emphasis on breeding and "background." Ginny Penn is an unabashed snob on the subject, and Capers Middleton has the gall to brag,
in the ninth grade, that his family arrived in America three years before
Jordan's did (1706 versus 1709). South Carolina, as the bastion of Confederate values, comes in for a share of censure for its uncritical attitudes
toward the Vietnam War and especially its reactionary, racist resistance
to integration. Conroy gives ample evidence of why Jack McCall, quite
aside from his personal problems, deplores the place of his birth. In spite
of its magnificent tidal landscape, it is a backwater politically and socially.

Another familiar Conroy theme is that of betrayal and, in *Beach Music*,
many instances of forgiveness. There are major acts of betrayal such as
those of Capers and Radical Bob. George Fox's participation in the Judenrat and Sister Magdalena's denunciation of Ruth and the nuns of her
convent to the SS are examples drawn from Europe in World War II.
Rembert Elliott could be said to have betrayed his role as father from
the moment Jordan was born. More specifically, on the pretext of wanting a reconciliation with his son, he tries to lure Jordan into the open in
Rome, when, in fact, he is trying to have him arrested. Capers and Mike
Hess are guilty of betrayal when for their selfish ends they have photographs taken of Jordan so as to flush him out of hiding. The Foxes
betray their better natures and their fidelity to Shyla by lying in order
to picture Jack as an unfit father. Even Jack says he is guilty of a kind
of betrayal by denying Leah her South Carolina heritage and telling her
stories that reflect only the sunnier aspects of that world.

Conroy links these stories to the major themes of healing and forgiveness through love and compassion. We are all, Conroy says, imperfect
and capable of betrayal, sometimes maliciously but sometimes uninten-
tionally by a confusion of values and mistaken priorities. At the same
time he shows that almost all these cases of betrayal can be forgiven if
we recognize our human frailty and are willing to rise above our initial
abhorrence of these acts. No example could better illustrate this principle
than Jordan's and Rembert Elliott's mutual willingness to make a new
start in understanding and love for each other.

With a broader definition of betrayal, Conroy introduces the whole
genocidal history of Nazi German and czarist Russian attacks on European Jews. Chiefly through the three long stories told by Max Rusoff and
Ruth and George Fox, Conroy brings the Holocaust into the novel in
excruciating detail. At first these set pieces of horrific description seem
tangential to the main characters, plot, and themes of the novel. Then,

near the end, as we learn about the effects of the Vietnam War on American values and attitudes, Conroy tells us that he sees a parallel between the effects of the Holocaust and those of the Vietnam War on the spiritual condition of our society. This is a tenuous linkage, but it is certainly an important plot element and thematic issue that Conroy wants to emphasize. Even if he is not completely convincing in this attempt, the stories, especially of Ruth and George Fox, are important in helping to explain their characters and Shyla's suicide.

Equally important is Conroy's presentation of a universal theme having to do with the individual and his or her past. As many philosophers and writers have observed, one cannot escape one's past, and an effort to do so almost inevitably ends in unhappiness, if not disaster. Jack attempts it and, not only does the past come crashing through his carefully constructed shield, he realizes that he has become a cold, withdrawn man because of his mistaken belief that he could close out his former life. Jordan, too, has attempted to run, and though there is no doubt that his religious devotion is sincere, he too is tracked down by figures from his past. Moreover, he increasingly feels the need to come to terms with himself, his family, and his friends. The past that Lucy has run from does not catch up with her in the same way that Jack's and Jordan's do, but from the beginning Ginny Penn has known that she is a phony, and Lucy spends a lifetime working to become the lady she has pretended to be.

Jack tells Leah that life is full of unexpected blows for which one cannot prepare. The only defense is to develop resiliency and an awareness that these unwelcome surprises will surely come no matter how we may try to protect ourselves against them. This wisdom comes, no doubt, from Jack's realization that his attempt to close a door on his past was a serious mistake. Jack's self-knowledge is a vital part of his rites of passage and coming to a fully mature manhood.

Conroy has touched on many of these themes before, but in *Beach Music* he explores several of them in greater depth than he has in the past. It is, without question, his most ambitious novel to date, and to the extent that it succeeds, the thematic level must be counted as one of its strongest elements. Conroy's hymn to love and family bonds, to compassion and forgiveness, to gallantry under extreme pressures is a powerful one indeed.

STYLE AND LITERARY DEVICES

From the first page of *Beach Music* to its last, no reader can fail to be struck by Conroy's extraordinary style. While there are not as many extended lyrical passages here as there were in *The Prince of Tides*, there are a great many long, descriptive ones. Almost any chapter offers an example: the lengthy description of Rome in Chapter Two; the sensuous description of the South Carolina low country in Nine; in Twenty-one that of Jordan Elliott's arrival in Waterford; or that of Lucy's elaborate party that takes up nearly half of Thirty-three. Conroy makes these descriptions come alive by the use of visual imagery, evocative adjectives and adverbs, and a keen use of unique detail.

Within these descriptive passages and elsewhere Conroy uses similes and metaphors with great fluency and poetic flourish:

> She [Shyla] had always prided herself in keeping her madness invisible and at bay; and when she could no longer fend off the voices that grew inside her, their evil set to chaos in a minor key, her breakdown enfolded upon her, like a tarpaulin pulled across that part of her brain where once there had been light. (3)

> I had not reckoned with Waterford's quiet stamina of insinuation, the muscular allure of spartina and azalea, storax and redbud. The town took you prisoner and never once considered amnesty or early parole. (418)

Indeed, so heavy is his reliance on this kind of writing that it is one of the things that his critics find excessive. But it is his rambling and sometimes contorted sentences that are most troublesome:

> From the smoke of a dream too dark to remember, I woke in the bedroom with my boyhood locked in fixed position around me as a timber-laden barge sounded its horn on the river, trying vainly to rouse the sleeping bridge tender. (122)

Often these sentences are evocative and produce the rich, lush prose that give Conroy his reputation as a master stylist, but occasionally, as Shone and other critics point out, they become cumbersome and pretentious.

Conroy is perfectly capable, however, of shifting stylistic gears. In

Ruth Fox's story he successfully uses rather clipped phrasing to imitate her halting command of English. He shifts back and forth from the past to the present tense, showing again, perhaps, her limited control of English but, more important, showing that although the events she is describing took place some forty years before, they are still as fresh and horrifying in her mind as if they were happening at the moment. This use of the present tense also serves to give immediacy to the story for the reader; the pace quickens and suspense is created as we wonder how Ruth will survive the many obstacles to her escape. Conroy's use of style to present George Fox's narrative is quite different. George is more fluent in English than his wife, but he is also more bitter and cynical. Once again Conroy shifts from past to present, but here the effect is of emphasizing atrocity more than it is in quickening the pace. George Fox's guilt and self-loathing are almost as terrifying as were his experiences, and Conroy's bleak style in this section helps to convey those qualities.

Style can also be used to create other special effects and emphases. On the night that the McCall house is attacked after Johnson Hagood's ruling on the desegregation issue, Lucy has planned a formal dinner party for several local politicians and their wives. She has been meticulous in the choice of menu and the candlelit setting of the table, and she watches proudly as the ladies are seated "as elegantly as monarch butterflies settling on peonies" (484). Immediately bricks come crashing through the windows and the ugly epithet of "nigger-lover" is hurled at Johnson Hagood along with a threat on his life. The juxtaposition here is stunning. It makes the desecration all the more crude and despicable. In a different way, style can be used for foreshadowing. On the night that Jack and his friends seal their friendship, Capers asks them each how they would commit suicide if the occasion arose. Jordan's response is an elaborate and carefully detailed plan of going to sea in a boat and, after slitting his wrists, slipping into the water so his father will be enraged by not having a body to bury. This passage prefigures almost exactly the faked suicide that Jordan uses to elude capture after the break-in trial. It might also be added that, after the others have said how they would kill themselves, Capers priggishly announces that he wouldn't commit suicide at all because it is a cowardly thing to do. This is a clear example of the one-upmanship that will become a hallmark of his character throughout.

While Jack's profession as a food and travel writer make it natural that he should speak frequently about victuals and wine, he does so at such length and in such sensuous detail that references to food become almost a motif in the novel. At times Conroy seems self-indulgent as when he speaks of rice and truffles forming a "silent concordat" (30) or when he rhapsodizes about the blend of tomatoes, garlic, and basil (85), but usually his descriptions, such as that of catching, cleaning, and cooking crabs (418) are charming and appropriate; in this passage he even gives us his recipe for the perfect crab cake! The description of the massive outlay of food and drink for Lucy's party, attended by scores of people in addition to the scores who were invited, comes close to a loaves-and-fishes story. So intense is Jack's interest in the good quality of food and beverage that, outraged by the cup of mediocre coffee that he gets from a machine, he thinks of writing an article urging coffee-exporting nations to boycott America unless we can learn to do a better job in processing the product.

Another motif in the novel is music, especially "beach music." This, it turns out, is the music, frequently played for dancing in pavilions on the beach by teenagers of the 1950s and early 1960s. The shag, a version of jitterbug danced to rock and roll songs, was especially popular in the South of this period, and the McCall brothers pride themselves in their expertise in this particular area of their southern heritage. They vie with each other in helping Leah to learn it. Central to this motif is the fact that Jack and Shyla danced the shag to "Save the Last Dance for Me" in the house that was crashing into the sea (mentioned in the Prologue and frequently thereafter) when they are first struck by a romantic interest in each other. It is some years later before that interest blossoms into love and marriage, but it is a transfiguring moment for them both. Of all the stories Jack tells Leah about her mother and himself this is her favorite. So often has she heard it that she corrects Jack when he makes slight errors of fact in the retelling. "Save the Last Dance for Me" becomes Jack's and Shyla's "song," and so well known is it to all their families and friends, that even when, at Jack's and Ledare's wedding the McCalls delight in teaching the Romans how to shag, they have diplomatically avoided including it in the repertory they bring on tape from South Carolina for the occasion. It is a reference to this song, and what it has symbolized for Jack and herself, with which Shyla ends the letter she writes to Jack before her suicide. She urges him to remarry, but to "save the last dance for me":

> Because she had promised it and because she had taught me
> to honor the eminence of magic in our frail human drama, I
> knew that Shyla was waiting for me, biding her time, looking

forward to the dance that would last forever, in a house
somewhere beneath the great bright sea. (628)

But *Beach Music* is full of music far beyond the shag and "Save the
Last Dance for Me." Some of the music in the novel, however, is disso-
nant rather than concordant. George Fox had been a concert pianist with
an international reputation before World War II. When he is conscripted
to play for the pleasure of a Gestapo officer, he does so with contempt
for the man but as a way, he hopes, of saving himself, his wife, and their
sons. This proves to be a vain endeavor and a major cause of his self-
loathing. In Waterford, although he continues to play privately, in his
bitterness he uses music as a way of breaking Shyla's spirit by forcing
her to play beyond her modest abilities. George Fox is a man damaged
almost beyond repair by his wartime experience, and it is a mark of his
warped psyche that he should use music, one of the greatest symbols of
harmony, in such a perverse way.

Much more frequently we find music used in its traditional sense. In
the sections of the novel set in South Carolina we are never far from the
sounds of the tides that lap the offshore islands. Lucy sings to call the
box turtles she keeps as pets in her beachfront home. Lucy and Leah
walk on the beach almost every day, and there is a metaphorical music
in Lucy's trying to maintain the natural rhythms of the life cycles of
loggerhead turtles when both man and nature seem bent on destroying
them. As the baby turtles instinctively move toward the waves, Lucy
says they are doing it because they are responding to "beach music"
(475). Conroy claims that Oliver Thomas, a child afflicted with Down's
syndrome who sings hymns to attract a porpoise, is based on a real boy
he heard about in his childhood (Carney 78). Ledare wants Leah to witness this ethereal communion of man and nature as the porpoise rises
from the water and emits sounds that mingle with Oliver's awkward
music.

The harmony that the McCalls and all of Jack's childhood chums feel
for the verge, with its bountiful fish, crabs, and shrimp is often in Conroy's limpid prose lifted to a kind of paean for the beauty of the beach.
Beach Music is, then, in both its narrow reference and its broader significance, a splendid title for this novel that by ending in concord and unity,
resembles the way in which a musical composition, after treating conflicting themes, returns to the "home key."

Conroy does not rely heavily on symbols. In *Beach Music* the mysterious "lady of the coins" is, if not precisely a symbol, a very important

element on the plot and character development levels. During Ruth's escape from Poland, she spends some time of haven in a Roman Catholic convent. While there she hides the dress, into which her mother has sewn eight gold coins, in a statue of the Virgin Mary. Ruth has told Shyla about this and has made the three remaining coins into necklaces for herself, Shyla, and Martha. Although a Jew, Ruth clearly sees the lady of the coins as protector, but for Shyla she becomes a confusing, ambiguous symbol. In her childhood Shyla has a hallucination in which the Virgin appears to her, presumably in a benign way. Just before her suicide, however, Shyla has another vision of the lady, but this time she seems to represent the Nazi Christians who revile Jews. In her cruelly disturbed mind, Shyla seems to think that by her suicide she will join the Jews who were tortured and killed by people who worshipped the lady of the coins. Nevertheless, she carefully removes the coin necklace before she jumps from the bridge and leaves it for Leah to wear. References to the lady of the coins occur throughout the novel because she is so central to Shyla's suicide, which Jack and her parents are trying hard to understand. Ruth blames herself for telling Shyla the story since it was the hallucination that was the immediate catalyst for Shyla's death. Jack tries to reassure her that it was not literally the lady of the coins that sent Shyla off the bridge but a whole syndrome of tormented ideas and images.

That bridge itself becomes for Jack a symbol of all of Shyla's pain and her death. Even in Rome several years later, when he crosses a bridge, he is reminded of *that* bridge and the loss it brought about. When, in being tested on her Christianity by an SS officer who demands that she name the twelve apostles, it is certainly symbolic that Ruth can name them all except Judas. And it is symbolic of his alienation that Jack's first sexual encounter after Shyla's death is an impersonal one with a masked woman who never reveals her name. In contrast, the wedding ring he wears at the end of the book is, like all rings and especially wedding rings, a symbol of wholeness and harmony.

If Conroy uses few specific symbols, he relies even more heavily on universal ones like water than he did in *The Prince of Tides*. Here water has its traditional dual associations of death by drowning on the one hand, and healing and life on the other. Shyla's death is by water, and it is at sea that Jack and his friends nearly perish during the ill-fated fishing expedition. But there are far more references to water as cleansing and life-affirming. Among the many references of this kind, none is more lyrically beautiful than the scene in which Jack and three of his brothers float naked in the river after John Hardin has forced them to jump off the drawbridge. This is a moment of great tenderness and release for them as they laugh and tell stories while they drift with the current:

> I listened to the small talk of my brothers and drew closer to them with every word they spoke. Through them, I could study some of the flaws I brought to bear in my own life. Like me, they had scratchy, muffled temperaments, but were courteous to everyone they met almost to a fault. . . . In a small armada of brothers, I stroked the waters that led to my father's house. (206)

When Shyla first menstruates, she is horrified and embarrassed (Ruth has told her nothing about the physical changes that come with adolescence), and Jack takes her to the river where they swim as Jack tells her that saltwater is a cure for everything (393). Ledare is like a Nereid (a mythological sea nymph) on water skis, and as she instructs Leah in the art, they become as fondly bound to each other emotionally as they are physically while Ledare stands behind Leah to guide her (380).

Jack, Jordan, Mike, and Capers seal their friendship in the summer before they enter high school as Jordan teaches the others how to use a surfboard. In the moonlit waters off the coast the four boys float among a school of porpoises and recognize (though as teenage boys they do not articulate it) that moments like this are rare and a gift from the sea:

> Each of us would remember that night floating on the waves all during our lives. . . . It was the purest moment of freedom and headlong exhilaration that I had ever felt. A wordless covenant was set among us the night of the porpoises. Each of us would go back to that surfboard again and again in our imaginations, return to that night where happiness seemed so easy to touch. (293)

And on the night before Jordan leaves to serve his sentence at Fort Leavenworth, the four men, some twenty-odd years later, recreate that moment, a symbol of their reconciliation and the reaffirmation of their love for each other:

> "Where were you going to send me, Capers?" Jordan asked. "Where is it you think I belonged?"
> We were floating in the Atlantic, holding on to the surf-

board, with another summer ending and the warm winds soft against the surface and the taste of salt in our mouths. We drifted in the deep currents on a moonless night and because we were low country boys we were not afraid. Then Capers summed it up by reaching out and rumpling Jordan's hair, saying, "Here. You belong here. With us. Always." (585)

It can hardly be accidental, however, that Conroy emphasizes the early scene's taking place under a full moon while the later one occurs on a night when there is no moonlight. And, significantly, Jack reminds the others that there are no porpoises (traditionally thought to be omens of good fortune) as they swim this second time. Perhaps, although there is a symbolic reenactment of the moment in which the boys' innocence and affection were so vividly demonstrated, there is a suggestion that time and experience have darkened these men's lives. It is good that they have been able to come together again, but their relationship can never be exactly as it was in their youth and the signs for their futures, while not necessarily dim, are not so bright as they once were. There is an elegaic tone in the description of the second scene. "Happiness" and "freedom" have been replaced by the ending of summer and salt in their mouths. "Floating on the waves" has become "drifting in the deep currents." "Exhilaration" has changed to not being afraid. Conroy's choice of words is exquisite as he depicts this bittersweet reunion of the four friends after years of separation and animosity.

In the last scene of the novel proper (that is, before the Epilogue) Jack and Leah go swimming immediately after Lucy's funeral. This is clearly another symbolic instance of water as a cleansing and healing element. But Conroy adds another dimension to the familiar pattern. Ledare arrives at the water's edge, still wearing her black dress, holding an albino loggerhead turtle that someone has found on the golf course. The turtle seems dead, but Jack and Leah take it out and release it beyond the breakers, where it comes to life and swims off to the open sea. The symbolic suggestions here are legion. First, it is Ledare who is the agent of lifesaving, just as she is, in a sense, for Jack on another level. Second, the juxtaposition of this episode with Lucy's funeral and the turtle's lifeless appearance suggests that being does spring from death. Furthermore, it is in water, which in many cultures is thought to be the ultimate source of all life.

The turtle is an albino, the only one Jack has ever seen. It is different in that respect just as it is in needing special care and attention after it has lost its sense of direction. John Hardin is, and Shyla was, also "different." (Lucy says that they are from the "same tribe" [603].) They need special care to survive. Fortunately, thus far, John Hardin has had it in the form of Lucy's and Dupree's love and understanding. Unfortunately, although Jack has tried to provide them, Shyla did not find them from her family during her early emotional difficulties and became too damaged to be saved. (Obviously there are other causes for Shyla's psychosis, but her parents, as they come to realize, have to bear a large burden of responsibility for her suicide.) That Conroy chooses this vignette involving the turtle to close the novel itself is surely his way of emphasizing his themes about the need for love and compassion and saying that in certain cases those qualities must be carried to special lengths for those among us who are hurt, disoriented, and different.

Finally, amid all the other symbols of harmony and rebirth in the Epilogue, at the celebration of Jack's and Ledare's wedding, the McCall brothers and Leah jump into the fountain of the Piazza Farnese and cavort in exuberance. So replete is the Epilogue with traditional symbols of harmony that it is reminiscent of the final scenes from Shakespeare's romantic comedies like *Twelfth Night, Much Ado About Nothing*, and *As You Like It*. There is, of course, a wedding. There is music, feasting, and dancing. There is joy and reunion after years of grief and strife. Obviously the past cannot be erased, but many of its wounds have been healed. All but a few of the major players in *Beach Music*'s drama are there, and those who are not, are present in Jack's mind. Jordan sends his blessing, and as Jack looks out on the Piazza after all the guests have gone, he feels at peace with himself and his world. Conroy ends the book with a scene brimming with symbolic harmony, a fitting conclusion for a novel whose characters have sought it so painfully and whose major theme is the achievement of it through compassion and love.

A NEW HISTORICIST READING

New historicism, as its name implies, is a methodology that reintroduces many of the critical considerations that were thought important by earlier historically oriented critics. The most central of these include a consideration of the author's physical, emotional, and psychological frame of reference as an influence on the work, its reflection of social and historical conditions, and to some extent, its ethical and moral stances. New historicists go somewhat further in that they adopt as well many of the positions taken by other relatively new schools of criticism such as feminist and deconstructive. The new historicist focuses, then, on the way in which a work of literature reflects, and is influenced by, a wide variety of autobiographical and sociohistorical factors and sees this material as important in helping us to a full understanding of it.

Like other specialized schools of literary criticism, the new historicists do not so much disagree with a close reading of the text as they are apt to place greater emphasis on certain aspects of it and factors outside it. Some of these critics such as Stephen Greenblatt have been influenced by the late Michael Foucault's theories about the interrelation of economic, social, and political variables as they influence historical events. Others like Jerome McGann have been more impressed by Soviet critics whose emphasis was on social class (Marx) and the way in which changes in language produce changes in meaning (M. M. Bakhtin). Still others have looked to Walter Benjamin's theories about art in a technological society. Thus, within the school of new historical criticism, there are individuals with different emphases. What they would agree on, however, is that a work of literature should not be read in a vacuum:

> [T]hey share a belief in referentiality—a belief that literature refers to and is referred to by things outside itself. . . . [They will] be interested in the work's point of origin and in its point of reception . . . as that body of opinion has become part of the platform on which we are situated when we study the book. (Murfin "New Historicism" 374–75)

The new historicist would immediately see the autobiographical elements in *Beach Music* as enormously important and fertile ground for helping to understand its full impact. Not only does Conroy base the five McCall brothers very closely on the five Conroys, he makes his mother's illness and death a central element in the plot. There are things here that the new historicist would pursue in greater depth than the general critic would in merely noting them. For example, in one interview, Conroy mentions his mother's death as one of the reasons for the novel's being so long delayed (Pitts and Robertson 12). In his lecture at the Smithsonian, Conroy described in great detail how, when in her final days, she lost control of her bodily functions, he bathed her in the shower. This scene in the novel is doubtless so vividly rendered because it is an exact transcript of what actually happened to Conroy as he helped his mother through the pain and humiliation of her dying days.

Another autobiographical element among many that the new historicist would find of interest, is Conroy's use of five brothers (and his dedication of the book to four of them) and the omission of his two sisters.
If an author is going to mirror the central family of the novel so closely
on his own, why, in what seems an arbitrary decision, does Conroy
choose the brothers and ignore the sisters? The ever-candid Conroy explains that:

> [M]y sisters carry the virus of my father's meanness. On the
> other hand, my brothers are filled with gentleness and a real
> capacity for love. (Pitts and Robertson 12).

His sister, Carol (whose portrait as Savannah in *The Prince of Tides* in-
furiated her), has only recently resumed speaking to him and his other
sister, Kathy, has remained very cool, presumably because of the way in
which he depicted their father in *The Great Santini*.

Perhaps the reconciliation of Jordan and Rembert Elliott in the novel,
which seems hard to credit after their years of enmity, may be less difficult to accept if one is familiar with Conroy's own reconciliation with
his father (described in detail in Chapter One). The inclusion in *Beach
Music* of so much material having to do with the Holocaust is explained
by Conroy's desire to use it for thematic and character-defining reasons,
but it may be, in part, the result of his mother's near obsession with the
subject. One of the first books she chose to read to the Conroy children
was *The Diary of Anne Frank* (Carney 78).

Beyond these comments on autobiographical material in *Beach Music*,
the new historicist would speculate on another: the way in which art and
life interact and influence each other. This is a matter that has been of
interest to literary critics and philosophers since the time of Socrates, and
it is a matter that Conroy addresses when he speaks frequently of his
visit to Asheville, North Carolina, to visit the home of Thomas Wolfe.
His high school teacher, Eugene Norris, insisted that in viewing the room
in which Wolfe's character, Ben Gant, died and that by eating an apple
from the tree in the yard as Wolfe did, Conroy would become more
aware of the relation between art and life (Logue 34). How much this
youthful episode is responsible for Conroy's extraordinary intermingling
of life and art is conjectural. What is absolutely certain is that, like his
exemplar, Wolfe, Conroy is an author in whose work biography and
fiction become almost inseparable. Ahrens quotes Conroy as saying that
like the tidal marshes of his home, where it is impossible to mark the

division of land and water, so it is for him with fact and fiction. Doug Marlette, who is one of Conroy's best friends and a collaborator with him on the screenplay *Ex*, puts it this way: "Between Pat's art and life there is a kind of seamlessness" (Ahrens C2).

Yet another autobiographical detail that would contribute to the art-life discussion of *Beach Music* is Conroy's deletion of the chapter in the book in which John Hardin commits suicide. After he learned of his brother Tom's jumping from an eighteen-story building in Columbia, South Carolina, Conroy could not bring himself to include that chapter. The new historicist would find this influence on the presentation of John Hardin's character important since, even before Tom's death, Conroy had worried about what effect his portrait in the novel might have on his disturbed brother, who was an avid reader and surely would have recognized himself in it (Berendt 110).

Among other matters that the new historicist would be vitally interested in is Conroy's attention to social and political events of the period covered in the novel and the way in which they help to shape major characters and themes. Most important of these would be the Vietnam War's polarization of American society, particularly as that was evident in the protests of those of college age and the angry, often repressive, response of those in authority. As the war dragged on, the protests escalated from sit-ins to vandalism at Selective Service Offices. Organizations like Students for a Democratic Society (SDS) created near constant tension for several years; and the protest at Kent State in Ohio, which ended in the National Guard's firing on and killing several students, precipitated the climax of the movement, as this overreaction had the effect of further inflaming the already overheated animosity.

Many historians and sociologists suggest that this division between so many young people and the establishment, as represented by authority figures like the police and an older generation of politicians had far more serious and broader effects on the American spirit than simply the protest of the war. Although there were certainly adults who protested the war, it became a generational conflict about the nature of authority and moral values. Conroy's depiction of all this in *Beach Music* is vivid and he uses it as a deciding factor in the destinies of Jordan Elliott, Shyla Fox, and Capers Middleton. The new historicist would cite this as Conroy's use of historical-social phenomena in shaping the characters and plot of the novel and might go on to analyze Conroy's fictional characters and their actions (including the betrayals by Radical Bob and Capers) by comparing them with real student activists of the period.

On the other side of the Vietnam War controversy, there were rigid defenders of the military intervention who denounced protesters as traitors and who, like Rembert Elliott, would disown their children for their anti-government sentiments. There have also been ambitious politicians who have tried to play on public sentiment, as Capers does, by exaggerating the hostility experienced by some veterans of the war. Conroy leaves little doubt about his sympathy for those who were opposed to the war, and the new historicist would note how, nearly thirty years after the events, passions are still strong on that subject—as has been evidenced by the controversy over normalizing diplomatic relations with Vietnam in July 1995.

Another polarizing event in American life that Conroy treats in somewhat less detail, but in a nonetheless memorable way, is the reaction of many Southerners to racial integration. In *Beach Music* Tony Calabrese is fired from his job in the high school for his classroom advocacy of integration. At the ensuing trial Johnson Hagood, in one of his finest hours, rules in Calabrese's favor and lectures the courtroom on the need for a change in old attitudes. This provokes not only an attack on the teacher by ten masked men who beat him, burn his house, and drive him out of the state, but on the evening after the trial the McCall house is stoned and fired upon by hoodlums who scream that Judge McCall is a "nigger lover" whom they pledge to kill. These actions and reactions were by no means unusual in the South of the 1950s and 1960s, and in many cases the results were even more dire. The new historicist would again note the way in which Conroy has incorporated historical material in the novel and how, while there was massive negative feeling among the white population of the time, a few brave and honorable men and women like Johnson Hagood actually risked their lives in the defense of their moral convictions.

Along with these domestic events of historical importance, Conroy introduces a scene of fatal terrorism at the Rome airport, a common enough phenomenon in Italy and elsewhere in the 1980s—and both before and since. Of even greater historical interest in the sections of the novel set in Europe are the stories of Jewish oppression. Conroy's descriptions are so graphic that even if the reader knew little about the Holocaust before, she or he would be shaken by Conroy's evocation of these horrors. Once again, not only does Conroy draw on historical evidence (he interviewed many survivors and pays homage to them in an Introductory Note to the novel), but he shows how these horrendous experiences have shaped the personalities, not only of those who under-

went the tortures, but also of their children like Shyla who has been
brought up in a household haunted by her parents' "ghosts." Thus, Conroy keeps the memory of the Holocaust alive at the same time that he
invites speculation, psychological and otherwise, about its effects on its
survivors and the world's need never to forget these atrocities.

Going outside the novel itself, a new historicist would see an important point made about American popular culture by the fact that in the
first week for which sales figures were available, *Beach Music* jumped to
the top place on the best-seller charts while the reviews of the novel
ranged from the almost entirely negative (*Newsweek*, *The New York Times*,
The Philadelphia Inquirer) to the guardedly favorable (*Boston Globe Books* ,
The Houston Chronicle, *San Francisco Chronicle Book Review*). There is obviously a wide gap between critical opinion and mainstream readership.
This gap is certainly not limited to Conroy; for example, authors like
Robert James Waller, whose *The Bridges of Madison County* was on the
best-seller list for over three years, and Danielle Steele are even more
roundly damned by the reviewers than is Conroy, but the new historicist
would find in this discrepancy a significant comment on the American
reading public. First, they are not much swayed by critical opinion. Second, they are swept along by characters, plots, and themes that touch
them, whether or not the author has presented these factors with economy and total credibility:

> Summer readers are always looking for the long, involving,
> entertaining book, the perfect mental escape to tuck into the
> beach bag or read in a hammock on the porch. (Larson D1)

Third, they are intrigued by set pieces of storytelling such as the Holo-
caust stories in *Beach Music*, the Great Dog Chippie fables that Jack tells
Leah, the southern-gothic exotica of Lucy's childhood, and the Jonah-
Moby Dick-like adventure of the great fishing expedition.

Conroy's characters in *Beach Music* (as they were in *The Prince of Tides*)
are larger than life; their emotions are powerful; and they are involved
in melodramatic situations. These seem to be the qualities that readers
of popular fiction crave. It must be said at the same time that Conroy's
unabashed willingness to speak so directly about nostalgia, love, and
compassion as healing qualities and about family reconciliation is part
of what makes him such a favorite. Several commentators have noted
that Conroy is one of our few male novelists who is willing to deal
openly and lyrically with emotion. Berendt claims that, while John Up-

dike writes of emotion, he does it in a clinical way, whereas Conroy "pours his heart out, unabashedly" (138) without sacrificing his male perspective.

All of this would lead the historicist critic to comment on the author's natural instincts in writing, but also on the fact that, if the reading public loved *The Prince of Tides*, then it serves him well to give them even more of the same in *Beach Music*. There could be a cynical view of this phenomenon, but in Conroy's case that would probably not be justified. If he were merely pandering to public taste, there would not be nine years between one novel and the next. Furthermore, through his many statements on his passion about writing and his willingness to rewrite *Beach Music* in the first person after having spent five years writing it in the third, there is a testimony to his integrity as a writer.

The new historicist, then, would find much from outside the novel itself to help in our understanding of it. Such a critic would note that there is a kind of illuminating interrelationship between the use of autobiographical and historical material in the novel and our knowledge of these things from other sources. That is to say, what is in the novel and what we bring to bear on it from outside reinforce each other in ways that a mere close reading of the text would not reveal.

Bibliography

WORKS BY PAT CONROY

Beach Music. New York: Doubleday, 1995.

The Boo. Verona, Virginia: McClure Press, 1970; Atlanta: Old New York Book Shop Press, 1981 and 1988.

"Death of a Marriage." *Atlanta Magazine* (November 1978).

The Great Santini. Boston: Houghton Mifflin Company, 1976.

Interview. With Charles Gibson, ABC Television, 28 June 1995.

Introduction. *Military Brats: Legacies of Childhood Inside the Fortress*. By Mary Edwards Wertsch. New York: Harmony Books, 1991.

Lecture. The Smithsonian Institution, Washington, D. C., 28 June 1995.

The Lords of Discipline. Boston: Houghton Mifflin Company, 1980.

"Pat Conroy talks about the South, his mother and *The Prince of Tides*." *Book-of-the-Month Club News* (December 1986).

The Prince of Tides. Boston: Houghton Mifflin Company, 1986.

The Water Is Wide. Boston: Houghton Mifflin Company, 1972.

WORKS ABOUT PAT CONROY

General

Abrams, Garry. "Novelist Turns Pain Into Profit." *Los Angeles Times*, 12 December 1986.

Blades, John. "What if . . ." *Chicago Tribune*, 25 September 1991.

"Conroy, Pat." *Major 20th-Century Writers*. Detroit: Gale Research, Inc., 1991.

Hopper, Leigh. "Writing Family Wrongs." *The Houston Post*, 16 November 1992.

Maryles, Daisy. "Book & Author Breakfasts." *Publishers Weekly*, 20 June 1986.

Max, Daniel. "Waves of Success for 'Prince of Tides' Author." *Variety*, 13 January 1992.

Romano, Lois. "Pat Conroy's Tide Comes In." *The Washington Post*, 9 March 1992.

Staggs, Sam. "Pat Conroy." *Publishers Weekly*, 5 September 1986.

Toolan, David. "The Unfinished Boy & His Pain." *Commonweal*, 22 February 1991.

York, Lamar. "Pat Conroy's Portrait of the Artist as a Young Southerner." *The Southern Literary Journal* XIX:2 (Spring 1987).

Biographical

Ahrens, Frank. "Tidal Recall." *The Washington Post*, 21 July 1995.

Berendt, John. "The Conroy Saga." *Vanity Fair* (July 1995).

Carney, Thomas. "Big Boy Is Back." *Men's Journal* (August 1995).

Epstein, Robert. "Magnolias, Palms: 'Tides' Author Meets Hollywood." *Los Angeles Times*, 26 December 1991.

Gorner, Peter. "An Author 'Blessed' by Unhappiness." *Chicago Tribune*, 25 November 1986.

Guthrie, Julian. "High Tide in the Low Country." *San Francisco Examiner Magazine*, 16 July 1995.

Klein, Julia M. "Larger than Life." *The Philadelphia Inquirer*, 31 August 1995.

Leviton, Joyce. "Shaping His Pain Into Novels, Pat Conroy Gets His Reputation, His Fortune—And His Revenge." *People Weekly*, 2 February 1981.

Logue, John. "Fearless Son of 'The Great Santini.' " *Southern Living* (July 1995).

Martelle, Scott. "The Pain of Truth." *The Detroit News*, 1 July 1995.

O'Neill, Molly. "Pat Conroy's Tale: Of Time and 'Tides.' " *The New York Times*, 22 December 1991.

"Pat Conroy Up Close." *The Literary Guild Entertainer* (August 1995).

Robertson, Brewster Milton. "A Life Tangled in Fact and Fiction." *Los Angeles Times*, 27 June 1995.

Stein, Ruthe. "Pat Conroy Reveals His Soap-Opera Life." *San Francisco Chronicle*, 26 November 1991.

Williams, Christine. "Fathers & Sons." *The Washington Post*, 23 October 1980.

Willingham, Robert, M., Jr. "Pat Conroy." *Dictionary of Literary Biography*. Detroit: Gale Research, Inc., 1980.

Wilson, Craig. "A Mother Mourned in 'Beach Music.' " *USA TODAY*, 6 July 1995.

REVIEWS AND CRITICISM

The Boo

O'Briant, Don. "More Valuable Second Time Around." *The Atlanta Journal*, 14 October 1990.

The Water Is Wide

Broyard, Anatole. "Supererogating Down South." Review of *The Water Is Wide*, by Pat Conroy. *The New York Times*, 13 July 1972.

The Great Santini

Burkholder, Robert. "The Uses of Myth in Pat Conroy's *The Great Santini*." *Critique: Studies in Modern Fiction* XXI:1 (1979).
Wertsch, Mary Edwards. *Military Brats: Legacies of Childhood Inside the Fortress*. New York: Harmony Books, 1991.

The Lords of Discipline

Crews, Harry. "The Passage to Manhood." Review of *The Lords of Discipline*, by Pat Conroy. *The New York Times Book Review*, 7 December 1980.
Dickey, James. Jacket blurb for *The Lords of Discipline*. Boston: Houghton Mifflin Company, 1980.
Faludi, Susan. "The Naked Citadel." *The New Yorker*, 5 September 1994.
Manegold, Catherine S. "The Citadel's Lone Wolf: Shannon Faulkner." *The New York Times Magazine*, 11 September 1994.
Rose, Frank. "The Martial Spirit and the Masculine Mystique." Review of *The Lords of Discipline*, by Pat Conroy. *The Washington Post Book World*, 19 October 1980.

The Prince of Tides

Bass, Judy. "A Prince of Pain." Review of *The Prince of Tides*, by Pat Conroy. *Chicago Tribune Book World*, 19 October 1986.

Eder, Richard. "The Prince of Tides." Review of *The Prince of Tides*, by Pat Conroy. *Los Angeles Times Book Review*, 19 October 1986.

Geeslin, Campbell. "The Prince of Tides." Review of *The Prince of Tides*, by Pat Conroy. *People Weekly*, 10 November 1986.

Godwin, Gail. "Romancing the Shrink." Review of *The Prince of Tides*, by Pat Conroy. *The New York Times Book Review*, 12 October 1986.

McCormick, Patrick. "Shame: To Thine Own Self Be Cruel." *U. S. Catholic* (September 1992).

Sheppard, R. Z. "The World According to Wingo." Review of *The Prince of Tides*, by Pat Conroy. *Time*, 13 October 1986.

Weeks, Brigitte. "Pat Conroy: Into the Heart of a Family." Review of *The Prince of Tides*, by Pat Conroy. *The Washington Post Book World*, 12 October 1986.

White, Robert A. "Pat Conroy's 'Gutter Language': *Prince of Tides* in a Lowcountry High School." *English Journal* 81:4 (April 1982).

Beach Music

Caldwell, Gail. "Flood Tide." Review of *Beach Music*, by Pat Conroy. *Boston Globe Books*, 25 June 1995.

Feeley, Gregory. "In 'Beach Music' Conroy Resorts to Familiar Themes, Melodrama." Review of *Beach Music*, by Pat Conroy. *The Philadelphia Inquirer*, 23 July 1995.

Fleming, Michael. "Buzz." *Variety*, 30 May–5 June 1994.

Harris, Mark. "Southern Discomfort." Review of *Beach Music*, by Pat Conroy. *Entertainment Weekly*, 30 June–7 July 1995.

Harris, Michael. "Bigger Than Ever." Review of *Beach Music*, by Pat Conroy. *Los Angeles Times Book Review*, 25 June 1995.

Larson, Susan. "Beached with Pat Conroy." Review of *Beach Music*, by Pat Conroy. *The New Orleans Times-Picayune*, 25 June 1995.

Lehman-Haupt, Christopher. "Lure of Entanglements Home-Grown and Lasting." Review of *Beach Music*, by Pat Conroy. *The New York Times*, 24 July 1995.

Pitts, Myron B., and Brewster Milton Robertson. "Author Pat Conroy's New Epic." *USA WEEKEND*, 30 June–2 July 1995.

Shapiro, Laura. [Untitled]. Review of *Beach Music*, by Pat Conroy. *Newsweek*, 17 July 1995.

Sheppard, R. Z. "First-Person Portentous." Review of *Beach Music*, by Pat Conroy. *Time*, 26 June 1995.

Shone, Tom. "You Can Go Home Again. And Again." Review of *Beach Music*, by Pat Conroy. *The New York Times Book Review*, 2 July 1995.

Spafford, Roz. "Land, Water and Memory." Review of *Beach Music*, by Pat Conroy. *San Francisco Chronicle Book Review*, 25 June 1995.

Warren, Tim. "Conroy Cranks up the Volume." Review of *Beach Music*, by Pat
    Conroy. *The Houston Chronicle*, 2 July 1995.
Weeks, Brigitte. "Where the Stories Sizzle." Review of *Beach Music*, by Pat Con-
    roy. *The Washington Post Book World*, 2 July 1995.

OTHER SECONDARY SOURCES

Guerin, Wilfred L. et al. *A Handbook of Critical Approaches to Literature*. 2d ed.
    New York: Harper & Row, 1979.
McMahan, Elizabeth, Susan Daly, and Robert Frank. *Nine Short Novels by Amer-
    ican Women*. New York: St. Martin's Press, 1993.
Murfin, Ross C. "What Is Marxist Criticism?" In *Hamlet*, edited by Susanne L.
    Wofford, 332–344. Boston and New York: Bedford Books *of* St. Martin's
    Press, 1994..
——— "What Is Psychological Criticism?" In *Hamlet*, 241–251.
——— "What Is the New Historicism?" In *Hamlet*, 368–376.
Pratt, Annis V. "The New Feminist Criticisms: Exploring the History of the New
    Space." In *Beyond Intellectual Sexism: A New Woman, A New Reality*, edited
    by Joan I. Roberts. New York: McKay, 1976.
Selden, Raman. *Practicing Theory and Reading Literature*. Lexington: The University
    Press of Kentucky, 1989.
Shor, Ira. "Notes on Marxism and Method." *College English* 34:2 (November
    1972).
Wasson, Richard. "New Marxist Criticism: Introduction." *College English* 34:2
    (November 1972).

Index

About the Author

LANDON C. BURNS is Professor Emeritus of English at The Pennsylvania State University. He maintains an active interest in the short story, mystery and detective fiction, and the popular novel. His paper on the mystery novelist Robert Bernard was presented at the Popular Culture Association Conference in March 1996.